Harvard Historical Studies · 161

Published under the auspices
of the Department of History
from the income of the
Paul Revere Frothingham Bequest
Robert Louis Stroock Fund
Henry Warren Torrey Fund

Woodrow Wilson
and the
American Myth in Italy

Culture, Diplomacy, and War Propaganda

Daniela Rossini

TRANSLATED BY ANTONY SHUGAAR

Harvard University Press
Cambridge, Massachusetts
London, England
2008

Originally published as *Il mito americano nell'Italia della Grande Guerra;*
© 2000, Gius. Laterza & Figli S.p.a., Roma-Bari. English language edition
published by arrangement
with Eulama Literary Agency, Roma.

Library of Congress Cataloging-in-Publication Data

Rossini, Daniela.
[Mito americano nell'Italia della grande guerra. English]
Woodrow Wilson and the American myth in Italy : culture, diplomacy, and war
propaganda / Daniela Rossini ; translated by Antony Shugaar.
p.   cm.—(Harvard historical studies ; 161)
Includes bibliographical references and index.
ISBN 978-0-674-02824-1 (alk. paper)
1. World War, 1914–1918—Diplomatic history.   2. World War, 1914–1918—Italy.   3. Italy—
Foreign relations—United States.   4. United States—Foreign relations—Italy.   5. United
States—Foreign relations—1913–1921.   6. Italy—Foreign relations—1914–1945.   7. Wilson,
Woodrow, 1856–1924.   I. Title.   II. Series.
D617.R6713   2008
940.3'2273—dc22   2007045079

To Franco, Francesco, and Giulia

Contents

Acknowledgments

The core of this book developed out of the many years of research I did at Harvard University, where I had an opportunity to consult American archives extensively and to discuss my ideas at length with American historians. Ernest May worked with me from the beginning in my efforts to reconstruct out of cold archival documents the personalities and conflicts of those years, while Akira Iriye was generous in helping me to interpret the political conflicts between nations as problems of intercultural communication, as well. I recall with fondness the other historians who worked at Harvard University's Warren Center on fellowships during the 1995–1996 academic year: Petra Goedde, Tom Knock, Tim Naftali, Phil Nash, and Rafia Zafar; they listened to lectures, read articles, and provided comments on central sections of this book. Both in America and in Europe, afterward, David Adams, James Burgwyn, Julie Jeffrey, Serge Ricard, and William Vance were unfailingly supportive and knowledgeable, good friends, and expert advisers. My gratitude goes out as well to my colleagues from the European Association for American Studies, among whom I should mention Nando Fasce, Sylvia Hilton, Steven Ickringill, the late and lamented Jan Willem Schulte Nordholt, Maurizio Vaudagna, and Cornelius von Minnen, who treated me with kindness and respect. I have a special debt of gratitude to Carlo Chiarenza, formerly the director of the Fulbright Commission in Rome, which partly financed my many trips to America, and to Bianca Maria Tedeschini Lalli, director of my department, which granted me a very long leave of absence.

After my return to Italy, I combined the American sources with the Italian sources. All of my work, from initial conception more than ten years ago to the publication of this book, was assisted and constantly encouraged by Lucio Villari, with his unfailing kindness. Also, many friends and colleagues, including Carlo Casula, Nando Fasce, Nadia Flores, Daria Frezza, Marta Francini, Stefano Lepri, Maria Lupi, and Caterina Ricciardi, patiently read and commented upon the manuscript, enriching it with observations and suggestions. Let me mention with special gratitude Beniamino Cadioli, who sent me invaluable American propaganda postcards from his collection, and Susan Hunt, administrator at the Warren Center, who helped me in a thousand different ways to work with Harvard professors and libraries. In both Italian and American archives, moreover, I met courteous and competent archivists, without whose help this book could never have been written. In particular, I would like to thank the archivists at the universities of Harvard, Yale, and Chicago, at Stanford's Hoover Institution, at the Library of Congress and the National Archives in Washington, D.C., at the Ufficio Storico dello Stato Maggiore dell'Esercito, the Italian Ministry for Foreign Affairs, the Archivio Centrale dello Stato, and the Biblioteca di Storia Moderna e Contemporanea in Rome. The rich and partly unpublished material that I was able to study helped me to reconstruct the shooting star of the American myth in Italy during the Great War, a phenomenon that is little known but significant, and which accompanied Italy's troubled entry into the era of mass civilization.

Woodrow Wilson and the American Myth in Italy

Introduction

The twentieth century was, as many have claimed, "the American century," and the year 1918 was unquestionably the first "American year" in Europe. The importance of America's entry into the First World War immediately proved to be fundamental, both in military terms and in economic and political terms. President Woodrow Wilson quickly rose to the status of world leader, the only head of state capable of confronting Lenin's simultaneously rising star. A full-fledged myth of America and of Wilson spread through Europe. That myth combined new and old elements: on the one hand, the myth of America as a "promised land," which had developed in the wake of the great Italian emigration and merged with the myths of American freedom and democracy that sprang up during the Italian Risorgimento; on the other hand, Wilson's political skill at managing and running a mass society. Wilson's charisma, in fact, both at home in America and around the world, was a product not merely of the magnetic attraction of his idealism, which captured the imaginations of the masses, but also of the modern use of propaganda, which he was the first to employ on an international scale.

The American myth was strongest in Italy, of all the nations of Europe, even though it lasted less than a year and was quickly transformed into its opposite in the wake of the clash between Italy and the United States during the peace conference—culminating in the explosive Fiume crisis. But in 1918, the myth of America and of Wilson ballooned into the ideological void of the aftermath of Caporetto, filling the vacuum of incompetence presented by the liberal political leadership, which was at a complete loss as to how to govern a society that the war itself had transformed into a mass society: "President Wilson is prompting expressions of the greatest support," as Antonio Gramsci recognized as early as March 1918.[1] In Italy, too, however, the popularity of the American president was not only a result of the modernity of his liberal and democratic message, but also a by-product of the grassroots propaganda campaign that he instituted throughout Italy, working through the Italian branches of the American Red Cross (an organization that the cream of American youth joined, including Ernest Hemingway and John Dos Passos), the Young Men's Christian Association (YMCA), the Committee on Public Information, and a number of representative institutions of the U.S. Army.

In 1918–1919, the myth of America manifested itself in Italy in intense and spectacular—if short-lived—forms. This marked one of the early chapters in the history of the myth of America, which would characterize Italian culture in various ways throughout the rest of the twentieth century. In this first phase, it was chiefly a folk myth, attaining high points that bordered on religious devotion; the Italian political forces used the leverage of that myth—in some cases sincerely, in others opportunistically—in order to survive the crisis of the aftermath of Caporetto. The myth, however, was not matched by a corresponding deepening in the political dialogue between the two distant allies. For different reasons, both American and Italian leaders chose to gloss over the evident incompatibilities between their foreign policies; they both elected to defer the thrashing out of differences—and likely ensuing standoff—until the peace conference. In this study, I have explored the underlying factors that led to the paradoxical behavior of the two allies, behavior that led to the equally paradoxical affair of the Adriatic question. Unable to come to an agreement, the two nations remained substantially and reciprocally alienated on a political basis, a situation that was both risky and fraught with consequences in the overwrought aftermath of the First World War.

Any search for the roots of this clash, however, should not be limited to the personalities of the political leaders themselves, as so many studies have done. Rather, we should look in particular to the cultural gulf between the two nations, a gap that sprang primarily from the unequal development of each country's civil society. Wilson's America, wealthy and up to date, was already familiar with mass consumption, modern means of communication, and mass politics; this made it very different from the elitist and repressive Italy of Orlando and Sonnino. The behavior of politicians and diplomats built up the wall of ignorance, misunderstanding, and prejudice that separated the two countries, instead of helping to break it down. Diplomacy, understood as the art of encouraging dialogue between different cultures and compromise between incompatible political objectives, was deplorably absent from the first encounter/clash between Italy and the United States during the years of the Great War.

Diplomacy may have been absent, but propaganda made an overwhelming entrance on the political stage and remained on that stage for the duration. In Italy, in 1918, the United States deployed its programs of relief and propaganda on a vast scale. The spectacular success of those programs was in part a result of the wealth of resources deployed and the efficacy with which they were administered, but it was also due to the growing ideological thirst of the Italian masses, both civilians and fighting men, and to the myth of America as a paradise for the common man, a myth that had developed in those parts of Italy that produced major flows of emigrants.

Now that the twentieth century is over, it is increasingly clear that events linked to the Great War profoundly influenced the century's history. In 1999, NATO nations bombed Belgrade at length, following years of bitter ethnic fighting that accompanied the dismemberment of Yugoslavia, one of the creations of the Paris peace conference. Many other European conflicts grew out of the 1919 peace conference. In particular, one of the problems that people were trying to answer at the time is still urgently relevant today: Should states be drawn according to ethnic lines of nationality? Can this principle be applied in the ethnic labyrinth of Europe?

But the controversial political map of Europe is only part of Wilson's legacy (and it is the part that was most greatly affected by compromises with the other Allies). Wilson was also the first president to ask the American people to become citizens of the world. He was the first statesman to call for the establishment of a new world order founded upon government action and the intermediation of an international body, the League of Nations. Even though Wilson's approach to internationalism was riddled with nationalist stances, linked in particular to the unique position that he believed the United States occupied in the international community, the fact remains that Wilson was one of the most influential proponents of those internationalist reforms that developed precisely as a reaction to the extreme nationalisms of the Great War. In this sense, the twentieth century can also be seen as the century in which—alongside the conflicts, wars, and genocides engendered by the thousand faces of nationalism—the drive for a new cosmopolitanism, an ideology better suited to the leadership of a progressively more global world, became increasingly powerful and self-aware.[2]

— 1 —

Reciprocal Images before the Great War

During the nineteenth century, Europe, and especially Italy, attracted a growing number of American visitors. Ever larger crowds of tourists were traveling the routes of the traditional eighteenth-century Grand Tour, on the one hand, fattening the revenues of the commercial tourism industry and, on the other, encouraging the development of a new sector of mass-market publishing: travel-based stories and reporting, feature articles, and the ever popular guidebooks. Thus, members of the well-to-do and educated classes in the United States not only took part in the well-established rituals of the "Italian journey" practiced by the European elite, but also went on to disseminate their impressions of the trip back home through mass-circulation periodicals and books.[1]

The eighteenth-century Grand Tour, which had attained its high point on the eve of the Napoleonic wars, entailed a unique blend of travel, education, and amusement for the scions of northern Europe's aristocracies, especially the British. Generally speaking, it involved about two years of travel by carriage along a route that traditionally ran through France, Switzerland, Italy, Germany, and the Netherlands. It followed the completion of one's youthful studies and was considered the necessary and crowning touch to the humanistic education that one would receive in one's native country. The journey was meant to prepare the youth of the upper classes to take on the responsibilities of the leadership role that awaited them upon their return. The Grand Tour, then, was a cultural rite of passage, a transition to adulthood, and an initiation into aspects of life that a more traditional form of education overlooked. Italy, with the wealth of its historic and artistic heritage and the beauty and diversity of its landscape, was the main venue for this sentimental and aesthetic education.[2] In the experience obtained in

Italy, the body of culture acquired through education would be enriched with sensations, emotions, and visual magnificence. This experience constituted the highest level of intellectual refinement and aesthetic enjoyment. Its vital importance as a stimulus to personal development is depicted in the writings of Goethe, Byron, Stendhal, and Madame de Staël, to mention only a few names.[3]

The American travelers who thronged to Italy in ever greater numbers in the second half of the nineteenth century slotted themselves perfectly into the English tradition of the Grand Tour, as modified by the new fashions and technologies of the bourgeois century. With steamships and the developing rail network, travel had become easier, faster, and cheaper. It no longer took two years to tour western Europe—it now required only a few months—and the overall cost of the tour had dropped to the point of affordability for the middle classes as well. In 1864 Thomas Cook inaugurated the commercial tourist industry with the first organized tour of Europe. Organized travel, tourist services, tour guides, and long-distance payment systems developed rapidly during the decades that followed, facilitating travel for a swelling flood of foreigners, with their colorful retinue of travel diaries, descriptive articles, prints, watercolors, photographs, and finally postcards. Thus, during the course of the nineteenth century, for a growing assortment of American artists, writers, architects, men of letters, art collectors, and the independently wealthy or comfortable, the Italian journey became an irreplaceable experience. The "Dream of Arcadia," as Van Wyck Brooks dubbed it, guided their pilgrimages; beginning especially around the mid-nineteenth century, the unique attraction that Americans felt for Italy accumulated an increasingly substantial place as an aspect of American cultural history.[4]

Traditionally, Italian art attracted painters, sculptors, and architects: leaving aside Thomas Jefferson's precocious love of Italian architecture, let us point to such sculptors as Horatio Greenough, Hiram Powers, and William Wetmore Story, or such painters as William Page and John Singer Sargent. In the second half of the nineteenth century, however, a new fever for all things Italian swept through U.S. architecture, with a profusion of public buildings in classical or Palladian style and princely private homes built in Italian style. To decorate these mansions, architectural elements and artworks were shipped in growing numbers from Italy to the United States. It was said that the eminent architect Stanford White kept a yacht moored off Leghorn (Livorno), loading it with the objects that he found and purchased during his stays in Italy: mantelpieces, stained glass windows, balconies, balustrades, and antique furniture of all descriptions.[5] And how could we forget the work done by the illustrious American Renaissance scholar Bernard Berenson, who lived most of his life in Florence as an expert adviser to American art collectors on their purchases? In several cases, he went so far as to assist in the illegal export of Italian masterpieces that became part of American art collections. Thus, between 1870 and the early decades of the twentieth century, most of America's great private collections and museums were assembled. The new tycoons of industry, trade, and finance were seeking to acquire a form of social legitimacy for their vast wealth, a façade that might conceal both their humble origins and their all-too-thin veneer of culture, in the magnificence and refinement of their homes. At times, entire *palazzi*—or significant sections of them—were dismantled in Italy and reassembled in America, as we can still see today in the Boston *palazzo*-museum of Isabella Stewart Gardner. An astonishing torrent of Italian art objects flowed toward America, passing, as it moved westward, a stream of artists and architects who were moving in the opposite direction as they came to learn the secrets of their profession in Italy. Out of this cultural panorama emerged the foundation of the American Academy in Rome. Plans for the American Academy's building were completed in the 1890s, and construction was finished just before the Great War, funded through sizable private donations.

Alongside the artists, writers were also influential in the construction of the learned, "high" image of Italy. In many cases, these were successful writers who lived in Italy for many years, savoring its flavors and penetrating the country's allure, and then popularizing them back home through their writings. Books and articles of this sort proliferated during this period, a result of the convergence of an expanding publishing industry and a growing tourist trade. The writers were leisurely tourists, in short, intellectuals who lived in Italy for long periods of time. They were the "happy few," as Edith Wharton called them, or the "passionate pilgrims" of Henry James.[6] It has been estimated that during the nineteenth century more than a hundred American professional writers (including much of the intellectual aristocracy of New England), and at least as many dilettantes, came to Italy and published books based on their experience there. As a result, nearly all major American novelists felt the powerful influence of the experience of the Italian journey. Among the best known, we should mention James Fenimore Cooper, Nathaniel Hawthorne, William Dean Howells, Henry James, and Edith Wharton, as well as other men of letters such as Charles Eliot Norton, James Russell Lowell, Henry Wadsworth Longfellow, and Henry Adams.[7]

Each of these "passionate pilgrims" added a tile or two to the great mosaic of an idealized image of Italy that was being assembled in American culture, a mosaic that was guiding the emotions and yearnings of U.S. readers and tourists. This was an Italy that existed primarily in the realm of the imagination, a literary construct, but one that played a role in American literature of the nineteenth century and the early twentieth century unrivaled by that of any other country.[8]

"Italy . . . haunts my dreams and clings to my ribs like another wife," and it is "the only region of the earth that I truly love,"[9] wrote James Fenimore Cooper, who lived in Italy for two years, from 1828 to 1830. Cooper was one of the earliest American writers to popularize among his fellow citizens the image of Italy as a land of Arcadian and sensuous charm: "there is no place," he wrote, "where mere living is such a luxury."[10] In his writing, the Italian way of life, focusing more on the pleasures of the senses and the mind, formed an antithesis and a remedy to the excessive and uncontrollable quest for wealth found among the Americans. His stay in Italy had modified his concept of civilization, leading him to criticize the prevailing materialism in American society. Life in a country in decline such as Italy appeared much more agreeable to him than life in a country on the rise, such as the United States.[11]

For Nathaniel Hawthorne, too, Italy was the only country "where life is . . . delicious for its own simple sake"; he, too, found that his lengthy stay in Italy had a considerable influence on his art: "no place ever took such strong hold of my being," he wrote, "nor ever seemed so close to me, and so strangely familiar."[12] This most introverted and puritan of American travelers saw in Italy possibilities of experiences and ways of life that were completely unknown in his homeland. The allure of the experience, however, intermingled with the risks that came with it: Italian beauty and spontaneity concealed abysses of corruption. The dilemma of how to open up to the Italian experience without allowing it to corrupt is the central theme of *The Marble Faun*, a work that immediately became, in Henry James's words, "part of the intellectual equipment of the Anglo-Saxon visitor to Rome."[13]

"If I ever come back, may I be born Italian,"[14] wrote Charles Eliot Norton, in a tribute to the Italians' nobility of soul, the product of centuries of cultural refinement. Norton was one of the most influential personalities in the Bostonian world of letters. He taught at Harvard for many years and,

along with Lowell and Longfellow, played an important role in popularizing the study of Dante and the Renaissance in America. (Among his many
achievements, Longfellow also translated the *Divine Comedy*.)

Henry James, too, often spoke of his "unspeakably tender passion for
Italy," "*quella terra santa,*" "that Paradise," "the most beautiful country in
the world—of a beauty (and an interest and complexity of beauty) so far
beyond any other."[15]

As Erik Amfitheatrof wrote, "the temptation of Italy was to remain a constant theme for Americans of the nineteenth century; a dream for many,
distant and beguiling; an undertow drawing the new citizen of the New
World back to the biblical stained-glass oldness of a Mediterranean time
and coloring, to art, to the stones of history."[16] The prevailing image was
that of an Arcadia, an idealized place, abounding especially in what an ambitious and pushing America most lacked: a sweet and sensuous landscape,
shaped by centuries of human labor, an unrivaled artistic patrimony, a natural bent for and love of art, a living presence of the past in everyday life, a
leisurely way of living that was pleasure-loving and thoughtful, less oriented toward materialistic values. This Italy was not so much a real place,
then, as it was an expression of an American intellectual need. As John Diggins pointed out, it was "in some ways a concept as much as a country . . . a
state of mind as well as a nation-state," "a humanistic fantasy born of the
frustration of all that seemed to be lacking in America."[17] The journey simply translated these ideas and needs into the feelings of the visitor.

This image was more widespread than one might at first have expected: it
was found not only among a narrow circle of intellectuals, but also in the
educated class at large, especially on the East Coast. Ugo Ojetti, for instance,
in his first-person account and survey of the United States, produced after a
long stay there, recalled meeting with four upper-class New Yorkers (of
whom three had been to Italy). They had a nostalgic and sentimental attitude toward Italy: "They spoke of my homeland with the fondness and
yearning that one normally reserves for a sweetly scented memory of the
love of one's youth. Art and flowers; sweetly mingling colors, sounds, and
scents, in a motionless crystalline air. This was Italy to them." Then, as he
toured the towns of New England, Ojetti found that "on every wall in every
home there hung the photographs taken the year before, or fifty years before, during a trip to Italy; and another visit to Florence or Rome, Milan or
Venice was in the hearts and on the lips of everyone the minute they were
introduced to you."[18]

The dream of Italy, then, was first and foremost an expression of a widespread American cultural need. One necessarily wonders about the nature of that need: why did Italy, to so much greater an extent than other countries, take on the role of the anti-America and the progenitor of western art? What was the reason for the urgent yearning that drove so many American artists and writers to go to Italy? Undoubtedly, Italy offered a temporary refuge from the all-encompassing materialism, the rigid moralism, the social climbing, and the rampant anti-intellectualism of America. The journey also allowed one to look back at one's own country from a distance, to compare and contrast very different ways of life and sets of values, and to understand more completely the elements of the culture of a nation still being formed and the role that intellectuals played there. To satisfy this need for distance and comparison, but also the quest for cultural roots, for the need to live temporarily in an atmosphere better suited to an artist and to artistic creation, what country could rival Italy, with its treasury of centuries of accumulated history and art? What place could be so alien and at the same time so familiar?

Let us consider Henry James, who so perfectly embodies this type of American intellectual in the decades prior to the First World War. Perhaps more than anyone else, he had a lasting attachment to Italy throughout his life. Italy for him was not only a continuous source of artistic inspiration, but also the fount of sweeping aesthetic experiences that verged upon veritable spiritual initiations. Italian material has a pervasive presence throughout James's work: "[T]he loved Italy was the scene of my fiction—so much more loved than one has ever been able, ever after fifty efforts to say!" he wrote in the preface to *Roderick Hudson*.[19]

Let us attempt to summarize, then, the components of the myth of Italy. One adjective that frequently recurs in the descriptions of these authors is "picturesque," a word used to describe the landscape or the inhabitants or Italy's ruins from the past or Italy's cultural traditions. The word is also used to refer to Italy's ability to evoke a complex assortment of feelings, emotions, and learned references: James called it "the Italian feeling," and Wharton called it "the Italian sensation,"[20] a difficult state of mind to attain, but once experienced, incomparable and priceless. Landscape, art, and history together evoked it, along with the sensitive and receptive nature of the observer himself or herself.

In the "picturesque" Italian setting, each author selected the aspects that best suited him or her. Howells, for instance, especially loved the scenes of everyday life that were so continuously laid open to the eye of the traveler. And so he described, with verve, empathy, and a fair amount of paternalism, the vignettes worthy of Goldoni that he glimpsed along the roadside. In these scenes, he perceived a deep-seated folk vitality that had been lost in more advanced societies, and he saw them as universal signs of the human soul. This quality, to him, made Italy "above all lands, the home of human nature."[21] Hawthorne, as reticent and diffident as he might have been toward the hedonism, the passionate nature, and the too-vivid colors of the Mediterranean world, was still fascinated by the art and emotional spontaneity of the Italians. Henry James and Edith Wharton were sensitive portrayers of the allure of the impalpable Italian atmosphere, in which the soul, besieged by a thousand sensory and mental stimuli, seemed to spread out to encompass broader and more spiritual panoramas.

All the same, contained in this positive image was a negative aspect as well. Many authors, in fact, noted that the Italian atmosphere could prove treacherous: it was possible to be infected by the excessive hedonism, and by torpor and apathy, which also concealed moral laxity and corruption. For Hawthorne, the atmosphere of Rome in particular seemed to have "a peculiar quality of malignancy";[22] for Howells, Venice was enchanting, but also stagnant and corrupt;[23] for James, Rome, "the Witch of the Seven Hills," enchanted, astonished, and enfeebled the visitor who yielded to its charms, falling into an embrace that could ultimately even prove mortal. The air itself, malarial and windless, that one breathed in the ruins of Rome was dangerous. It was fatal, for instance, to the young Daisy Miller, protagonist of the novel that bore her name. Italy was an arena in which visitors could broaden their spiritual horizons, it was a place that facilitated inner growth and artistic creation, but it was also a reality that concealed a thousand pitfalls for the naïve visitor. Italy had a corrupt and corrupting side, as does anything that lives in symbiosis with the past and with death. Many of the characters in the novels dating from this period came to Italy to suffer; they exposed themselves to knotty moral and existential dilemmas; they grew spiritually, but they ultimately became unhappy. Thus, after abandoning themselves at first to the various Italian initiations, there resurfaced a need for critical detachment, for distance, which was also an affirmation of American moral superiority over Old World morality.

This need for distance and detachment manifested itself especially in the attitude toward the Italians. It was a myth of Italy, not a myth of the Italians. There was an intense relationship with the artworks, with the enchanting ruins of the glorious past, with the sensuous landscape, occasionally even with Italian literature. The inhabitants of the land, however, remained distant, perhaps picturesque, but fundamentally alien, with questionable values and incomprehensible, at times unacceptable, codes of behavior.[24] Indeed, the imposing magnificence of the classical ruins took on stature and drama precisely in contrast with the backwardness and mediocrity of contemporary Italy. In travelers' letters and memoirs, there are endless comments on the distance between Italy's glorious and creative past and its miserable, vulgar present.[25] While Byron believed that this distance reflected the paradoxes of man's fate, for most American travelers the causes of Italy's present-day decadence could be traced back—in a much more straightforward manner—to the Italians' many defects, their indolence and passivity, their inability to rein in their passions, the moral laxity of the Roman Catholic religion, and the absence of civic spirit among the country's ruling class. To American intellectuals in search of their own artistic and national individuality, Italy offered historic, artistic, and literary traditions, but also allowed them to establish a cautious distance from the country's present-day reality.[26]

Filth, superstition, servility, poverty, and a lack of emotional self-control could be seen everywhere. It was easy to realize that the Italians lacked the Puritan virtues of industry, rationality, and civil and moral probity. In the end, the image of a free and democratic America emerged as stronger and more valuable. Through frequent distinctions between Italy and the Italians, we perceive the other face of the myth of Arcadia: like a glove turned inside out, the mythical image of Italy could be reversed, producing its opposite, a negative image of the Italians, clearly serving its essential function in the construction of an American national identity. As the profoundly American Emerson wrote: "We go to Europe to be Americanized."[27]

Negative Images

The negative image of Italy, lurking subtly in the attitudes of so many Romantic pilgrims, became dominant in America in the decades before and after the turn of the century, when Italian mass immigration exploded. Even intellectuals who had admired and praised the Italian people for their humanity, spontaneity, and cheerfulness were shocked and disgusted by the horde of poverty-stricken, filthy, ignorant individuals who now crammed into the outskirts of American cities. "It has undergone the same sort of malign change here that has transformed the Italians from the friendly folk they are at home to the surly race they mostly show themselves here," wrote Howells in 1896.[28] What an abyss between the literary myth of the Arcadian Italian people and the reality of the ragged masses of immigrants! It was impossible to reconcile the two realities: the allure of Italy itself, which continued to capture the imaginations of the educated class, and the average American's rejection of the overwhelming waves of Italian immigration.

Along the same shipping lanes, plied by the luxurious ocean liners that ferried American tourists traveling to Italy and Italian art masterpieces destined for American collections, there also sailed huddled masses of Italian peasants, abandoning the most backward regions of the Italian peninsula. The flow of immigrants, which began in the 1880s, had grown steadily, reaching high points of nearly 300,000 Italian immigrants annually in the years just before the Great War. Between 1900 and 1910, more than two million Italian immigrants passed through American ports, bringing the percentage of Italians out of the total number of foreigners present in the United States up from 5 to 10 percent.[29]

It was during the last decades of the nineteenth century that European agriculture—faced with the challenge of a new competitor from across the Atlantic Ocean, rendered especially redoubtable by the widespread use of machinery and by the recent revolution in transportation—turned in upon itself, attempting to protect itself with trade barriers and state funding. As a result, European agriculture slid into a state of general inefficiency and chronic crisis from which it never fully emerged. During a phase of destabilizing economic transformation, it did, however, play an important role as a social and political stabilizing agent. That is, now European agriculture, became the sector that supplied capital formation and manpower for industrialization. Thus, the countryside of those European nations that came late to the table of industrial development became reservoirs of manpower for the industrial sectors that were developing elsewhere, either in the same country or abroad.[30]

America, like some giant magnet, attracted growing masses of these Italian, Russian, Hungarian, or Polish peasants who were no longer able to survive in their homelands. It was an exodus of biblical proportions. In this period, major American corporations introduced the subdivision of labor and the assembly line. Ordinary production turned into mass production. This type of simplified and automated production no longer demanded skilled workers, the members of the American labor aristocracy; preferable were the new European immigrants: unqualified, underpaid, nonunion-ized. A new compatibility arose between large U.S. factories and illiterate, semifeudal European peasants. Those peasants willingly accepted living and working conditions that were unimaginable for American workers. And so peasants who back home had rarely if ever set foot in a city, now packed into the squalid and unhealthy slums of America's industrial mega-lopolis. Countless "Little Italies" sprang up in those years in American cities. These "rootless ones" did their best to protect themselves from their traumatic impact with a hostile and alien reality through solidarity with their fellow compatriots.[31]

The wave of immigration triggered a violently xenophobic reaction in American society. This horde of those "unlike us" constituted a threat to America's traditions and free institutions. The prevailing attitude shifted from one of celebration of the melting pot to an urgent impulse to protect the predominantly Anglo-Saxon society of the early immigrants. Already in the 1880s, proposals were discussed and bills drafted to restrict immigration.

This led to the formation of a dominant ideology, strongly oriented to-ward racism, which united politicians and intellectuals of various stripes; this ideology offered a clear and consistent vision of the world and Amer-ica's place in it. It was based on a hierarchy of the races, with the highest position assigned to the Anglo-Saxon peoples, who were seen to be histor-ically summoned to the mission of civilizing the other races. In this way racism reinforced the vigorous American expansionism of those years and justified traditional British imperialism, while withholding any acknow-ledgment of a comparable degree of civilization for other countries. Wil-son's fundamental underlying concept of America as the "redeemer nation which could purify the entire world" originated, on the one hand, from his profoundly Calvinist belief that both he and America were chosen by God as instruments of His will in the world, and, on the other hand, equally deeply and solidly, from America's new industrial identity. This new iden-tity, which developed alongside the country's tumultuous process of in-dustrialization, had come to portray industrialism as the new frontier. This new perspective necessarily entailed an ideology that was no longer isola-tionist but instead focused on international expansion and involvement. Let us not forget that Wilson, prior to America's entry into the First World War, had intervened frequently and substantially in Latin American na-tions, in some cases for the sole purpose of "teach[ing] the South American republics to elect good men."[32]

The *Dictionary of Races or Peoples,* published by the U.S. Immigration Commission in 1911, ranked the immigrant "races" in a specific hierarchy, topped by the Anglo-Saxon people, descending through the Hebrews and northern Italians, all the way down, at the bottom of the list, to the southern Italians, allegedly "violent, undisciplined, and incapable of genuine assimilation."[33] Of course, in American society taken as a whole, African Americans occupied even lower rungs of the social ladder, since they were thought to be by their nature disinclined to think rationally and behave morally, but they were not considered immigrants. In the overall hierarchy, the "Latins"—that is, the Spanish, French, Italians, and Latin Americans—occupied a position somewhere in the middle between the two extremes.[34]

Thus, American society furiously rejected the Italians. Several episodes of social violence in the 1890s, such as lynchings in New Orleans or Gunnison, Colorado, generated scandal and tension in diplomatic relations between Italy and the United States.[35] Those episodes were merely the visible tip of the iceberg of a widespread situation of intolerance and discrimination. Wilson himself, in a book that he wrote many years before entering politics, referred to the wave of immigration that began in the late nineteenth century and specifically described Italian immigrants as "men out of the ranks where there was neither skill nor energy nor any initiative of quick intelligence"; it was "as if the countries of the south of Europe were disburdening themselves of the more sordid and hapless elements of their population, the men whose standards of life and or work were such as American workmen had never dreamed hitherto."[36] The southern Italian peasant was the prototype of the immigrant that Yankees wanted to banish from their country. The prevailing image portrayed this immigrant as ignorant and semibarbaric, dishonest, vindictive, and dominated by the obscurantism of the priests. To many Americans the word "Italian" immediately summoned up images of "the stiletto, the Mafia, the deed of impassioned violence . . . an Italian vendetta." On the eve of the First World War, hostile attitudes toward the Italians could be found everywhere, in social behavior, in cultural stereotypes, and in folklore. A negative image of the Italians was spreading rapidly through America.[37]

As is so often the case, the social stereotype had some basis in reality. The murder rate in southern Italy was the highest in Europe.[38] At the same time, the social hostility that the new immigrants encountered in America reinforced both a tendency to react violently and a search for forms of individual self-defense through the protection of locally and ethnically based bosses and organizations. As a result, this period witnessed steady growth in the power of the bosses and of the new urban political machines that drew their strength from the loyalty and votes of immigrant communities. In this context, the Mafia boss was a degenerate mutation of the political system that had emerged in response to the immigrants' most urgent needs. Americans whose forebears had immigrated long ago looked with disgust at the rapidly spreading phenomenon of the new immigrants, their living and working conditions, their profoundly alien habits, customs, and religious practices, their ignorance, and their questionable physical and moral cleanliness. The response of these older American classes was, both defensive, in the form of a groundswell movement in favor of closing the borders to immigration, and reformist, with the rise of the Progressive movement. Among the Progressive crusades were the fight against corruption in the municipal administrations, the battle to clean up the slums, and the quest to Americanize the immigrants. In any case, this response shows that the Progressive Era also featured attitudes that we might today consider anything but progressive.[39]

In reality, as Hofstadter has shown, it would be hard to imagine two more different codes of political ethics than those that were taking form in the new American urban reality in the decades prior to the Great War. On the one hand, Progressive reformism took its inspiration from the high moral values of the urban middle classes that had immigrated long before. On the other hand, the political system based on bosses relied on the party faithful (immigrants for the most part), whose allegiance was to their leader and to their group and consisted of personal bonds of loyalty and self-interest. Since each segment emerged not only from different visions of politics, but also from differing needs and moral values, the typical Progressive and the typical immigrant were not only manifestations of different worlds, but also were intensely antagonistic and incapable of genuine dialogue. The Progressive movement, which we will analyze shortly, took its inspiration from the ideology of individualism and the Protestant values of abstract justice and responsibility of the individual citizen; it dreamed of an impersonal society, dominated by the rule of law and by efficiency. In contrast, the peasant masses from southern and eastern Europe, who had no familiarity with independent individual political action, were better able to grasp ties of loyalty based on authority, devotion, and hierarchy. They simply assumed that political and civic relations necessarily sprang out of the network of needs, emotions, and obligations that linked individuals, families, and groups. They therefore had a more personal and utilitarian vision of politics and placed the values of loyalty to the chief and personal ties above any abstract codes of morality. They asked society and politics for humanity rather than for efficiency. Out of these masses emerged the urban political organization dominated by the new figure of the boss, viewed by Progressives as an unfailing fount of corruption in municipal administration and of pollution of the founding values of American society.[40]

Beginning at the close of the nineteenth century, Progressive ideology became hegemonic. It dominated the Progressive Era, a period that extended up to the Great War. This ideology is of particular importance for our story because it constitutes the context from which emerged both the figures of Wilson and many of his followers and the spirit of a global mission that was such a distinct feature of American intervention in the First World War. This crusading spirit, which was undergirded by a substantial dose of self-congratulation over America's political and moral supremacy, proved costly to the Italians. The costs were incurred both inside the United States, where the Italians were an ethnic minority characterized by differing political and social models, and on the international stage, where Italy was gradually shunted aside as the black sheep of the Allied forces and the Treaty of London became a symbol of the deplorable Old World in need of reform.

American Ignorance of Italy

Especially in the period that we are studying, U.S. relations with Italy reflected the paradox that Stuart Hughes has identified for the entire recent history of both nations: the Americans viewed Italy as a profoundly familiar country, while in fact it was almost unknown to them.[41] The positive or negative stereotypes about Italy and the Italians that we have analyzed in this chapter were the product of a profound ignorance concerning contemporary Italian realities. In neither set of images, good or bad, was there room for a nation that, with a substantial baggage of contradictions and limitations, was undergoing a process of modernization.

The cultural distance became evident, for instance, when one considers the indifference of most Americans to the Italian Risorgimento. With only rare—yet significant—exceptions (such as Margaret Fuller),[42] not only was the Risorgimento of no interest to Americans, but also it often prompted complaints about the loss of the "picturesque" aspects of Italy entailed by the Risorgimento, along with the modernization that came with it. Typical in this connection was Henry James's nostalgia for that "old all-papal para-dise" of Rome prior to national unification.[43] Paradoxically, the attraction to the evocative rituals and ways of the Roman Catholic religion went hand in glove with a sharply negative opinion of the Church of Rome, a perpetual source of indignation to Protestant and forward-thinking travelers. For centuries Americans had looked upon St. Peter's in the same way that they would view the Kremlin in the twentieth century.[44]

American indifference and even hostility were even more marked with respect to Italy's prosaic post-Risorgimento period. With the sole, notable exception of the work of William Roscoe Thayer, whose superb study of Cavour was published in Boston in 1911,[45] prior to the Great War no stud-ies were published in the United States on the Risorgimento. Even after the war, the interest of American historians in Italy's unification and modern-ization remained episodic.[46] The search for the "eternal Italy" got in the way of any real contact with the young Italy that was laboriously freeing itself from the weight of an underdeveloped political, social, and economic orga-nization. The prevailing image was that of a backward country, dominated by the Catholic Church, immobile and semifeudal.[47]

In the decades before and after the turn of the twentieth century, then, the image of Italy in American culture was a strong one, charged with intense im-agery and associations, depicted in bright light and dark shadow. For many members of the well-to-do and educated classes, it was a land of dreams and ideals, an Arcadia, an aesthetic, cultural, and emotional paradise, while the av-erage American identified Italy with the backwardness and defects of the hordes of Italian immigrants. In both cases, these were stereotypes that had lit-tle to do with the reality of Italy, which was undergoing profound transforma-tions in those years, both because of the intense, if localized and unequal process of industrialization, and because of the ensuing social and political changes that reached a crescendo during the years under Giolitti (1903–1914).

These elements—idealization, rejection, and ignorance—exerted a pro-found influence on relations between the United States and Italy during the war years. A number of examples can help to explain the importance of these factors for the topics we will be exploring. We will find an idealized image of Italy held by the throngs of university students and intellectuals who volunteered for war duty in Italy. (The ambulances of the American Red Cross on the Italian front were driven by, among others, students from elite American universities, as well as Ernest Hemingway and John Dos Passos.) In contrast, a negative image, underlay the spirit with which many

Americans committed themselves to action in Italy in the wake of Caporetto: for these Americans, Italy was a country that needed to be changed through the proselytizing of a new gospel, that is, "the American way of life." Paradoxically, we find the greatest ignorance in the work of those American experts on Italy who surrounded the American president during the war years. It was difficult to find experts on America in Italy. While American academia abounded with experts on the Renaissance and the Roman Empire, there were no specialists on contemporary Italy. In the end, William Lunt was appointed as the sole full-time expert on Italy. Lunt was a university professor of English history who had lived in Italy and learned a little Italian in the course of his studies on Anglo-papal relations during the Middle Ages.

As we will see, much the same thing could be said for Italy. There, however, ignorance of the United States was especially common in the upper and middle classes, while the lower classes had a much clearer idea of the way things really stood in the United States. And, in Italy as well, a medievalist was assigned to write the entry for *Stati Uniti* (United States) in the respected *Enciclopedia Treccani;* clearly, this medievalist could not be an expert on the New World. Even in the world of Italian academia, it was difficult to find a scholar familiar with the contemporary situation in the United States.

Images of the United States in Italy

Until the final year of the war, the ignorance and indifference of the Italian ruling class toward the United States were astonishing, as Thomas Nelson Page, the American ambassador to Italy during the war, never tired of pointing out:

> I would say that the feeling towards America is rather one of complete indifference, based for the most part on complete ignorance of what America is and represents. . . . *The great body of the people who represent Italian life make no distinction between the United States and the states of South America.* . . . They have hitherto thought of it only as perhaps a larger Brazil or Argentine or Mexico and they have not got very far yet with this idea.[48]

Few observations can adequately portray Italy's cultural distance from the United States. Before the war, none of the major daily newspapers, not even the leading Italian news agency, the Agenzia Stefani, had a full-time correspondent in the United States. The few news reports concerning North America were copied from French or British news agencies. The Italian public had only limited interest in the United States. Even the best informed political observers considered the United States to be a distant country whose influence on the European balance of power was negligible. Only a very few people, even among the educated classes, knew English. Orlando's complete ignorance of the English language, which caused him so much trouble at the peace conference, was a very common condition. American history and culture were almost never taught at Italian universities. Similarly, in diplomatic circles, Washington was considered a second-choice posting, far from the power centers of international politics [49]

Ignorance about the present-day United States astonished Americans then living in Europe. Norval Richardson, first secretary of the American embassy in Rome, recalled:

> One of the most puzzling sides of my diplomatic education was the constantly recurring incidents which showed me more and more the gulf of misunderstanding between America and Europe. Writers are always stressing the point that we do not understand Europe; I wish some one would accentuate the fact that Europe does not understand us. I am inclined to think that we understand Europeans much better than they do us; at least we know something of their history, their customs and their ways of living; but they accept without question anything that is told them of us.[50]

In particular, the United States was beyond the political horizon of Italian leaders. As late as January 1918, as far as Sidney Sonnino, minister for foreign affairs and symbol of the Italian war, was concerned, the United States practically did not exist. When Page referred in a conversation to changes that were revolutionizing the world, Sonnino simply replied: "I shall not see them. I am too old."[51] In reality, it was difficult for any European leader to fully anticipate the impact of the American intervention in the European war: opposing positions could be maintained with equal credibility.[52] But the Italian elite's stubborn refusal to take the American intervention into account was a sign of its overall inability to perceive the outlines of the society emerging in that period. In a word, it was a sign of the ideological obsolescence that conservative and radical politicians seemed to share.

This ignorance and indifference was often accompanied by mistrust. Like its European partners, Italy considered America's extended neutrality to be the selfish stance of a country interested only in exploiting the war as the source of huge profits. At the end of 1916, for instance, many Italian newspapers criticized Wilson's appeal to the warring nations, branding it a "mercantile document" of the sort that might well be expected from a nation so distant spiritually from the European mentality.[53]

A Violent and Mercenary Country

For a broad array of judgments of the United States, we must turn to the newspapers of Europe in 1898. In that year,[54] the Spanish-American war—that short but crucial conflict that suddenly put the United States in the international limelight—brought to the surface an assortment of latent images of the United States held by the Old World's social elites. In all the countries of Europe, the press—whether favorable or opposed—had reacted vehemently to the changes which this new non-European world power brought to the international stage.

A careful study of the Italian press confirms how limited and ideologically slanted its coverage and analysis of the United States were. For nearly all Italian observers, America was a distant, vaguely understood phenomenon; it was easy to make the United States into a vast grab bag from which each observer could draw all the elements desired to support his or her view, praising or demonizing various aspects as a function of a personal vision of the domestic political context. That was especially true in 1898, that white-hot year of violent popular unrest and equally violent repression.[55] This is not to say that Italian observers failed to perceive the irrepressible rise of American world power; many observers were keenly aware of it. Lacking were adequate analysis and familiarity with the factors responsible for that rise. They therefore failed to grasp the underlying general trend lines in the new international phase, and they also overlooked the possibility of a profitable interaction with the Italian situation. Ignorance and provincialism seemed to be the common hallmarks of the various components of the Italian political world, ensuring that each component reacted in the same stereotypical way to the news reports that arrived from across the Atlantic. The image of the United States, therefore, was ultimately formed and then caught in a limbo, midway between reality and mythification, subject to all sorts of political manipulation.[56]

Traditionally, the most vehement critics of the new American developments were to be found in conservative circles and tended to be hostile to the republicanism, egalitarianism, and democracy of the United States. For parallel reasons, the most enthusiastic supporters were found in the democratic, radical, and socialist sectors of Italian politics. Conservatives emphasized that it was money—not the people—that ran things in American society, with all the corruption, cynicism, and social alienation that this entailed. In 1897, for instance, *La Tribuna,* at that point a publication aligned with Crispi's positions, published an article headlined *La repubblica decadente* (The Decadent Republic): "The great American republic, rather than embodying the ideals of democracy, offers a spectacle of plutocratic despotism without rivals on earth."[57]

In that article, the American republic was called "the most corrupt, and the most contemptible of all forms of government, as well as the most susceptible to the abuses brought about by selfishness and covert personal interests." Previously, Scarfoglio, in the pages of the *Corriere di Napoli,* had sung the praises of Europe in contrast with America:

> As tattered, aged, and feeble as you may find us, we have a world that is incomprehensible to those men, ravaged even now by the thirst or frenzy of wealth, a madness that first led them to abandon their homeland. We have an inalienable patrimony that is our glory and our consolation: a sense of beauty and virtue.[58]

Especially interesting were the Italian Catholic leadership's reactions to the Spanish-American War. The Vatican in particular watched with concern the rising of the American star over the international horizon. The victory of this Protestant nation over Roman Catholic Spain set a new world stage in which the influence of Europe and the power of the Vatican, as traditionally understood, were threatened. But there were other, more subtle reasons for worry. The Church was suspicious of the American model. The United States presented itself as a dynamic and self-centered society, one that would be very difficult to influence. The example of the United States could have a negative impact on the fights that the Holy See was conducting in European political systems in general and in the Italian political system in particular. Alongside the traditional battle against the liberalism, positivism, and materialism of the bourgeois century, the Vatican was now involved in a sharp struggle with the Italian state, which had recently put a violent end to the Vatican's temporal power. The Vatican refused to accept its new confinement to the spiritual sphere, condemned the new political regime, considered the pope to be a prisoner of the Italian state, and exhorted all

Catholics to refrain from participating in the public life of united Italy. It therefore appears quite evident that the harmonious separation of church and state in the United States, with each contentedly relegated to its own sphere of influence, would naturally upset conservative Italian Catholics.[59]

Apparently, moreover, the United States had a distinctive variety of Catholic clergy with strong national sentiments. In the last five years of the nineteenth century, two encyclical letters from Pope Leo XIII attempted to remind the American clergy of the importance of strict obedience and submission to the Catholic faith as promulgated by Rome.[60] Thus, when, in 1899, La Civiltà Cattolica, the authoritative periodical published by the Jesuit order, published a series of articles on the "perils of Americanism," the Church's chief concern was not so much the emerging phenomenon of American imperialism, but rather the excessive independence of the Catholic clergy in the United States.[61]

For the entire course of the Spanish-American War, the Vatican had of course supported the noble, chivalrous, heroic, and courageous Spaniards, while describing the United States as a vulgar nation where money was "the standard for everything" and where most of the population betrayed "a monstrous indifference to religion."[62] Spain was a Catholic country, a traditional Vatican ally, both in Europe and in the colonial world, where for centuries the mission of civilization had been carried out, from throne and from altar.

Throughout 1898, La Civiltà Cattolica published articles sounding the alarm over the fate of Spain, a noble nation whose basic rights were being threatened by the United States' aggression. American greed for Cuba and, later, for the Philippines, proved the vast scale of American colonial ambitions. L'Osservatore Romano, the Vatican daily newspaper, was also decidedly on Spain's side and opposed to the United States' arrogant brute force.[63] The newspaper urged Europe to shake off its apathy in the face of so vast a "holocaust." It was not Spain alone, but all of Europe that was threatened by the emerging wave of jingoism.[64]

That was the position of the hard-line Catholics, but the conciliatory Catholics, or Christian democrats, held different opinions; they looked with interest to the American context, curious about how the country had established a form of harmonious separation between church and state and intrigued by its openness to scientific research and engagement in social reform movements, so closely aligned with their concerns. The attitude of Catholics, then, was not unified but quite diverse.

This same narrow-minded rejection of the American world was to be found in a variety of sectors, some quite surprising. For instance, the revolutionary trade union organizers, described the United States in 1909 as follows in its publication, *Il Divenire Sociale*:

> This country which does not exist, which is not a people, has no name, has no history, in short, which has no past, which is a motley rabble of impertinent shopkeepers operating under a social logic devoid of any content but money, and we might say that it has no present, or rather that it has a single present, which is the present of finance and business. . . . Let us imagine that the conquest is successful, and we shall see the world become one giant fair, whose symbol will be the flag of the United States: an enormous advertising billboard.[65]

Thus, the rough outline set forth above, arraying the Progressive alignment and pro-Americanism against the conservative alignment with anti-Americanism, is accurate only as a first general approach. Actually, there were major exceptions in each of the two camps. In those same years just before and after the turn of the century, for instance, the growing and riotous Italian nationalist movement had begun to praise the dynamism, the will to power, and the expansionism of the young American nation (Theodore Roosevelt and his "strenuous life" represented one of the myths of this political formation).[66] In contrast, reports of the marginal conditions in which most Italian emigrants lived in America had led a number of left-wing leaders to criticize the racism, classism, and plutocracy of American society: "The America that you see from a distance, with the eyes of dreamers and fighters on behalf of civilization," wrote one recent emigrant in a Socialist journal, "the America that I hoped to find . . . is no longer either the America of your dreams, nor the America that you believed existed."[67] Praise or condemnation of the United States, then, ran transversely across political alliances and formations and amounted to an ideological filter, primarily intended for internal use.

The Promised Land and the Home of Freedom

In the decades before and after the turn of the century, a positive image of the United States developed in Italy as well. This image was composed of two main currents that remained independent of one another because they were expressions of social classes and affiliations that hitherto had existed largely in a state of reciprocal alienation. On the one hand, a full-fledged myth of America had spread through the Italian countryside, both in the north and in the south, and had accompanied the exodus of growing numbers of peasants to the New World. On the other hand, in numerous sectors of the governing classes, particularly in radical segments that included republicans, Socialists, bourgeois progressives, and nationalists, the image of the United States had a distinctly mythical hue. We will now analyze these two schools of thought that developed and disseminated a positive image of America. In the later years of the Great War, this image would constitute a fertile substrate for the birth and rapid spread of the myth of America and of Wilson in Italy—a spread that would otherwise be inexplicable.

In the last decades of the nineteenth century, the myth of America spread throughout the Italian countryside concurrent with development of the phenomenon of trans-Atlantic emigration. As a result, a composite image of the "New World" that was deeply rooted in magical and religious beliefs and in the millenarian expectations of the peasant population became a growing presence in the popular culture and the popular imagination. This presence, also contained quite practical and concrete ideas that provided useful guidance to those peasants who were about to make a move in the vastly expanded second wave of western industrialization.

These ideas flowed along alternative channels, circumventing the realm of "high" culture entirely and often in clear opposition to that culture. First the emigration agents, and later the letters from the emigrants were the principal vehicles conveying that information, and they culminated in the creation of a widespread network that circulated reports from the New World. Particularly remarkable was the fact that this network was used and developed primarily by the illiterate or only partially literate, individuals who were apparently the last people one would expect to make use of such a system. Also noteworthy is that this network remained quite separate from the official, bourgeois, and city-centered circuits of information, and instead worked through the effective channels of an oral culture that was still very much alive in the countryside. We can therefore safely say that in the decades leading up to the Great War, the myth of "La Merica" in Italy was essentially a peasant phenomenon, while the cities and the traditional governing classes continued in general to remain indifferent to and cut off from the vigorous phenomenon developing on the far shore of the Atlantic Ocean. With respect to the United States, Italy exhibited two opposing attitudes, specifically differentiated according to the originating social class. The barriers to communication that separated the classes allowed this dualism to survive and endure. The war only amplified it: the positive feelings of the lower classes reinforced the myth of America and of Wilson, while the ignorance and mistrust of the governing class often translated into a rejection of the American message of democracy.

The fertile soil in which the myth of America grew and flourished was a product of the increasingly hard times afflicting Italy's rural masses following unification: in both northern and southern Italy, small landowners, tenant farmers, and farmhands shared a common plight of poverty, malnutrition, and exploitation. This state of affairs made the new taxes levied by the liberal Italian state all the more hateful, in particular the unpopular milling tax on flour. These peasants, untouched by the Italian Risorgimento, felt no attraction for the liberal ideology or the liberal saga; they felt no bond with the new postunification governing class. Indeed, they often yearned for the previous regimes that, if nothing else, had ensured some form of traditional and paternalistic protection: "If our Germans were so much trouble, where are the wonders and pleasures that Victor Emmanuel brings, with the Italian plutocrats? Won't we peasants only lose by the exchange?" sang the protagonist of a Venetian folk opera composed around 1867; the actor went on to list the taxes imposed upon or feared by the rural classes of the region.[68] Peasants not only rarely ate meat, but they rarely ate white bread. According to the clerics, pellagra was the "terrible disease that followed behind the banners of liberalism."[69]

The first emigrants to set out at the end of the 1870s were poor peasants from northern Italy, who were already accustomed to temporary stints of emigration to the neighboring countries of central Europe. The force driving them away from the land of their birth was the clearly proven impossibility of survival, for self and family. This is what they continued to explain to the public authorities who attempted to stem the mass exodus: these emigrants were not certain of making their fortunes in America, but it was still better than starving to death in Italy.[70] They made their preparations for departure in great secrecy in order to elude the restrictions of the authorities and the opposition of the landowners. At least at the beginning of the mass emigration, there was a general climate of extreme class hostility. A Friulian newspaper in 1878 pointed out that the cry of "Viva l'America" ("Long Live

America!") was invariably followed by the shout of "Morte ai signori" ("Death to the Landowners").[71]

The American destination and the means of reaching it, however, remained quite nebulous. The earliest emigrants departed on the basis of fragmentary information conveyed by emigration agents. The job of emigration agent was often held by well-known and respected local figures, who had traditionally served as intermediaries between illiterate peasants and official public institutions. Among those likely to fill this role were the local innkeeper, artisan, curate, school teacher, or a peasant who was particularly astute, well informed, and outgoing. These intermediaries would gather their information, from shipping companies, from nearby American consulates, or from advertisements published in local newspapers or magazines. These reports assured one and all that in America (and at this early date there was no distinction made between North and South America) one could find plenty of work for everyone, good wages, and land for the taking. In some cases, the reports even claimed that life was easier in America, that with very little work one could live comfortably, and that it was a sort of "*Bengodi*" (an Italian term for the mythical Land of Cockaigne, or land of plenty) where anyone who wished to could become a prosperous landowner. The peasants believed these stories about the "New World" because they trusted the intermediaries who purveyed them. In contrast, they put no credence in the opposing claims made by the press and the authorities. They presumed that the newspapers and the government were trying to discourage them in order to protect the best interests of the landowners and upper classes, who were being harmed by the emigration of poor laborers.

The governing classes and the local administrations indeed opposed the mass exodus and did all they could to block it, or at least limit the departures. They issued emigration documents only on certain conditions, they charged emigration agents with fraud and "instigation to emigrate," and they tried to mount counterpropaganda campaigns in the rural areas. In the landowner-controlled press, which reflected the traditional attitudes of the Italian upper classes toward the "bumpkins," articles proliferated describing the peasants as a mass of gullible simpletons, taken in by the glittering and absurd promises made by dishonest charlatans. The urge to emigrate was variously, described, as a "frenzy," "lunacy," "craving," and "mental hallucination" that would bring the naive peasants "to almost certain ruin."[72] neither the public postings, the newspaper articles, nor the speeches of the authorities had much effect. They ran headlong against the peasants' firm and widespread determination to emigrate, and were further undermined by the emigrants' inherent mistrust of "*i siori*" ("gentlefolk"). The emigrants viewed all of the ruling class's efforts to dissuade them as simply arguments on behalf of the landowners' interests.

In the decades that followed, in a movement that rose to a crescendo in the years just before the First World War, the exodus of emigrants leaving Italy for America was drawn primarily from the countryside of southern Italy and increasingly focused on the United States instead of South America. Once this flow of emigration had stabilized, the *lettere americane* (letters from America)—that is, the letters sent to friends and family by those who had emigrated—became the chief source of information, feeding the myth of America and coaxing more peasants to emigrate. These letters found a vast audience in the villages back in Italy. They were often read aloud in public, described to one's neighbors, passed from hand to hand, and discussed in the public venues for socialization in the village, notably the tavern, the marketplace, and the church courtyard. They often included a cash remittance and sometimes a prepaid transatlantic ticket, giving evidence of the truthfulness of what the letter stated. Later, photographs and illustrated postcards also served as evidence, feeding the collective imaginations in the so-called emigration zones.

So it was that a myth of America sprang up, a myth that was destined to endure in the Italian countryside: "America ultimately came to assume the form of a real and alternative world in which, alongside the misfortunes and exploitation that had always existed, . . . there could also coexist, even for the bumpkins, the possibility of social elevation and economic betterment that were wholly unthinkable in the shadow of the bell tower under which one had been born."[73] This image of America was based on the traditional aspirations of the peasants to attain social status and financial prosperity through work and the ownership of property. The American myth sprang up just when all hope of attaining these goals in Italy had been abandoned. A folk song from the Cilento nicely conveys this state of mind: "What happiness in this land now that everyone can go to America, passage by ship is cheap, and poverty and suffering are over."[74]

A broadsheet from the Veneto reflected the same hope for a better life through emigration. Such a path would hardly have beckoned had living conditions at home been better:

> The discoverers of this land were Columbus and Amerigo
> And people go to America to earn a living
> Singing: Let's go to America to work
> Because there's nothing left to do here but sigh!
> We're not making this journey to become wealthy lords
> But just to live better, with less toil
> If the masters of Europe will raise the daily wage
> Then no one will go to America.[75]

A folk song quoted by Franzina offers a good example of the content of this myth of America and emigration as the only way out of poverty that condemned any hopes for a better life. The emigrant says to his betrothed, if in America "things are going well for me," "in the home of my folks/we are going to be married;/there will be wine by the bucketful/ and chickens to be slaughtered." Other dreams mentioned in the songs are the hope of owning "a little home," "a patch of land," and having a crowd of children.[76]

The myth was based on concrete evidence provided by the reports that echoed back from the far shores of the Atlantic Ocean or the stories told by emigrants who came back home. These reports, however, were swollen out of proportion by the exaggerations that inevitably crept into the accounts as they passed from person to person. The image of the Promised Land was also supported by the amplification effects linked to oral transmission and the characteristics of a folk culture that were still very much present in the Italian countryside.[77] This was, a period of rapid cultural transformation of the Italian peasant world, which was undergoing a transition in which old and new cultural media coexisted and reciprocally reinforced one another: the "rumor" and "gossip" intrinsic to the oral tradition alongside the early development of written documents. Thus, in this phase it is possible to identify the characteristics and effects of oral culture through study of written documents, primarily the letters from emigrants.

The inability to read or write was never an insurmountable obstacle for the emigrants or their families to using this basic means of communication. If someone did not know how to read and write, it was always easy to ask the help of a better educated acquaintance. But the real resonance that the letters generated when they arrived derived from the effectiveness of oral transmission. The letters that spoke most enthusiastically of the possibilities available to immigrants in the lands across the ocean circulated not only privately, but, as noted earlier, often prompted the ritual of a public reading and became the frequent subject of conversation among the peasants. The letters, working their way through family and community networks in the villages, often prompted new waves of emigration, mirroring the grid of those relations. A child of Italian emigrants in Colorado, speaking of the time prior to their emigration, recalled:

> Each month one or the other of my father's brothers sent a letter home. They were letters which my father read avidly—as, for that matter, did all the villagers. They used to gather in my grandfather's house whenever one of those magical missives from the New World arrived, listening again and again to the incredible accounts of America which the letters contained, nodding to themselves, muttering aloud, occasionally giving vent to delighted, incredulous exclamations.[78]

The observation made by an American writer in Italy in 1917 is quite pertinent: "the humblest emigrant knew more of the political importance and potential power of the United States than Italy's Foreign Minister."[79]

For the Italian rural masses the letters were symbols of attainment of territorial mobility. These missives established a significant network for transmitting information between the two continents and served as a "bottom-up" regulator for the spontaneous flow of migration. More important than the advertisements by emigration agencies, shipping agencies, and banks working in the field of emigration, the letters were vehicles for countless direct appeals from across the Atlantic. They proved crucial factors in countless decisions to leave. In this way, letters often triggered veritable "migratory chains," based on relations of kinship or neighborhood. Statistical studies done in other European countries have shown a close relationship between letters and a spatial and temporal mapping of the first flows of emigration, as well as parallels between the curve of postal deliveries and the pace of emigration movements.[80]

The "American letters" had such a powerful grip on the rural masses that even emigration agencies, at least until the 1880s, distributed for marketing purposes hundreds and even thousands of copies of particularly evocative letters from emigrants. Whether they were genuine or fake, these letters sparked great interest among the peasants. In an attempt to break the migratory fever, even the composite front of opposition to emigration chose the same approach and tried to circulate letters discouraging emigration. According to Franzina, those anti-emigration initiatives, while they may have managed to squelch some of the emigration agencies' efforts, did nothing to stem the influence of letters sent back by emigrants to their home villages; the credibility of those letters was too great.

Alongside the letters, and as a product of the progress of spreading literacy in the Italian countryside, the rich production of the popular press and cheap pamphlets served as a crucial vehicle for spreading this most recent folk myth. With their attractive array of illustrations, almanacs, pamphlets, astrological charts, newspapers, and popular periodicals influenced the image of the New World that was spreading through the masses of potential emigrants. Even the demand for education, observed a local director of education in the southern Italian provinces, was stimulated far more by the urgent advice that relatives sent back from America in their letters than by any regulations issued by the Ministry of Education:

> Peasants travel great distances to attend school, and they crowd into the classroom benches to learn to read and write, and not because of the law on obligatory schooling, which everyone ignores, but only because the emigrants urge them to learn quickly, or they will be unable to leave. For the Basilicata all the way down into Calabria, America is seen as the promised land. One of those letters, filled with mistakes, and passed from hand to hand, is much more influential than all the circular letters sent out by the minister for education.[81]

The image of the emigrant that emerges from these studies is quite distant from the picture of the foolish and ignorant *villano* (Italian for "bumpkin") easily swindled by dishonest emigration agents, which was so commonly purveyed in the landowner-controlled press and public relations of the time. On the contrary, one has the impression of crowds of peasants who may well have been illiterate but who were cautious and perceptive in their decision making, capable of operating in a rapidly changing transnational scenario, primarily through a network of personal relationships that spanned the oceans. In the background, powerful, deep-rooted, and commonly accepted, was the myth of America as the emigrant's Promised Land.

Although the American myth was primarily a myth of the working classes, it had a grip also on the imaginations of a part of the ruling class. To the republicans and the patriots of the battles of the Italian Risorgimento, the United States had always appeared as a blessed island, a country free of the antiquated institutions of the *ancien régime,* capable of solving the problems of social and productive modernization and of encouraging individualism and democracy. Following Carlo Botta's school of thought, both

Giuseppe Mazzini and Carlo Cattaneo had sung the praises of the United States of America, Mazzini because of his pursuit of republican ideals and Cattaneo because of his wish to import the U.S. federal system to both Italy and Europe. In general, the United States was seen as sympathetic to the struggles of European patriots fighting for unification and hospitable to their exiled heroes, from Garibaldi to Kossuth. There formed in Italy a liberal-democratic opinion that saw America as the mythical—though also remote and alien—land of liberty and republican institutions.[82] For others, including many nationalist schools, America was a land of rampant individualism and unbridled vigor. Therefore, this sector inherited from the Risorgimento a vision of the United States as the land of liberty and democracy, but it was also influenced by the new cultural climate of decadentism and irrationalism, which permitted the exaltation of American vitalism and expansionism.

Even the European Socialists were susceptible to pro-American sympathies. Engels himself, in 1887, admittedly with a number of reservations, described himself as an optimist concerning the future development of the political organization of the proletariat in the United States.[83] In terms of the gradualist vision of reform Socialists, moreover, the United States represented a pure bourgeois society, free of all the aristocratic, monarchic, and feudal encrustations that still burdened Europe, providing a marvelous social laboratory in which to explore the clarity of class relationships, as well as the image of a potential future for the underdeveloped Italian society, which was preparing its own transition to Socialism.[84] In this attitude the Socialists resembled the representatives of the most well-informed and far-sighted sector of the Italian bourgeoisie. At first, it may seem surprising to find that many of the most perceptive articles about America in such Socialist publications as *La Critica Sociale* and *Avanti!* were written by bourgeois intellectuals of the stature of Olindo Malagodi or Angelo Crespi. All of them pointed out the progressive nature of American society, a model for a welcome new direction in development. In different ways, Filippo Turati, Gaetano Salvemini, Leonida Bissolati, and the young Antonio Gramsci all shared in this hope and looked sympathetically upon the political program with which the American president became involved in the European war. Indeed, the reform Socialists were among the earliest and most sincere supporters of the Wilsonian democratic message and remained faithful to it until the end of the war. "I had always placed my hopes in Wilson," Anna Kuliscioff wrote to Turati as early as March 1917, "because he alone can hold high the principles of democracy at the future peace conference."[85] Once the war was over, Turati declared these same ideas before the Chamber of Deputies: "In the application of Wilson's principles, we see salvation from the dangers of victory. But these principles must be put into practice with full sincerity."[86] As Piero Melograni recalled, " 'Wilson or Lenin': this was the formulation repeated frequently at the end of the war. In 1918 the Italian masses and the reformers chose Wilson."[87]

— 2 —

Two Parallel Wars

The First World War marked a watershed between two profoundly different eras: the peaceful, optimistic, and rational nineteenth century and the violent, pessimistic, and irrational twentieth century. The twentieth century, "the short century" as Eric Hobsbawm described it, began historically with the First World War, while the long nineteenth century—with its baggage of economic progress, liberalism, positivism, and Eurocentrism—extended until 1914. The war, which to many arrived like a bolt from the blue, lasted five interminable years, deeply marking the peoples caught up in it. For European countries in particular, emerging from the golden atmosphere of the Belle Époque, the war was a traumatic event, a clear boundary between eras. After the war, with its burden of the dead and the mutilated and the vast swath of destruction, who could still believe in progress and in the rationality of human actions? Both the cultural and political climate and the social and economic terrain emerged profoundly transformed after the war.[1]

Europe had just experienced a century of peace. The nineteenth century had seen no major wars fought upon its soil. The continent had been swept by waves of liberal uprisings, but these disturbances, even though they occurred on a pan-European scale, had involved only narrow sectors of the population. The only extended, bloody war that was massively destructive of human lives and resources, the only war that could be said to foreshadow the horrors of the wars of the twentieth century, the American Civil War (1861–1865), had been fought on a different continent.

With the long-lasting peace came unprecedented economic progress. Industrialization and the transportation revolution had spread prosperity to broad sectors of the population. Indeed, a constant decline in prices had accompanied the spreading industrialization, allowing most of the population to adopt customs and forms and styles of consumption that had previously been the privilege only of the wealthy.

Over the course of the century, based on this foundation of peace and increasing prosperity, liberalism and positivism had spread across the continent—ideologies full of faith in progress, science, and reason. Even opponents of the bourgeois system, the utopian and "scientific" Socialists, still operated in the context of an all-encompassing optimism. Bourgeois and Socialist ideologies shared the same conception of history, understood as humanity's march toward ever higher goals. Growing wealth, welfare, and positivism advanced arm in arm, painting the future in shades of pink (though now and again with a more violent revolutionary rupture), as a destiny of continual progress.

In the nineteenth century's final years, few were able to foresee the danger of the growing friction that was developing among the European nations in the economic, diplomatic, and colonial sectors, or the risks of the irrationalist currents that, while remaining firmly in the minority, began to undermine the great edifice of positivist and liberal thought. Economic growth had also ground to a halt during the long period of stasis produced by the depression of 1873–1896. This extended depression had been a period of overall shuffling and reshuffling of the cards in the western world; it had coincided with the second wave of the industrial revolution. During this depression, new sectors of manufacturing emerged (the electric, steel, and chemical industries), along with new industrial organizations based on mass production and new industrial powers (Germany, the United States, and Japan). Alongside those three powers, other nations, though not with equal success and impetus, had begun their own industrial development. Italy, having laboriously attained national independence and unification, was one of these nations.

Within the European nations, the extended depression of the late nineteenth century had redefined the roles of social classes and production sectors. In many of those countries, the depression had finally ordained the downgrading of agriculture as the principal productive sector and its shift to a subordinate status with respect to the industrial sector. From that time on, the condition of chronic underdevelopment and overpopulation of such a major portion of European agriculture came to be seen as a necessary stage, linked primarily to the need for social stability and domestic politics. The mass exodus from the countryside and the vast trans-Atlantic migrations that ensued were the sole response that the poor peasants of the Russian, Polish, Hungarian, and Italian countrysides could muster.

On the international stage, the fragmentation of the nineteenth century's unified framework was taking place. Instead of a landscape centered around Great Britain, with its City of London, banker to the world, the pound sterling as the sole international currency, Britain's unrivaled military and commercial fleet, its boundless colonial empire, its liberal and free-trade ideology, the world stage now became polycentric, as new powers attained greater international importance. The three protagonists of the second wave of the industrial revolution—Germany, the United States, and Japan—in ways specific to each country, sought to expand their "living space" on their own continent and in colonies. The expansionist fever also infected less developed powers, such as Italy, Russia, and the Austro-Hungarian Empire. This led to a progressive exacerbation of conflicts over the control of markets, colonies, and spheres of influence. In the years before and after the turn of the century, friction increased in Africa, Asia, the Americas, the Middle East, and the Balkans.

At century's end, then, Great Britain was no longer the sole, unrivaled, and hegemonic world power, nor was it any longer the only beating heart of European industrialization. Although Britain preserved its supremacy in the colonial, naval, commercial, and financial spheres, it began to feel growing competition from the increasingly efficient industrial systems of the emerging powers, especially within the new powerful and dynamic sectors of the economy. Conflict with Germany became especially acrimonious, inasmuch as the rise of this new industrial colossus was taking place in the heart of Europe and therefore immediately began to undermine the carefully poised equilibrium instituted during the Bismarck era.[2]

The German push to broaden its sphere of influence in Europe and in the colonies was the chief destabilizing factor in the European political situation. Germany felt that it was surrounded and hemmed in by the other industrial powers, which had attained industrialization and colonial conquests before Germany. The simultaneous expansion of Japan in Asia and of the United States in Latin America and in the Far East appeared worrisome but peripheral to the chief interests of the traditional European powers. All the same, the political climate, heated up to the point of incandescence because, whether it was a matter of conquering "living space" or defending established positions, all the European powers viewed the conflict as a struggle for national survival.[3]

The European War

The assassination of the prince and heir presumptive to the Austro-Hungarian throne, which took place in Sarajevo in June 1914, was a spark in a powder keg. For years, the military high command of the European states had carefully prepared plans of attack to be implemented immediately upon the outbreak of hostilities. These plans were all based on the element of surprise and rapidity of execution. Similarly, nearly all of the political and military leaders in Europe expected that, once war broke out, it would be a rapid war of maneuver and that victory would therefore belong to whoever managed to mobilize and attack more quickly than his adversary. Upon Austria's declaration of war against Serbia on 28 July 1914, there thus followed within just a few days the intersecting mobilizations and declarations of war of Russia, Germany, Belgium, France, and Great Britain. All agreed that the war would be a short one: "The point about all of these war plans was not merely that they appear, in retrospect, like a line of dominoes which would tumble when the first one fell. What was also important was . . . [t]he notorious miscalculation that the war begun in July/August 1914 would be 'over by Christmas.'"[4]

"You will be home before the leaves have fallen from the trees," the Kaiser had told the troops leaving for the front in the first week of August. In St. Petersburg, the question was not whether or not Russia would win, but only whether it would win in two months or three. A short war of maneuver, therefore, was what all the European strategists had in mind. As in every nation and every era, the generals were preparing to fight the last war.[5]

It was also a war loudly acclaimed by the urban petty bourgeoisie and a war to which many members of the middle classes marched off with a song on their lips, seeing it as the heroic experience of a lifetime. University students enlisted en masse, their heads filled with vital myths of nationalism that hailed war as an intoxicating and purifying ritual, which would spiritually transform both individuals and peoples. The heroic and inebriating war of D'Annunzio, Marinetti's war, "was the sole hygiene of the world." "We love war," wrote Papini in 1914, "and we shall savor it as connoisseurs as long as it lasts."[6]

United States Neutrality

The sudden outbreak of war in Europe and its rapid spread to most European nations, as well as Japan, the Middle East, and the colonies, had a profound impact on American public opinion, which was still psychologically dwelling in the reliable and safe international community of the nineteenth century. Most Americans were profoundly indifferent to the war, which they saw as the product of the deplorable power politics of the European countries; they opted with great determination for neutrality. Wilson personally shared this perspective, and, after the outbreak of hostilities, he urged his fellow citizens, most of whom were of European descent and many of whom still had ties of language, tradition, and emotions with their homelands, to remain impartial—in thought and action—toward the two warring blocs.

America remained neutral for quite a while, until the beginning of April 1917. Its neutrality, however, underwent changes during this period, and from strict neutrality in the early phase of the war, the country progressed to growing involvement in favor of the Triple Entente, to which it sent shipments of arms and raw materials as well as increasing amounts of financial aid.

At the beginning of the war, especially during William Jennings Bryan's term in office as secretary of state (until June 1915), various measures were adopted to preserve an impartial stance toward the two warring blocs. There was, for instance, a prohibition against exporting parts of ships or submarines, as well as a regulation forbidding American banks from making loans to the warring powers. The American government also worked energetically to keep the shipping lanes open to American vessels and goods, in open conflict with the naval blockade that England was attempting to maintain around Europe as well as with the German U-boat war. The naval blockade, was one of the chief elements in Britain's war strategy, and its central objective was to prevent supplies from reaching the Central Powers. As a result, at first, there was a certain degree of friction developed between the United States and England. The British, however, managed to keep that friction from exploding into open differences.

In time, the American government came to accept British control of the open seas and increasingly directed its foreign trade toward the Allied nations. This trend became even more pronounced once Bryan left the State Department. Bryan was replaced as secretary by Robert Lansing, in the aftermath of the sinking of the passenger liner *Lusitania* in May 1915; that event triggered a wave of outrage in American public opinion against the German submarine strategy. The financial business followed the same routes as national exports, and America began to become the warehouse, banker, and arsenal of the Triple Entente. At the same time, American foreign policy increasingly converged with British foreign policy.[7]

Italy and the Treaty of London

When war broke out, Italy hastened to declare neutrality, despite the fact that for some thirty years it had been a member of the Triple Alliance, along with Germany and Austro-Hungary. Formally, Italy justified its decision by stating that the Triple Alliance was an exclusively defensive alliance and accusing Austria of failing to comply with the requirement to provide advance notice in the event the decision was to go to war. Basically, the war had exacerbated disagreements between Italy and Austria, especially because it stimulated the expansionistic ambitions of both countries in the Balkans. Moreover, Italy's "Risorgimental" claims to territories still under Austrian rule remained unresolved and the source of much anger (the "Italia Irredenta" of "Trent and Trieste").

Most Italian parliamentary forces were opposed to intervention. The Giolittians believed that Italy could obtain *parecchio* ("quite a lot") from Austria simply by remaining neutral. Socialists and Catholics were pacifists, though for different reasons. Moreover, many of the leaders of the moderate alliance feared that the state of white-hot social unrest—manifested in all its seriousness by the disorderly mass demonstrations during the "red week" of June 1914—would make a new war full of risks, in the wake of the war that had just been waged for the conquest of Libya.

During the months of neutrality, however, an interventionist front gradually formed in support of the Triple Entente, drawing adherents from all political alliances. This front was made up of groups that ranged from interventionist Socialists and revolutionary union organizers all the way across the spectrum to "irredentists," the so-called democratic interventionists, and the most radical nationalists. The nationalists ultimately succeeded in winning control of the street and seizing dominance over the movement at large.

During the period of neutrality, Italy secretly negotiated with both blocs, attempting to size up the extent of the concessions it could win in exchange for its own intervention in the war. The goal of Italian diplomacy, supervised in this phase by Baron Sidney Sonnino, was to obtain for Italy—a country that had just attained the status of industrial power following a decade of economic development under Giolitti—a rank among the major

European powers. To do so, according to the political ideology then common throughout Europe, meant conquering new territories, new markets, and new colonies. Specifically, the objective was to extend Italy's sphere of influence into the Balkans and across the Mediterranean basin, or at least preserve the status quo, thus averting the risk that the war might lead to a further expansion of the Austrian, French, English, or Russian spheres of influence in those areas. Both the objectives and methods of Italian diplomacy derived from the Bismarckian school of nineteenth-century diplomacy, founded on a balance of power and secret negotiations.

Despite the genuinely "Risorgimental" component in Italy's territorial ambitions, the foreign policy of the liberal-conservatives then in power clearly foreshadowed an emerging Italian imperialism, the product of the country's new industrial might as well as of a vitalist and nationalist cultural climate then spreading rapidly through Europe. This Italian imperialism was relatively feeble and open, however, at least in comparison with the far more solidly based and structured imperialism of France and England, which had already split between them most of the world, or the equally recent but far more aggressive imperialism of the German empire.[8] The recent debut on the international stage of American imperialism, moreover, with its economic and technological superiority and its ideological modernity, rendered obsolete both the goals and methods of all European foreign policies. At the same time, it gave new direction to the political management of the war and the development of international relations.

Italian neutrality ended on 24 May 1915, when the country declared war on the Triple Entente side. One month earlier, the Italian government had signed the Treaty of London with Great Britain, France, and Russia. Those nations had showed great generosity in ceding Austrian territories to Italy as the price for ensuring Italy's almost immediate entry into the war, which they considered crucial at that juncture. The treaty promised Italy a sharp expansion of its northern and eastern boundaries, at the expense of the Austro-Hungarian Empire, in particular, Trentino and Alto Adige all the way to the boundary at the Brenner Pass in the north; Trieste, Istria, a sizable portion of Dalmatia, including Pola, Zara, and Šibenik, but not Spalato (Split), and Vlorë (Valona, in Albania), as well as the Dodecanese, already under Italian occupation, and other possessions, left vague, in Asia Minor and Africa. In the crude, unadorned language typical of the secret diplomacy of the nineteenth-century school, the pact promised Italy a territorial expansion that went well beyond its ethnic boundaries.

Most of the secret pacts that held the two opposing alliances together contained imperialistic objectives very similar to the Italian war aims. The Treaty of London was certainly not the principal treaty, much less the only treaty, that pointed to the imperialistic ambitions of the signatory nations. The Allies had concluded at least ten of these treaties, though only six of them were discussed at the peace conference, since the others had been abrogated by the preceding Treaty of Brest-Litovsk, which established a separate peace between Germany and Russia. Among those treaties, the Treaty of London—which subsequent heated debates with the Allies and in particular with the United States proved by far the most controversial—was not the most ambitious.[9]

Italy, too, expected a short war. This expectation is clearly documented by the minimal size of the loan that Italy requested from England in the Treaty of London: 50 million pounds (compared with the 120 billion pounds that were ultimately spent), a figure that was sufficient to cover the country's credit requirements for just a few months of war.[10] At the time, the war was expected to be not only brief in duration, but also so contained that it would not substantially alter the balance of European power. Fiume (Rijeka), for instance, had not been included in the list of Italian demands because its role as a port was considered to be essential for the kingdom of Croatia and therefore for the entire Austro-Hungarian interior. Moreover, all the boundaries that Italy demanded were meant to establish easily defended frontiers or ports useful to control of the Adriatic Sea in the context of an entirely anti-Austrian defense posture. The Italian negotiators' political scenario had no conception of the possibility of the dismemberment, and therefore, disintegration of the Austro-Hungarian Empire.

Italy's intervention was not simply a cold-blooded decision on the part of the Italian government, which had evaluated the costs and benefits of that decision primarily in terms of the territorial expansion it offered. Intervention was also being demanded by a vast campaign carried on by interventionists in the streets and piazzas of all Italy. The interventionists were in the minority, but, in part because their position tended to coincide with decisions the government had already reached, they conveyed the impression that they had brought about Italy's entry into the war by popular acclaim, in the face of an apathetic parliament, as indecisive as it was indifferent. Vitalism and irrationalism—which had developed rapidly in the years just prior to and after the turn of the twentieth century and were signs of a widespread malaise afflicting much of the Italian petty bourgeoisie, threatened by the complications attendant to Italy's slow and problematic industrial development—acquired new strength and contributed decisively to the most extreme nationalism.

Mass demonstrations in May 1915 were hailed by the nationalists as a signpost of the new Italy then coming into existence, freeing itself from the constraints of a fifty-year period that had been devoid of ideals. The nationalists envisioned the war as a revolutionary act. According to the account written by the historian Guglielmo Ferrero in that period, it was as if an avalanche of hatred had burst down onto Giolitti and the parliamentary system with whom Giolitti was identified. And suddenly, the entire edifice of the Giolittian system—which had governed Italy successfully for more than a decade, providing economic progress and considerable social stability—collapsed. The interventionist line prevailed, even though it was opposed not only by Giolitti and the Italian parliament, but the Socialists, the Vatican, and the majority of the Italian people as well.[11]

A Long War of Exhaustion

Lightning war, that is, a war brought quickly to a conclusion through skillful maneuvering and rapid, overwhelming victories by military strategists, was a short-lived dream. Soon enough, the conflict froze into place along miles and miles of unmovable trenches.[12] Neither side was capable of inflicting rapid defeat on the other. Consequently, it became clear that victory would fall to the bloc with greater economic strength, superior organization, and greater capacity for long-term endurance; the side better able to produce and deliver the enormous flow and assortment of resources demanded by the brutal forge of war would prevail. The economic front, the front for planning national mass production and distribution, became a second front, backing up and reinforcing the military front.

It was in the economic front that American power began to manifest itself. The United States represented a crucial reservoir of resources; it was able to supply vast quantities of foodstuffs, raw materials for energy and industrial production, weapons and munitions, as well as the financial credit to make the necessary purchases. It was here that the fundamental strategic importance of the control of the seaways became clear—control that the British navy managed to maintain throughout the war, in the face of the increasingly menacing attacks by German submarines. Despite American neutrality and efforts to maintain an equal distance between the two warring sides, the United States increased exports to the Allies at a dizzying pace, while its exports to the Central Powers dwindled to a negligible trickle. The United States became the supply center of the Allied war effort.

Contrary to all predictions, then, the war proved to be long and all-encompassing; it became a war of exhaustion that demanded and devoured all human and material resources available. Each warring nation was transformed into an enormous war-making machine controlled by the state, a machine that drew the entire population into its workings, even the rural outliers that had traditionally been excluded from the national political life. Millions of soldiers and immense quantities of resources were poured into the European fronts in a destructive struggle that, especially after the first few years, seemed to feed on itself parasitically, in a manner that defied all logic.

During the war and in part "by virtue" of the war, a new mass society emerged in Europe. For many of Europe's infantrymen, this was a traumatic transition from the preindustrial reality of the countryside to the collective, impersonal, and merciless reality of the trenches. For them, the emerging mass society took form, first and principally, in the uniformity of the two sides, locked in combat, and in the atrocious universe of the vast cemeteries of war. For everyone, soldiers and civilians alike, the war meant subordinating individual needs and ambitions to the domestic and international goals of the nation. The "minimal state" idealized and advocated by liberal ideology vanished and transformed itself into its opposite: the planned state par excellence, the greatest conceivable collective organizer. Few spheres of daily life fell outside of state control: not only did wartime production and military operations come under its jurisdiction, but the state also dictated the percentage of white flour to be used in making bread, controlled the press, and even censored the mail of private citizens. At the same time, public opinion, though subject to repression, still expanded its realm, and the experience of war—through the changes and the very demands that it posed on a daily basis—expanded the horizon of the masses and transformed subjects into citizens who demanded a greater say in the political management of the country.

In the face of this profound transformation of society, the leadership of the European liberal classes soon demonstrated its inadequacy. It was incapable of orienting such an expansive public opinion. Both at the war front and in the country, the leadership's watchwords no longer had any impact on the masses, while its conduct of the war remained elitist and based essentially on repression.[13] As the conflict dragged on, the European ideological void became increasingly evident, a desert landscape over which the new stars of Wilson and Lenin were about to rise.

Economic Warfare

In a war of exhaustion, each belligerent nation's capacity to resist was measured primarily in terms of its productive potential. Measured in that way, Italy and the United States were clearly different. Quite soon, Italy found itself depending on supplies from the United States for its wheat, steel, armaments, and other essential goods. The Italian manufacturing base fell far short of its American counterpart. This aspect is of particular importance because it casts light not only on how the war was conducted, but also on the differences between the two civil societies that lay behind the political leaders of the two countries.

First and foremost, we should remember that both countries began their industrialization process belatedly, for the most part arriving with the second wave of the industrial revolution in the last decades of the nineteenth century. Prior to that time and as a premise to that development, both Italy and the United States had experienced a painful process of domestic unification: Italy's wars for independence and unification, and the U.S. Civil War. Both nations had had to deal with the thorny and complex problems of unifying a more modern North that was oriented toward industrialization with an agrarian and culturally traditional South. The phenomenon of the transoceanic flows of migration in the decades prior to and following the turn of the twentieth century had also affected both countries on a massive scale, though in opposite ways.

The similarities end here, however. Instead, we should attribute more importance to the vast differences in the respective processes of development. American industrialization had been a broad-ranging process, nourished by an abundance of raw materials and a plentiful flow of manpower and capital, as well as a vast domestic market. Once industrialization was underway on this broad productive foundation, the flywheel of manufacturing began to spin at increasing velocity and, thanks to the existence of virtuous circles, in just a few decades the United States had become the world's leading industrial power. Suffice it to consider that in 1901 steel production by the United States Steel Corporation alone was equal to England's entire production, or that in 1913 energy consumption from modern fuels in the

United States was equal to that of England, Germany, France, Russia, and Austria-Hungary combined.[14] The flourishing growth of the American industrial sector went hand in hand with the presence of a modern and strongly competitive agricultural sector, as well as a vast and efficient sector of transportation and communications, fed by sizable flows of foreign investment. As early as the late nineteenth century, American hyperproductivity began to flood the domestic and international markets with cheap merchandise: the United States balance of trade, which became positive in those years, remained in surplus until 1971, a year that American public opinion viewed as the end of an era.[15]

In comparison with the scale and energy of the American process of industrialization, the Italian picture is far less easy. Even though economic development did lift Italy out of a general situation of underdevelopment and chronic stagnation and transformed the country into a significant presence on the European stage, Italian industrialization had to reckon with strong structural obstacles, and it succeeded in overcoming those limitations only in part. Its scarcity of raw materials and capital, combined with the limitations of the domestic market, made it possible to only partially exploit the vast domestic reservoir of manpower; it was from this point onward that mass emigration became an Italian phenomenon. Industrial growth was thus limited, both qualitatively and quantitatively. Crucial sectors were able to develop only with massive state protection in the form of contracts, funding, and tariffs or with the assistance of foreign patents, know-how, entrepreneurship, and capital, especially from Germany. The gap between north and south, moreover, far from mending, grew and became the foundation for the power bloc comprised of Italy's northern bourgeoisie and southern agricultural interests, a bloc that dominated so much of Italian history. An underdeveloped agricultural sector primarily served the interests of social and political stabilization. Modernization of the economy and of society was therefore left unfinished. The old and the new intertwined in various ways in different zones of the peninsula. Even the postunification governing class reflected this dualism in its personnel: alongside the liberalism and enlightened reformism of the more advanced sectors, there was the dead weight of the backward conservatism of agrarian landowners, bureaucrats, and industrialists working in the sectors that enjoyed state protection.[16]

All these elements led to sharp differences in the rates of growth of the two national economies: in the period from 1870 to 1913, for instance, the gross national product grew at an average annual rate of 1.4 percent in Italy and 4.3 percent in the United States, while the figures for annual growth of productivity per worker were, respectively, 0.8 percent and 1.9 percent.[17] Thus, "Although Italy marginally entered the listings of Great Powers, . . . every other of these powers had two or three times its industrial muscle; some (Germany and Britain) had sixfold the amount, and one (the United States) over thirteen times."[18]

The differences that emerged between Italian society and American society prior to and following the turn of the century were considerable. In those years the two countries reached a high point of divergence. America was a wealthy, dynamic society in a state of continuous expansion, a society that had already reached the stage of mass consumerism. In contrast, Italy, although it was developing, remained unable to pass through certain bottlenecks and could only partly rid itself of the burdensome heritage of its history.

Statistics document the differences. Let us take a look at several statistics that provide a cross section of the two countries, in both economic and social terms. First, Italian per capita income was $108 in 1914, while American per capita income, at $377, was triple that amount. The urban population as a percentage of total population in 1913 was 11.6 percent in Italy and 23.1 percent in the United States. That same year, the per capita rate of industrialization, if English industrialization in 1900 was 100, was 26 for Italy and 126 for the United States. Total energy consumption (expressed as millions of metric tons of coal and equivalent) was 11 for Italy and 541 for the colossus on the far shore of the Atlantic Ocean. This gap is not surprising when we consider that American standards of living before the war were the highest in the world and that certain consumer goods, which would not become common in Europe until after the war, were already widely used in America. For instance, in the United States there were already 18 million electric lightbulbs in 1902, 902,000 automobiles registered in 1912 and 8 million in 1920 (Italy had barely 20,000 registered automobiles in 1917), and 10 million telephones in 1914.[19]

Similarities and differences characterized the field of education as well. In Italy, the illiteracy rate as documented during wartime conscription was very high: a whopping 33 percent compared with 6.8 percent in France and the astonishingly low 0.1 percent in Germany.[20] The Italian statistic reflected primarily the social underdevelopment of the countryside. Surprisingly, we find a similarly high percentage in the wealthy American society: there was an illiteracy rate of 31 percent among young people between the ages of 21 and 31 called to arms in 1917—1918.[21] In America, too, then, broad swaths of the population (rural population in the southern states, ethnic minorities, recently arrived immigrants) were still being largely left out of the process of economic growth and social modernization. The most substantial social difference between the two countries, as we will see in greater depth in the following chapter, lay in the vast and well-to-do American urban middle class that served as the context for the Progressive Era. That class had fed the substantial increase in secondary education that went hand in hand with economic development: the number of public high schools in America, for instance, rose from 160 to 6,000 between 1870 and 1900.[22]

Italy up to Caporetto

The years 1916 and 1917 were especially difficult war years in Italy. Instead of the short war that had been expected, the conflict had turned into a grueling war of position, with no end in sight. It demanded a tremendous price, in terms of both the country's productive effort and human lives, in the continuous and futile offensives launched against machine guns and barbed wire. It truly seemed like a "perfect abattoir."[23] The casualty lists of the dead, wounded, mutilated, and missing grew longer and longer. In May 1917 alone, the Italian army lost more than 127,000 men, either dead or wounded. At the same time, there was a glaring increase of crimes committed by soldiers, such as insubordination, desertion, mutiny, and intentional self-mutilation, with a corresponding escalation in the harshness of repression in its crudest forms, such as execution by firing squad, with many summary executions and even a few savage decimations. The upper ranks of the Italian army apparently believed that the soldiers' bravery and initiative would be proportional to the ferocity with which they were treated.[24]

A widespread and powerful sense of lurking discontent pervaded the countryside as well. Basic necessities were running scarce, and popular unrest often manifested itself in the long lines for foodstuffs. Opposition to the war thus broke out into small and spontaneous explosions, often under the leadership of women. It was like "a continuous creeping succession of brushfires," culminating in the full-fledged revolt of Turin in August 1917.[25] That same month, to the shock of the liberal class then in power, the pope described the war as "a useless slaughter."[26]

The governing class, frightened by the social situation that appeared to be teetering on the brink of collapse, managed no better response than an increased crackdown and further repression.[27] The governing class was completely unfamiliar with the use of propaganda, taken in its broader sense as an attempt to involve the subordinate classes in the war and to explain Italy's war on an international stage. Sonnino, in particular, was unflaggingly opposed to propaganda and managed, with his skepticism, to paralyze the three governments that ruled Italy in succession during the First World War. The chief of staff, General Cadorna, shared that opinion and never understood, for instance, the benefits of allowing foreign journalists to report from the front. Those foreign journalists might have helped to generate an understanding and appreciation of the Italian war effort in the international, and especially American, public arenas. Instead, journalists were met with open hostility, and only a very few managed to secure permission to go to the Italian front. This is how an American journalist commented on the behavior of the Italians in early 1917:

> They [the Italians] are only just commencing to realize the political value of our national maxim: "It pays to advertise." . . . Instead of welcoming neutral correspondents and publicists, they have, until very recently, met them with suspicion and hindrances. What little news is permitted to filter through is coldly official, and is altogether unsuited for American consumption. The Italians are staging one of the most remarkable and inspiring performances that I have seen on any front—a performance of which they have every reason to be proud—but diffidence and conservatism have deterred them from telling the world about it.[28]

In part because of this introverted and mistrustful attitude, the Italian government soon faced, along with the growing domestic instability, increasing difficulties first with their European allies and later with the United States. In 1916–1917 Italy was suffering from a profound and deepening political isolation within the Allied coalition. The danger of this isolation had been present at the outbreak of the war, when Italy seemed to have sold its intervention to the highest bidder and to have thus abandoned, out of mere self-interest, its traditional partners in the Triple Alliance. That isolation was destined to grow. On the one hand, the European Allies were increasingly disappointed by Italy's contribution to the war, and on the other hand, the intervention of the United States was diminishing Italy's contribution to the war and pushing the Allies to feel less and less willing to pay the "price" agreed upon in 1915 with the Treaty of London.

The American intervention had also shifted the conflict onto a more ideological plane, making Italian territorial aspirations appear to be far more out of tune with the emerging values, and seemingly deplorable because of the aggression against nations struggling for independence from the Austro-Hungarian Empire. The Italian liberal-conservative coalition's narrow and mistrustful political management of the war only deepened this isolation, practically glorifying it with slogans such as "sacred selfishness" or "our war"—as if the Italian war against Austria was only tangentially linked to the Allied war against Germany. Italy's slogans were not likely to win points with American public opinion, much less with Wilson. Nitti recalled his awkward embarrassment in answering the first question that Wilson asked him during their meeting in America in the spring of 1917: "Exactly what does the expression 'Sacro Egoismo' ('Sacred Selfishness') mean?"[29] In reality, the idealistic and emotional reasons that prompted much of the Italian bourgeoisie's support for the war were never known or understood in America. The Americans only knew about the motives of the Italian governing class, expressed in the chilly language of secret agreements.[30]

In comparison with the American ally, there was a disconnect linked to the respective belligerent states. In the United States, while public opinion was strongly opposed to autocratic Germany, the attitude was one of indifference, if not veiled sympathy, for the Hapsburg Empire, viewed romantically as emblematic of the old European courts. The Italians, in contrast, felt no special hostility toward Germany, the ally of their recent economic development, but they saw the Italian territories still under Austrian dominion as one of the chief motives for Italy's declaration of war. It followed that Italy was late in declaring war on Germany (August 1916), as was the United States' declaration of war on the Hapsburg Empire (December 1917). Therefore, even after both nations entered the war, public opinion and the governing classes in the two countries were moving on different political and emotional planes.

In any case, Italy's isolation was also due to structural factors. It was a newcomer in the narrow circle of the leading European nations, and the established industrial powers were hardly pleased to witness an expansion of Italy's sphere of influence—at their expense—in the Mediterranean, in the Balkans, or in Asia Minor. This had been the root cause of Italy's growing difficulties with Austria-Hungary within the Triple Alliance, but it was also the source of discord with the countries of the Triple Entente. The ambiguous attitudes of Italy's leading allies toward the Austro-Hungarian Empire (consider, for instance, their secret attempts to broker a separate peace with the empire) accentuated Italy's suspicions and misunderstandings. From this point of view as well, the United States' entry into war had only increased the difficulties facing Italy. Almost until the summer of 1918, Wilson continued to hope to broker a separate peace with the Austro-Hungarian Empire and, with this goal in mind, continued to encourage bilateral negotiations. It is easy to imagine how threatened Sonnino must have felt by the prospect of such a peace, established between Italy's chief enemy and an ally that proved to be so profoundly alien to the idea of recognizing Italy's territorial ambitions. Sonnino responded with a stubborn attachment to the Treaty of London, which he considered the sole certainty in such a dangerous and confusing international setting.

In this sense, the Italian war, fought primarily against Austria, and the American war, waged principally against Germany, were two parallel wars. Not only were the enemies different, but the rhetoric and the emotions tied up with the state of war were quite distant as well, as was the vision of the international situation that would emerge from the war. The policies of both countries were discordant, and, given the lack of effort to harmonize these policies, they moved blindly along a fateful collision course.

The military situation, too, mirrored Italy's growing isolation. Especially after the United States entered into the war and Russia withdrew from the conflict, the main focus of military action became the western front. Contrary to the Italians' growing hopes and expectations, Wilson refused to commit part of the two million U.S. soldiers who landed in France to the Italian front. Italy was considered to be on the sidelines of the main event, and, correspondingly, Italy showed only a secondary interest in events on the French front. Thus, during 1917, the Anglo-Franco-American management of the war was accentuated, a result also of the new ally's greater familiarity with its two major European partners.[31]

Gradually, during the period of American neutrality, Wilson had acquired international stature as a defender of the rights of neutral nations and, later, as a mediator among the contending powers. In the face of the barbaric senselessness of the war, in whose coils Europe seemed to be ineluctably wrapped, Wilson had attempted to preserve a role as a nonpartisan referee, as a guarantor and protector of the highest values of western civilization. He unfailingly attempted to preserve a stance of clear-eyed impartiality. For instance, he refused to listen to reports or read articles about German atrocities in Belgium or about the horrors of submarine warfare, subjects that had so greatly influenced the emotional involvement of the American public.[32]

Wilson's last effort to reconcile the warring blocs came just shortly before the American declaration of war. In December 1916, immediately following his reelection to a second term as president, in an attempt to broker a peace, he had asked the two alliances to state specifically their war aims. Since his message came just a few days after a similar move by the Central Powers, and since those powers had just conquered territory and strongholds along all fronts, the Allies looked askance upon Wilson's initiatives, and, after feverish meetings in Rome, they responded to his request with a terse note declining his offer to mediate. In reality, both blocs were committed to the annihilation of the enemy, not a compromise peace, and certainly not a "peace without victory," as Wilson had proposed.[33]

German recourse to unlimited submarine warfare beginning at the end of January 1917 and the ensuing torpedoing of a number of American ships brought the situation to a head. America broke off diplomatic relations with Germany and issued an ultimatum declaring that it would no longer accept the sinking without warning of American ships or the ships of other neutral nations. This led quickly to a U.S. declaration of war against Germany on 6 April 1917.

Ideological War

If the Great War was the watershed between the nineteenth century and the twentieth century, 1917 was the turning point of the war itself. In 1917 the war changed face. The intervention of the United States transformed the European conflict into a world war, putting an end at the same time to Europe's traditional centrality. Moreover, this event and the simultaneous Russian Revolution shifted the war onto a more ideologically driven plane: it was as if a third front had opened, running parallel to the military and economic fronts—the front of propaganda and mass politics. The year 1917 was therefore a revolutionary year—not in Russia alone but around the world. In order to respond to the domestic transformation that the war had accelerated, such as the growing politicization of the masses, and in order to offset the powerful appeal of the Soviet regime to broad sectors of the civilian and combatant population, all the western governing classes were obliged to change their watchwords and their political style. At times the change was purely superficial; at other times it was more substantial.

Wilson and America, in addition to massive economic and military aid, offered the contents and techniques of a new liberal-democratic form of mass politics. Wilson was the great propagandist of the Allied front, the only one capable of halting the ideological avalanche emerging from eastern Europe.

In the last few days of October 1917, a vigorous Austrian offensive managed to break through the Italian front near the small town of Caporetto. The Italian retreat lasted more than two weeks, until a new front could be organized along the banks of the river Piave. At that point, the entire Friuli region and the eastern portion of the Veneto fell into Austrian hands, and the loss of men, weapons, and materiel seriously undermined Italian military potential.[34] The defeat was a brutal shock to the Italian governing class, which feared not only that the defeat would prove fatal and definitive, but also that the Italian masses might *fare come in Russia* ("do as in Russia")— that is, transform the military rout into a social revolution.[35] The fear was not unfounded. As Leo Valiani observed, "the only moment in which a revolutionary uprising would have been objectively possible in Italy, during the war, was after Caporetto."[36]

More than the American intervention of the preceding April, the defeat of Caporetto marked a turning point in the Italian war. Domestically, it obliged the governing class to recognize the dangers of a thoroughly antiquated leadership. The defeat proved that it was impossible to lead a mass army with only discipline and repression: both soldiers and civilians needed ideals that could motivate them. Similarly, the gap between the masses and the governing leadership had to be reduced, if there was to be any hope of preventing military collapse and social revolt. Caporetto, then, obliged the governing class to attain a rapid new awareness and an equally rapid change of course. Caporetto thus marked the beginning of an overdue rethinking of relations between government and the governed, an attempt to heal over that age-old division between governing class and popular political base that the first years of the war had only served to worsen. The Orlando administration—which replaced the Boselli government at the end of October 1917, just as the first reports were arriving of the collapse of the front at Caporetto—managed to deal with the emergency by assembling the support of diverse social and political forces and issuing a number of orders that pointed to a change of direction. Among them were replacement as supreme commander of Cadorna by Diaz, who arranged for a number of social benefits to be made available to the soldiers (life insurance, improvement of rations and shifts, more frequent leaves, bonuses and subsidies for the families, etc.); encouragement of the development of agencies for assistance and civilian propaganda; and formulation of a foreign policy that would be more in tune with that of the Allies, at least during the difficult months until the summer of 1918.[37]

Propaganda, hitherto overlooked, if not rejected, by the Italian political and military leadership surged impetuously into the programs of the government and the new Comando Supremo (Italian chiefs of staff). In the context of government makeup, Romeo Gallenga Stuart was put in charge of foreign propaganda, while Ubaldo Commandini was made the director of domestic propaganda. Throughout Italy there sprang up, both spontaneously and through the efforts of central and local authorities, a myriad of patriotic and relief committees (such as the Opere Federate, Unione Generale degli Insegnanti, Opera Nazionale Invalidi di Guerra, and various other charitable institutions and associations for civilian relief). In the months following Caporetto, a structure was organized at the front that was devoted exclusively to generating propaganda among the troops (the so-called *Uffici "P"*). Among this welter of initiatives designed to motivate the social political base and to join it more closely to the governing class, the white-collar, intellectual, and professional petty bourgeoisie acquired a new and crucial role as a social link. This was largely the same urban petty bourgeoisie that had been so interventionist in 1915 but that over the long years of trench warfare had lost both its enthusiasm and sense of social influence that had been one of the especially intoxicating elements of the *maggio radioso*, or radiant May of 1915, as noted above. The propaganda initiatives that were developed as a reaction to Caporetto restored to this class a crucial function in society: a role of apostleship toward the demoralized masses, who were now easy targets of pacifist, subversive, or Bolshevik propaganda. It was precisely this attempt to repair the ideological bonds between government and nation that was initiated in the wake of Caporetto, with its emphasis on the role of the petty bourgeois intermediate cadres. This marked the beginning of a new phase of Italian politics, though with all the contradictions that Fascism displayed soon thereafter.[38]

In the field of international relations, in the first phase of the Orlando government and again as a reaction to Caporetto, an attempt was made to bring Italy's war goals into line with those of the Allies. The most important initiative was the Congress of Nationalities Oppressed by Austria-Hungary, held in Rome in April 1918, which briefly kindled hopes that Italy might become the spokesman for the peoples struggling for independence from the Hapsburg Empire. This initiative, carried on in a less-than-straightforward manner, petered out. Orlando supported it "unofficially," while Sonnino, who opposed it, remained firmly in control of Italy's foreign policy. Sonnino's stubbornness lay at the core of the Italian problem: social instability, the fragility of the governing coalitions, and international isolation kept Italy from participating in the general, continentwide shift of the domestic political alignment from the conservative wing to the liberal wing of the governing alliance, from the so-called forces of order to the forces of mobility, which took place during the course of 1917 in the leading European nations.[39] This shift in ideals led to an accentuation in liberal rhetoric, stimulated by the radical changes that had occurred on the international stage. As for how it affected Italy, however, it meant that the language, methods, and objectives of its foreign policy would appear increasingly tone-deaf with respect to the new ideals that were sweeping through the western world. All of this was developing at a time when a broader public opinion, expanded by the effects of the war, was establishing itself as one of the forces of political orientation of European societies. The Italian liberal class proved its historical obsolescence precisely in its inability to grasp the depth of the changes that the war brought about in the domestic social field and in the international political arena. With immense shortsightedness, that class continued to fight with outmoded weapons to obtain a choicer position for their country in the context of a system of power destined to decline.

Bipolarism between the United States and the USSR Begins

Where Italian American relations were concerned, Caporetto provoked the U.S. declaration of war against Austria-Hungary (December 1917), together with a vast activation of the American system of humanitarian relief and propaganda, which we will analyze soon. All the same, despite repeated requests from both Italian politicians and American representatives in Italy, Washington did not respond to the Italian crisis by sending troops. Throughout the war, Wilson chose to concentrate the American army on the French front. Even in the summer of 1918, when the American army was millions strong, with nearly two million men already in France, the United States sent to Italy only Red Cross and YMCA aid, a cluster of propagandists, and a handful of soldiers who toured Italy for propaganda purposes. The twofold response of material aid and propaganda allowed the American leaders to help their distant ally to overcome what they saw as a basic collapse of morale without becoming too deeply involved in a war being fought for questionable aims.

Thus, in 1918 the Italian and American governing classes joined forces to spread propaganda among the demoralized and often hostile Italian masses, putting off to a more tranquil future any discussion of their conflicting war aims.[40] The Italian governing class soon discovered the power that the myth of America and Wilson exercised over the common folk and exploited it fully in order to create consent and to increase the Italians' stamina and resistance. Numerous local and national committees now began to spread Wilson's words among soldiers and civilians. Even the conservatives, frightened by the specter of the Bolshevik revolution, began to borrow Wilson's attractive formulations. For nearly a year, various components of Italian society—some in all sincerity, others opportunistically—adopted the Wilsonian credo.

Over the course of 1918 in Italy the press, the political world, and public opinion in general became increasingly focused on the new and powerful ally. In less than a year the distant and unreliable partner had become the symbol of the ideals of freedom and democracy for which the European peoples were fighting.[41] This phenomenon, though in part spontaneous, was largely the creation of a new force that was emerging in that period: propaganda.

American intervention in the war therefore provided the western bloc not only with military and economic assistance that appeared to be limitless, but more importantly with powerful weapons for ideological warfare. The Allies had urgent need of those weapons. Never as keenly as at war's end did the new society that the war had forced into being require more modern political tools and relations between those who governed and those who were governed. In Italy, "for the first time, great masses of working-class people, along with considerable sectors of the middle class, finally emerged from a centuries-old state of passivity, expressing their own orientations and ideals in forms that were, perhaps, muddled, but certainly autonomous and positive. Wilson and Lenin, in keeping with an impulse that is anything but new to give concrete form to historical phenomena by identifying them with major personalities, were the two points of reference in which the rejection of the old pre-war world joined with aspirations for a new society."[42]

Mass warfare demanded a mass ideology. As the historian Guglielmo Ferrero observed at the time, the armies that had been facing off for years along miles of unmovable trenches appeared to be "millions of bayonets in search of an idea."[43] During 1917, new ideals and foreign myths came to fill the European ideological vacuum: in a short period of time, Wilson and Lenin—democratic America and revolutionary Russia—became the ideological poles of the war. In Italy, in particular, on the basis of still-fragmentary reports that were arriving from Russia, since the spring the myth of Lenin had been spreading through the trenches and behind the lines. As in other European countries, Wilson' s democratic message and the nascent myth of America proved to be the sole ideological barrier capable of stemming the crashing propagandistic wave sweeping in from revolutionary Russia.

The decline of Europe, then, was not only military or economic in nature, but also primarily ideological. It was at that point that Russian and American bipolarism began on a global level and went on to characterize the history of the twentieth century, until our most recent past. Western Europe, until then the center of the world, remained compressed and marginalized between the two new colossi. The European liberal class lost its ideological wartime leadership. Even in the crucial realm of ideologies, Europe lost its supremacy, handing it over to the two hegemonic powers of the twentieth century in an apparently lasting manner. This planetary bipolarism developed in 1917, when a new phase, not just of the war, but of contemporary history, began. It was a phase that encompassed nearly the whole century, lasting at least until the fall of the Berlin Wall.

Propaganda was the chief product of the shift in direction of the war that came in the spring of 1917 with American intervention and the Russian Revolution. On this new front, the American liberal-democratic message and the Soviet credo competed with each other to win the support of those masses whom the war had suddenly hurled onto the national and world political stage. Within a few months, Wilson and Lenin became the new stars in the international spotlight, and their personalities rapidly took on the characteristics of myths.

— 3 —

Woodrow Wilson, World Leader

The Wilson presidency (1913–1921) witnessed the rise and rapid fall of the Progressive movement. Wilson won office with the votes of a coalition that brought together Progressives from a variety of political affiliations, and during his first term Wilson's political platform was responsive to many of the hopes of Progressive reformers. In Wilson's second term, however, once the United States entered the war, the domestic reform movement was almost entirely abandoned, though it was in part rechanneled into the zeal that so many Americans expressed for the undertaking to make the world "safe for democracy." The experience of the war itself, however, with the intolerance and irrationalism that it generated, dealt a fatal blow to enlightened rationalism and the Progressive reform movement. As Diner points out, the war first co-opted the Progressive movement and in the end destroyed it.[1] The "age of innocence" was over. When the reformist spirit finally reappeared, it took the more pragmatic and concrete form of the New Deal. This is not to say that Progressivism failed to exert a powerful influence on American politics throughout the Wilson presidency. Indeed, we must understand the Progressive movement if we hope to grasp the spirit in which America launched its first international crusade. In particular, it was often Progressives who worked on behalf of Wilson's "missionary" propaganda. Just as frequently, it was individuals with Progressive beliefs who took part in the Italian campaign of 1918.

In the decades prior to American intervention in the world war, years of substantial and growing prosperity, a groundswell of civil engagement and reformist fervor swept over the United States in the period known as the

Progressive Era. Progressivism, more than other phenomena of the period, opened a window onto the social transformations that accompanied the tumultuous growth of American industry. Not only was Progressivism a distinctly urban movement, mirroring the growth of American cities and, in those cities, a broad-based and vigorous middle class, but also its leadership and membership, means, and goals were all indicators of the great modernity of American society in the broad dissemination by the press, the presence of mass labor unions, and women's emancipation movements, as well as the various forms of grassroots democracy. This distinctly American social background we should be compared with the sharply differing context of Italian society at the turn of the century. This difference in social context, more than any other factor, explains the difference in political language and the obstacles to intercultural communication that led to the clash between Wilson and the Italian governing class.

Today historians avoid the term *Progressive movement* primarily because so many diverse components made up the movement.[2] The large array of goals and methods adopted by the different segments of the movement does make it difficult to provide any general definition of Progressivism. The evils that the Progressives hoped to combat and reform were varied and in some cases diametrically opposed. Some considered the unbridled power of monopolies to be the chief problem plaguing the new and developing industrial society, whereas others focused on the corruption that was rife in municipal governments. Yet others targeted the decay and squalor to be found in the slums of large cities or the discrimination and exclusion of minorities or women from political activity. Thus, the movement was a coalition of reform movements, some of which were in open contradiction with each other—for example, the struggle of the labor movement as against the excessive power of the labor unions; the fight against trusts, either on behalf of free-market individualism and competition, or, alternatively, in favor of a more determined government regulation. In brief, this was not a single unified movement. To a certain extent, it was a continuation of the populism of previous decades, and from the Populist movement it inherited the farmer's indignation over the corruption and decadence of the cities. Its center, however, was no longer rural. Its leaders and adherents had a solid urban base. The evangelical revival, too, provided ideas and themes, as did the growing influence of the new social sciences and the rationalism that went with these ideas.

Heterogeneous though it may have been, this political movement still had certain common features. First, it was national in character in a way that very few American reform movements have been. The "Progressive impulse," as some historians suggest calling it, gradually became a prevailing ideology, recruiting adherents from both traditional political affiliations, and the ranks of the Socialists. Moreover, as Hofstadter points out, it was generally an urban, Protestant, Anglo-Saxon, middle-class movement.[3] Its leaders were for the most part journalists, educators, social workers, intellectuals, and professionals of all sorts. Through investigative journalism, public denunciations, civic engagement, and the encouragement of philanthropic and social initiatives, they hoped to combat the most harmful effects of unbridled industrial capitalism and the chaotic and growing new cities. American society was already riddled with glaring contrasts between the wealthy and the poor, natives and immigrants, whites and "colored," in a stark departure from the egalitarian society, which was so much a part of the American myth and which had made such a strong impression on European visitors in the early nineteenth century.

A typical representative of the Progressive movement during Wilson's presidency was the investigative journalist, or "muckraker," who managed to create scandals by digging up news that could help to sell thousands of copies of his or her newspaper. Other typical figures in the movement organized homes for the poor (or settlement houses) in large cities, social workers, or suffragettes. The common objective was to hold up to the purifying and moralizing view of public opinion the darkest and most infamous pockets of the new urban reality: the decay and squalor of the slums, the inhumane exploitation of child and female labor, the corruption of politicians and union leaders, the unbridled power and sybaritic luxury enjoyed by the industrial and financial plutocracy.

The movement was not immune to yearnings for a mythical past characterized by small, independent and egalitarian communities in which representatives of the middle classes had traditionally always played a decisive leadership role. In this aspect, it is easy to identify the struggle of the bourgeoisie to maintain its own social status in a society that was increasingly wedging the middle class between its two opposing but complementary faces: large-scale industry and labor unions on the one hand and mass parties and teeming throngs of immigrants on the other. The movement had a genuinely reformist aspect that did much to mitigate the harshest features of American capitalism and individualism, turning it into something that approached the twentieth-century welfare state.[4]

The social base of the Progressive movement consisted of the traditional middle class, joined by the rapidly expanding "white-collar" class and the urban petty bourgeoisie (technicians and clerks in industry and the services, businessmen and teachers, and so on), whose presence in the total population had increased eightfold (rising from 756,000 to 5.6 million) from 1870 to 1910. In contrast, farmers in the same period had merely doubled in number and laborers had tripled.[5] These classes struggled to maintain and improve their social standing in a rapidly changing society riven with conflict and contrasts, but also a society that was open, wealthy, and offering an array of opportunities, perhaps not for everyone but for many. This diverse economic and social background explains many of the differences in political and cultural attitudes found in the American middle class compared with its European counterpart. Optimism, rationalism, civic engagement, trust in one's fellow man, democracy, and the future were opposed to the irrationalistic, pessimistic, and elitist currents of the European shores of the Atlantic Ocean.

Throughout the western world, the first decades of the twentieth century were a time of insecurity, dissatisfaction, and unrest for the middle classes. The rise in prices that began at the close of the nineteenth century had become one of the distinctive features of the twentieth century, in contrast with the steady price decline that had accompanied the first wave of industrialization and the phase of competitive capitalism during the nineteenth century. Inflation, the dark side of a world of organized interests and swelling concentrations of economic power, was undermining the prosperity and social importance of the petty and middle bourgeoisie. Thus, a sense of precarious vulnerability in terms of one's own social ranking (the "status anxiety" described by Hofstadter) underlay many of the political and cultural attitudes of the end of the nineteenth century.[6] In America, that anxiety took the form of a widespread indignation over social ills and a diverse and warlike reforming impulse, which, however, was perhaps more earnestly concerned with defending the social standing of the reformers than the genuine interests of the subjects of reform. This would also help to explain the partial ineffectuality, contradictions, and inconsistencies of the Progressive movement that have been noted by several historians.[7]

It was especially members of this energetic urban petty and midlevel bourgeoisie that lined up in favor of intervention as war approached and who later worked on behalf of the various forms of wartime assistance and propaganda, much as their European counterparts did. Among them were many Progressives, who brought to their war work their moralistic attitudes, missionary spirit, and slightly naïve trust in the efficacy of reformist intervention. When war came, however, as we have already seen, the radical and reforming impulse was lost, and this phase of American political history came to an end. Not only did the focus shift from the domestic situation to the international stage, but with mobilization repressive measures were introduced and emotional, irrational attitudes were stoked in public opinion, feeding the reactionary hysteria that followed the war.[8] Therefore, Wilson, despite his best intentions, ultimately sapped and defused the impetus of the Progressive movement.

The presidential election of 1912, which carried Wilson to the White House, demonstrated the surprising popularity that Progressive ideas had attained in the country. In fact, three of the four candidates for the presidency—Theodore Roosevelt, Woodrow Wilson, and the Socialist candidate, Eugene Debs—appealed to reformist voters. Even the fourth candidate, the incumbent president, William Taft, would have rejected the label of conservative. Wilson won with less than 42 percent of the total number of votes because the Republican vote split between Roosevelt and Taft. The Socialist candidate Debs, moreover, had received nearly a million votes, signaling an extraordinary moment in U.S. political history.[9] After a long interval (since 1860, with the sole exception of the two Cleveland presidencies), a Democrat became president, as well as a man from the South, though the fact that most voters and the majority of Congress were Republicans created considerable problems for Wilson.

Wilson would have lost the election if the former president, Theodore Roosevelt, had been running alone against him.[10] Roosevelt had been one of the country's most popular presidents and had maintained a strong hold on the hearts of the American public, even during the presidency of his protégé Taft, toward whom he developed a growing sense of hostility and whom Roosevelt saw as increasingly conservative. It was specifically in opposition to Taft and the Old Guard of the Republican Party, once his political home, that Roosevelt in 1912 founded a third party, the Progressive Party, which he hoped would attract Progressive voters from both the Republican and Democratic parties. This move failed because Wilson managed to keep his Democratic electorate while running on a Progressive platform. The two leading candidates were therefore competing for the same shares of public opinion and were running on similar campaign platforms, precisely because each candidate was positioning himself as a progressive. Despite the careful distinctions listed by Arthur Link and John

Milton Cooper, we can agree with Allen White: it was difficult to distinguish between Wilson's New Freedom and Roosevelt's New Nationalism.[11]

Wilson led the United States from 1913 to 1921, eight crucial years in American and world history. For America, this was a period of radical transformations on both the domestic and international stages. Domestically, the Wilson presidency attempted to channel the actions of powerful private interests into the context of a social and political democracy. In this regard, we might mention the creation of the Federal Reserve, social legislation (eight-hour working day, regulation of child labor, etc.), and women's suffrage. On the international stage, Wilson led the American people through the tempest of the Great War, setting aside traditional American isolationism and instead winning leadership of the world liberal-democratic movement.

Wilson's Idealism

"We are in many ways heirs of Woodrow Wilson," states Dutch historian Jan Willem Schulte Nordholt in his fascinating biography of Wilson.[12] The modern world has deep roots in the Wilsonian period. Aside from all the possible misgivings we might have about Wilson as a historic figure, if we wish to understand the origins of the fundamental dynamics of the international system in the twentieth century, we must delve into the key years of his presidency and the characteristics and consequences of U.S. involvement in the European war, and examine both the modernity and limits of his administration's approach to foreign affairs. Wilson was the first western leader to mobilize the masses ideologically; he was the first American president to urge his compatriots to become citizens of the world; he was the first statesman to propose a supranational political organization, the League of Nations; he was one of the chief masterminds behind the map of Europe, which, with all its virtues and defects, was with us for most of the past century.

Wilson led the United States in the transition from its provincialism and isolationism toward international engagement and world political leadership. Yet he himself, much like his country, felt unprepared for the new role. It is often noted that, before moving to the White House, Wilson commented to a friend: "It would be the irony of fate if my administration had to deal chiefly with foreign affairs."[13] His extended academic and scholarly training had made him an expert on the American political system and a chief executive especially well suited to promote domestic reforms, as he did during his first term as president. The world outside of America was outside of his field of interest, as it was for most Americans.

Once international problems surged to the forefront, however, Wilson became the chief strategist of American international action and took direct control over the development of foreign policy, delegating both the secretary of state and the entire American diplomatic corps to the job of carrying out his instructions. The power of his leadership was based principally on the impact that his words seemed to have on American and international public opinion and on the charisma that he managed to project with the rising masses. In the brilliant essays that he had written many years before on the American political system, Wilson had stated that a president's power of leadership was based primarily on his ability to appeal directly to public opinion. If the president wins "the admiration and confidence of the country," he believed, ". . . no single force can withstand him, no combination of forces will easily overpower him."[14] In particular in the field of foreign affairs, he believed that "the initiative . . . , which the president possesses without any restriction whatever, is virtually the power to control them absolutely."[15] As Link has correctly noted, in the field of foreign policy Wilson believed that the president of the United States almost had the powers of an absolute monarch and was answerable not to Congress but only to national public opinion.[16]

Wilson's charismatic hold over public opinion—first in America and later around the world—was one of the most modern characteristics of his role as a political figure. Precisely to obtain the support of public opinion for his program, he broke a tradition that was over a hundred years old by delivering many of his speeches to Congress in person. These speeches were in general short, clear, and delivered in a masterly fashion; they were obviously meant as much for the public as for Congress. The brevity of his messages ensured that they would be quoted in their entirety in the leading daily papers.[17] His closest collaborators, such as his secretary Joseph Tumulty and his adviser Edward House, kept him briefed on the direction of public opinion.[18] Until the end of the war, Wilson's skill at shaping and using public opinion proved to be his most effective tool.

Wilson's idealistic internationalism guided the Americans through the massacre of the Great War. In a very brief period of time, he succeeded in transforming a neutral and isolationist nation into a giant war machine. Mobilization involved most of the national human and material resources.

American soldiers were rapidly equipped, both physically and ideologically, to go to fight in the European trenches. It was a notable undertaking and could never have been accomplished without strong and inspired leadership.

The American intervention provided Wilson with a global stage. His rise as a world leader was closely linked to his skill in providing the demoralized European masses with new, attractive ideals expressed in concise slogans. America wanted to make the world "safe for democracy," fight "a war to end all wars," launch "a people's war" against all the forces of the past that were trying to hinder the advance of democracy. It was with these goals that the United States had entered the war: not out of self-interest but out of pure idealistic and moral necessity. This transformed the U.S. intervention into a crusade for democracy; it put the United States on a different plane from the other warring nations, conferring upon the American president the nonpartisan role of arbiter of the peace.

The Fourteen Points, presented in a speech delivered on 8 January 1918, are a renowned example of Wilson's style of conducting foreign policy and the distinctive characteristics of his international leadership. The political manifesto of the Fourteen Points set out clear, concise, and advanced goals for a war that increasingly appeared to be bloody, interminable, and senseless. It thus helped to stem the ideological offensive being promoted by Soviet Russia, which in that period had launched the watchwords "peace without annexations or indemnities." At the same time, Wilson was attempting to shift the foreign policy of his recalcitrant European partners toward more liberal objectives. The Fourteen Points included five initial points elucidating general principles—international liberalism and free trade (open diplomacy, freedom of navigation, freedom of trade, reduction of armaments, and equitable adjustments of all colonial issues)—followed by eight points involving the disputed territorial questions (restoration of Belgium, restitution of Alsace-Lorraine to France, creation of Poland, Italian frontiers "along clearly recognizable lines of nationality," and so on). The final, fourteenth point, called for the creation of a supranational organization: the League of Nations. The Fourteen Points made a major impact and immediately became the banner of the international liberal-democratic front.

Wilson's powerful influence over public opinion was a product of the idealistic content of his political message. As has been noted, "idealism was the main drive of Wilson's thinking about international relations": its foundations were fundamentally ethical and religious and solidly rooted in American political traditions. The belief that foreign policy should be guided primarily by moral considerations was joined to an equally stalwart faith in democracy, considered to be the most elevated form of government. It was from the Christian optimism of the nineteenth century that Wilson drew his trust in the goodness and perfectibility of man, while social Darwinism provided him with his faith in the superiority of Anglo-Saxon civilization. In his vision of the future, Christian ideals and democracy, once they had triumphed everywhere, would produce a peaceful and enlightened world community.[19]

The League of Nations was intended to be the form of government capable of encouraging and governing this new, more advanced system of cooperation among nations. It became the pivot around which all of Wilson's vision of the postwar world revolved. The first and fundamental objective that Wilson set for himself at Versailles was to persuade his European partners to accept the central role of the new international organization in the very language of the peace treaty. For him this was the only tool capable of resolving the inevitable compromises, wrongs, and mistakes that might emerge from the peace negotiations, carried out in an atmosphere still ridden with violent hatreds and bellicose nationalisms.

The concept of the League of Nations made Wilson one of the most forward-thinking and innovative statesmen of the twentieth century, but it also revealed the limitations of his political method. Why on earth, one wonders, did Wilson—who fully understood the vital importance of the role the League of Nations would play in the world that was emerging from the war—fail to properly prepare American and international public opinion for this project? As Knock acknowledges, "Yet his effort was much too little, much too late."[20] In Italy, too, where he implemented a vast propaganda campaign, the subject of the League of Nations remained marginal to the glorification of the image of American society and the American president. During the war years, Wilson seems to have kept the project in his vest pocket for the time of peace: a tool to be presented in the aftermath of the war, not a driving idea with which to appeal to the imagination of the masses during the actual conflict. The path to achieving this dream ran straight through the field of his personal leadership, not through the pressure of world public opinion.

In general, Wilson put off too many problems until the peace conference. In his relations with the Italian political class as well, we find the same stance: he postponed the solution of thorny territorial problems until the peace conference. By this time, in the wake of victory, the nationalists' appetites had become far more voracious, and Wilson was gradually beginning to lose his aura as the savior of civilization and peacemaker.[21]

Thus, Wilson found himself dealing with knotty problems and launching crucial initiatives at the very moment when he had the least power both at home and abroad. His supporters, too, came to the moment of peace with insufficient preparation: the international system that they hoped to bring out of the war had not been sufficiently developed, negotiated, or popularized. Thus, Wilson found himself in deeper and deeper trouble, not only because his opponents were growing stronger, but also because his supporters had no clear strategy with which to oppose their adversaries. The democratic, peaceful, open world that was supposed to be born out of the war still had excessively vague outlines, and in the diverse realities of the European nations, it was unclear who would carry that world forward.

The last, but certainly not the least important, element of Wilson's internationalism had to do with the role the United States had been summoned to play on the international stage. He believed that America was a unique nation, the vanguard of humanity: whatever happened in the United States prefigured and influenced what would follow in the rest of the world. Moreover, he believed that his country occupied a special place in the historical implementation of divine plans: "Providence has presided over our affairs with a strange indulgence," he had written in 1893.[22] Naturally, as a people chosen by God, Americans had certain great responsibilities, a veritable mission to be achieved in the context of universal history. The American nation was destined to become the messenger of freedom, the model of democracy, the champion of peace and progress throughout the world.

Placing the United States on so much higher a plane than all the other nations, however, did nothing to encourage cooperation, especially with countries that were culturally different. Wilson's diplomacy, superb in its enunciation of principles and general objectives, was very poor in the more prosaic arts of dialogue and compromise. As a result, mutual mistrust and ignorance prevailed, and rendering the political dialogue especially difficult, in some cases impossible. Thus, Wilsonian exceptionalism, which was nothing more than a special kind of nationalism, wound up hindering the internationalist component of his program.[23]

As far as relations with European nations were concerned, the ambiguity of Wilson's attitude began to insinuate itself into the very first efforts at mediation between the two opposing blocs. Detectable from the very beginning and later quite evident during the peace negotiations was that the American president did not consider himself *unus inter pares* (one among equals) but instead aspired to a position *super partes* (above all parties) for himself and his country—the judge's role due to American moral superiority. In the long term, this attitude created substantial problems; the Europeans rejected it, and it was also objectively difficult to simultaneously play the roles of referee and player in the same game.[24]

Of course, the very position of "associate power," not ally, which Wilson had chosen for his country when he took it to war, reflected this attitude. For the same reason, he was unwilling to discuss with the Allies the many secret treaties and agreements that formed an intertwining labyrinth of mutual promises binding the nations of the western bloc. Walter Lippmann was right when he pointed out that the failure to strike an advance agreement on the contents of the Allies' secret treaties had undermined the subsequent success of relations between the United States and the European Allies.[25] We should add, however, that during the war Wilson's exceptionalism was broadly shared by most of his colleagues, including Lippmann himself. In this sense, Wilson was doing nothing more than translate into words and political measures something that was already a widely held belief in America, and one of the basic underlying characteristics of the United States' first venture into world politics.

Wilson had overlooked the need to explain that America had gone to war primarily to safeguard its national interests, which would have been threatened by a German victory. In the end, his elevated idealism also failed to explain to Americans their interest in the peace treaty and especially in the system of international cooperation under the leadership of the League of Nations. As Lippmann pointed out in an article in the *New Republic:*

> [Wilson] had not convinced . . . the American people, that his so-called idealism was as vital an American interest as any strategic frontier in Europe or concession in Asia. He had said many times, but he had never digested the idea, that a stable peace in Europe is the first and most important line of defence for the American democracy, that a democratic settlement there meant more to the security and prosperity of Americans than anything else in the world.[26]

The compromises of the peace conference increasingly spread the impression that Wilson's nebulous idealism was based not on the nation's interest but on some ethereal ideal or distant abstract moral principle. As a result, in the 1920 elections, Americans repudiated Wilson, the U.S. Senate refused to ratify the peace treaty, and, in the wake of that development, the United States did not join the League of Nations. Instead, in Seymour's effective turn of phrase, "Comfortably and blindly the United States fell back into the spirit of isolationism."[27]

The most disconcerting aspect of the splendid edifice of Wilsonian politics is the realization that behind the imagination-capturing slogans of wartime there had been absolutely no adequately organized effort to translate those slogans into practical terms in the postwar years. Entirely lacking was the slow and laborious diplomatic and political effort to bridge the gap between the diverging positions of the Americans and their European allies. There was no campaign to promote support for continuing American international engagement following the wartime emergency, and there was no effort to demonstrate to the world the benefits of a new international system guided by a supranational institution. When peace came, therefore, it laid bare the fragile foundations of Wilsonian foreign policy. Over the course of a year, his vast political project was dashed on the rocks. The man who had been the idol of the masses in 1918 was a political leader without a following by the end of 1919, as well as a seriously sick man. He had in fact suffered a stroke during an exhausting speaking tour that he had imposed upon himself in the hope of persuading the Americans public to follow him on the road to international engagement. His sudden and dramatic collapse endowed his personal and political story with tinges of tragedy.

We should add, however, that even though the years following the First World War witnessed a sharp return to American isolationism, the change in course that Wilson introduced to the foreign policy of his country was more enduring than might have been apparent at the time. International commitment was destined to reemerge and to characterize American history in the twentieth century.[28] The greatest significance of Wilson's idealism lies in the fact that it was the forerunner of fundamental developments of the century regarding the masses, ideologies, and internationalist impulses; this was what his greatest biographer rightly termed his "higher realism."[29]

Wilson's Realism

Wilson's realism stood out in particular in the unprecedented propaganda campaign that he organized in the United States and around the world immediately following the decision to intervene in the war. The Wilson who organized the Committee on Public Information (CPI) and then carefully monitored its activities in the months and years that followed was no politician in blind pursuit of abstract principle. Realism and idealism merged in the work of the first state agency for propaganda.[30]

Wilson's presidency and the intervention of the United States in the First World War came just a few years prior to the mass diffusion of radio, one of the most important instruments of mass communications of the twentieth century. By an ironic twist of fate, Wilson, who owed so much of his charismatic appeal to the hold his words had on the masses, did not make his first radio broadcast until 1923, three months before his death, when he was no longer president but a politically isolated private citizen. The dissemination of his words throughout the United States in the final phase of the Great War, capturing the imagination of the whole world, had been entrusted to relatively rudimentary means of communication. This fact has led historians to wonder what would have become of Wilson's reputation if he had been able to use the mass media that technology would make available just a few years later. Let us think, for instance, of the exhausting trip out West that Wilson made in 1919 to persuade the American people to follow him on the path of international engagement, as envisioned in the peace treaty and in national participation in the League of Nations. The long journey and the dozens of speeches contributed to the stroke that virtually paralyzed Wilson and from which he never fully recovered. Obviously, radio would have made it much easier and more effective for him to communicate with the further reaches of the American countryside, as shortly thereafter President Franklin D. Roosevelt's would be able to do with his popular "fireside chats" broadcast on the radio.[31]

One of the stumbling blocks of the Wilson presidency, then, was the problem of communications between the center and the outlying areas, between the leader and the masses, between the central government and the boundless American heartland. U.S. society was already a full-fledged mass society that demanded modern leadership tools. One of Wilson's most distinctive characteristics, the source of positives and negatives in his political leadership, was his understanding of the need for a strong, direct relationship with the masses. He attained this relationship repeatedly and successfully, in some cases by going over the heads of the Democratic Party leadership, the United States Congress, or the governments of the European nations. This made him a precursor of twentieth-century politicians.

American intervention in the world war accentuated these dynamics. Modern war required not only the obedience of the soldiers, but also the participation and support of both soldiers and civilians. Wilson was extremely aware of this aspect of war, and he soon became the chief propagandist on the Western Front, winning the role of spokesman for world liberal-democratic opinion. As Harold Lasswell observed,

> If the great generalissimo on the military front was Foch, the great generalissimo on the propaganda front was Wilson . . . this mysterious figure in the White House . . . who spoke in elegiac prose of a better world. . . . For a few brief months . . . [Wilson] was raised to a matchless pinnacle of prestige and power, and his name was spoken with reverence in varied accents in the remotest corners of the earth. . . . From a propaganda point of view it was a matchless performance.[32]

In a clear demonstration of his practical realism, just a few days after the declaration of war on Germany, Wilson created the first public organization for propaganda, the Committee on Public Information (CPI), which soon grew to enormous size. It was one of the most original and controversial creations of America under arms. The CPI organized the first mass propaganda campaign in history. In this way, Progressive America led the way for Europe's totalitarian regimes, and Wilson was a forerunner of Mussolini, Hitler, and Stalin. In the short period of its operations (April 1917–December 1918), the CPI obtained spectacular results. Domestically, it rapidly transformed a fundamentally indifferent and pacifist nation into a giant war-making machine; overseas, in both belligerent and neutral nations, it effectively promoted the image of America and its president.

Even if it is true that in certain aspects of its censorship and propaganda activity the CPI prefigured the ministries of propaganda in the European totalitarian regimes that followed, it was first and foremost a very specific creation of Wilsonian America, an America that had enthusiastically transplanted the Progressive faith into the new context of the war. Like a magnet, the CPI attracted into its ranks Progressive writers, artists, journalists, scholars, and advertising experts who eagerly devoted themselves to spreading the new gospel and organizing the new crusade for democracy, this time, with the entire world as a background. This, too, was emblematic of the Wilson administration's shift "from indrawn pacifist reformism to Progressive nationalism" that took place during the war.[33] The naïveté and passion with which many CPI employees transformed themselves into government propagandists would make them blush in the disenchanted postwar years. However, it is important to remember how different the intellectual climate of the preceding years had been. Propaganda was a new phenomenon and had not yet acquired the sinister connotations it would during the decades between the two world wars. It was a tool for shaping public opinion, but it was also the daughter of "publicity," a moralistic medium *par excellence* of the American Progressives. In their minds, a simple exposition of the facts was sufficient to win over the support of their listeners. It was not, therefore, really propaganda, but simply information, instruction, and education.[34]

The background against which we should set the operation of the CPI extends over an area far greater than the immediate context of wartime emergency. It should include the development of the Progressive movement, which, as we have seen, reached its apex and began its decline in the years of the Wilson presidency. The history of the CPI fits into this arc perfectly and matched the arc of so many American intellectuals who, over a brief space in time, moved from reformist enthusiasm and faith in the war as a crusade for democracy to the bitter disillusionment of the 1920s. Indeed, the very success of the CPI's work, its clear capacity to determine how people thought, helped to undermine the Progressive faith in the rationality of public opinion and to foster the apathy and skepticism of the postwar years.[35]

During the war years, in contrast, the very name of the CPI reflected its organizers' faith in "public information," while their work postulated the validity of American democratic values and ideals for bettering the world at large. It was a short but intense period, a time when propaganda had not yet become the nightmare of democratic thinkers. Thus, not only the need to shape public opinion in a state of wartime emergency, but also civic engagement and Progressive enlightened reformism were all protagonists of the first major mass propaganda campaign.[36]

The CPI succeeded in its goal of "selling the war" to the American people.[37] Domestically, it was a major vehicle of the nationalization of the masses: it encouraged the formation of a mass ideology prior to the spread of the most powerful communications media of the twentieth century. In the way it overcame the technological handicaps of the time, the CPI proved to be imaginative and effective in developing new instruments or adapting existing communications networks and media. Through numerous ingenious methods, it allowed the federal government to communicate with virtually every citizen, in even the most remote corners of the boundless American heartland. It was, therefore, an essential element linking Washington with the rest of the vast American nation.

The CPI was created by presidential order in mid-April 1917, a few days after the United States went to war. Its two institutional responsibilities were censorship and propaganda. The agency grew until it had a staff of some 400 permanent employees, supervising from Washington the work of tens of thousands of volunteers scattered both inside and outside of the United States.[38] The structure of the CPI was changed continually as it adapted to the input and needs of the moment. One element, however, that remained reasonably stable was the internal subdivision between the Domestic Section and the Foreign Section. In this chapter, we will focus exclusively on the CPI's Domestic Section, and we will devote extensive space to the CPI's Foreign Section in the chapters that follow.

George Creel, a Progressive journalist with boundless energy and absolute devotion to Wilson, was appointed president of the CPI. Creel started his career as a reporter, first in Kansas City and later in Denver; with hard work and personal sacrifice, Creel steadily climbed the many steps that finally made him the editor-in-chief of a number of provincial dailies. He was a man of impulses and passions more than a heavy thinker, and he launched many sensationalist campaigns, invariably championing the oppressed and the defenseless. Despite the effectiveness of his language and the tireless zeal with which he fought his battles, he never managed to win the respect of the more refined, but equally Progressive, East Coast journalists: As he wrote to the intellectuals of the *New Republic* in March 1915, in response to an attack by that publication against him, "You, on the other hand, are academic products, who have become commentators by virtue of self-election, based upon self-evaluation, aided, I believe, by an endowment fund that spares you the fear of existence. The antagonism between us, therefore, is as instinctive and inevitable as that of the house cat for the street dog."[39] Creel's new job as the organizer of all government propaganda reinforced the scorn of the world of American journalism to such a degree that a new verb was coined—"to Creelize"—referring to the process of editing an article, film, or anything else in order to make it more acceptable to a regime's ideology. In reality, Creel was a prodigious organizer, driven by a boundless faith in his cause—support of the American model of government in its latest Wilsonian version; he was a genuine product of his time. Today, perhaps with a more disillusioned view than that of our parents, who lived through the propaganda excesses of Europe's totalitarian regimes, we can see his merits more clearly and recognize that he was responsible for much of the unprecedented success of the work of the CPI, "a social innovation brilliantly conceived and in many ways brilliantly executed."[40]

A quick glance at the overall structure of the Domestic Section gives a sense of its range of activities on the domestic front. The Committee worked in every sector that was linked to the formation of public opinion. One of its first creations was the Division of News, designed to feed information to the press through the mass distribution of agency dispatches and the *Official Bulletin,* the first government daily newspaper, which soon reached a daily circulation of about 100,000. The Division of Civic and Educational Publications printed and distributed millions of pamphlets on the progress and aims of the war, as well as on the president's speeches. The Division of Speakers staged assemblies, lectures, and exhibitions around the country. The Division of Industrial Relations oversaw propaganda in the factories, while the Division of Work with the Foreign Born reached out to recent immigrants and the Division of Women's work organized and promoted the contribution of American women to the war effort.[41]

Separate mention should be made of the work done by the Division of Pictorial Publicity and the Division of Films. Both posters and films were distributed in large numbers and proved to be effective media for disseminating government propaganda throughout the country. The Division of Pictorial Publicity, directed by Charles Dana Gibson, one of the most famous illustrators of the time, created posters that are still symbols of the Great War—for instance, the picture of Uncle Sam, pointing his forefinger at the public and saying: "I want you for U.S. Army," or the young woman who says: "Gee!! I wish I were a man. I'd join the Navy!" These posters appeared in every corner of the country. One needed only go to the post office or the local grocery store to be exposed to their powerfully emotional message. The movies, moreover, had already become a major form of mass entertainment, and a network of movie theaters had developed in America in a way that had no parallels anywhere else on earth.[42] But American posters and films, however effective and broad scale in their distribution, were hardly a uniquely American creation. All the warring nations produced them, and a great many were quite well done.

In the dizzying array of propaganda initiatives undertaken by the CPI, many of them had been expressly designed to reach the indifferent, remote, outlying citizen who did not read the daily papers, much less government brochures, and who never went to patriotic gatherings or exhibitions: "Our idea," Creel recalled, "was that the facts and necessities of war must be carried not only to every home in the cities and towns, but to hamlets and the most remote farm-houses as well."[43] In this field, we find the CPI's most original initiatives, those that give us a sense of just how advanced Wilson's America was as a mass civilization. Let us examine a few of them.

The Four Minute Men formed a veritable army of volunteer speakers who, during the year and a half that America was at war, acted as spokesmen for the government, disseminating its messages throughout the national territory. In accordance with instructions from Washington, the Four Minute Men delivered short speeches (four minutes long, of course) about crucial aspects of the war, in varied gathering places, primarily movie theaters, but also schools, churches, synagogues, universities, private clubs, and workplaces. Their number swelled rapidly, with "the sweep of a prairie fire," to use Creel's words. From 2,500 speakers in July 1917, the organization grew to 15,000 in November 1917, 40,000 in September 1918, and 75,000 by war's end. At that last high point, Four Minute Men were present in every state of the Union, as well as Alaska, the American possessions of the Panama Canal Zone, the Philippines, Hawaii, Guam, Puerto Rico, and even American Samoa. All told, it is estimated that they delivered about a million speeches to a total audience of about 400 million. It was unlikely that an adult American citizen had failed to hear at least one of these propagandistic appeals.[44]

As has been observed, the remarkable success of this initiative can be attributed to three factors: first, to the sincerity and conviction of the speakers, warranted by the fact that they were volunteers for the most part; second, to the use for brief periods of existing and ready audiences, such as those in movie theaters; and finally to the control and direction carried out by the chiefs of the organization in Washington, D.C.

The name "Four Minute Men" referred both to the Minutemen, volunteer soldiers during the American Revolution, and to the binding limit of four minutes: their speeches could be no longer. The work of the Four Minute Men was organized in campaigns, each of which lasted one to four weeks. The topics of the campaigns were decided and developed centrally and could deal with fund-raising for national loans, the Red Cross, the draft, saving food and energy, and so on. The topics were illustrated in a pamphlet and distributed to all the organization's members, through the organizers of the individual states, counties, and cities.

An examination of the content of the bulletins tells us a great deal about how the organization functioned in practical terms. Every issue began by explaining the current theme in words that were not rhetorical but punchy and accessible, peppered with quotes from famous individuals. Chief among them were quotes from President Wilson. There followed instructions and practical advice on the best way to present the subject of the campaign to the public. Also offered were suggested outlines of the main points to be expanded upon, potential opening phrases and other effective slogans, and finally, two sample four-minute speeches that the speakers could use. Individual tailoring was encouraged in order to make the appeal more personal to the audience. Throughout the bulleting there were continuous reminders not to go over the maximum time limit of four minutes, at the risk of being expelled from the organization. This limit was carefully timed to correspond to the normal duration of the intermission between movies, but it also comported with the demands of effective propaganda. Each speech was to be preceded by the projection of the same standard CPI slide, so that it was clear that the speaker was there as a government spokesman.[45]

It is easy to see how close the organization of the Four Minute Men was to radio broadcasting: for the duration of each campaign, almost simultaneously tens of thousands of mouths repeated all across the country a substantially standardized message, drafted and fine-tuned in Washington, D.C. The network of Four Minute Men combined centralization with distribution to the outlying areas, and the slogan elaborated by the top leadership had the human warmth of the individual appeal. The Four Minute Men acted as "so many separate loud-speakers, reproducing with greater or less fidelity the words of Woodrow Wilson as interpreted by the CPI." In short, this group was a forerunner of radio, which piggybacked on the network of another form of mass communications, the movies, which had only recently been invented but were already present on a grassroots level throughout the United States. At that point in history, the United States was already in the vanguard of the film industry. It is estimated that in 1917 and 1918 millions of moviegoers attended a movie theater on a weekly basis. During the intermission that followed the projection of the first reel, the piano-player would generally play the notes of a patriotic song, while the standard CPI slide would appear on the screen giving the name of that evening's speaker. At this point, the Four Minute Man would step up to the podium and speak for four short but intense minutes.[46]

With their appeals, the Four Minute Men managed to reach remote and indifferent small towns that other types of propaganda failed to touch: they were a legion of thousands of men "carrying the message," who could "drop a thought, a pebble, . . . in an ocean of minds, one thought each time, until the wave of right thinking rolls up to overwhelming might!"[47] Their work was nicely representative of the CPI's efforts of, which its enthusiastic director described as "the fight for the *minds* of men, for the 'conquest of their convictions' " in which "the battle-line ran through every home in every country."[48] In this way, the Four Minute Men, with the carefully calibrated development of their message, its studied brevity, simplicity, and focus, spread the words of the government to the most remote and undeveloped areas of the United States.

Another distinctive creation of the CPI was the Bureau of Cartoons, which was an office in the Washington headquarters that worked strictly to influence the work of cartoonists. With the development of photography and movies and with the spread of high-circulation publications, the image was becoming the predominant medium of mass communications in the twentieth century. The propagandists of the CPI were well aware that "a picture is worth ten thousand words."[49]

The background of the work done by this division was the enormous circulation that the press enjoyed in the United States in those years. In 1914 there were more than thirty newspapers with a daily circulation of over 100,000, while the *New York World* had already exceeded a daily circulation of a million copies by 1897. Alongside these major newspapers with national circulation (the *World,* for instance, already had 1,300 full-time employees by the mid-1890s), there existed a myriad of local newspapers, midsized, small, and tiny. Indeed, the vitality and sheer number of these local enterprises was one of the distinguishing characteristics of the Progressive Era. The greatest number of daily papers was reached in 1914 (2,250), after which a process of concentration prevailed in the daily press. According to the data provided by De Fleur, in the decade 1910–1920, there was almost a newspaper and a half every day for each American family.[50]

Cartoons, in particular, were very popular. Their message reached nearly every newspaper reader, even the less educated one, and for that specific reason cartoonists were especially targeted by the executives of the propaganda organization. "Your patriotic cartoons . . . have done an infinite amount of good in arousing the true American war sentiment," wrote Carl Byoir, associate chairman of the CPI. The executive offices of the Bureau of Cartoons echoed Byoir: "The importance of 'picture messages' at this time can not be overestimated." "Cartoonists are molders of public opinion and therefore have an important part to play in the winning of the war. Fight on, cartoonists, with your pens and crayons." "The world is much too busy to stop and listen to the orator, or even to read all the stories of the war that crowd every printed page," wrote George Creel, speaking to the cartoonists, "but you never lack for an audience. Your constituency includes every reader of your particular newspaper. Your appeal is irresistible, and if your subject is wisely selected and handled with skill and force your success is instantaneous."[51]

A bulletin was created for cartoonists—the *Bulletin for Cartoonists*—and it was sent out weekly to 750 of the best known cartoonists in America. It called the cartoonists' attention to a dozen key events and phrases that the government wanted to popularize at the moment. The purpose and themes were similar to those of the Four Minute Men: to launch full-fledged national campaigns on select topics, so as to spread the messages of the executive branch in a widespread manner. Cartoonists were seen as crucial factors in the "persistent public education" that the government considered an integral component of the war effort. They were told: "Your work in this world war has a threefold value. You can expose wrong and injustice by a dramatic condemnation; you can furnish a gentle enlivening humor to irradiate the dark days of those who are prone to despair. But far more important, you can excite to patriotic emulation those who need the stimulus your gifted pencils provide."[52]

The Division of Syndicate Features was in charge of encouraging the composition of short stories, novels, and reporting about the war by the finest writers of the time and then distributing the resulting creations to the mass readership, especially through the Sunday editions of the daily newspapers. The Sunday editions had especially high circulation. For the war years, it is estimated that between 16 million and 19 million copies of Sunday papers were sold every week.[53] Even then, the Sunday edition of major dailies came with a number of supplements on all sorts of subjects.[54] Therefore, there was space for the publication of short stories, novels in installments, or eyewitness accounts that might influence the way that readers who preferred fiction to the news reporting of newspaper articles saw the war. The work of this division, as in the other cases, was designed to reach sectors of public opinion that were not touched by the normal channels of propaganda. This work was guided by the belief that a fictional war story, written in a patriotic spirit by a skilled author, might have elevated powers of persuasion.

Prior to June 1918, when the work of this division was drastically reduced because of budget cuts, the essays and stories that it distributed reached an estimated 25 million people each month.[55]

Some of the most popular writers of the time, including Booth Tarkington, Meredith Nicholson, Will Irwin, John Spargo, and Mary Roberts Rinehart, were involved in the work of this division. Overall, some fifty writers, essayists, and university professors volunteered to work for it. Even a Socialist writer like Upton Sinclair suggested that Creel publish a novel that he was writing, which was "exactly what the Government needs in order to win and hold the radical part of labor." After showing some initial interest in the proposal, Creel declined the offer. In this and other cases, the desire to be useful among many reformist and radical intellectuals was even greater than the government's needs.[56]

One of the most innovative and successful of the CPI's publications was the *National School Service* (NSS), a biweekly, usually sixteen pages long, that was sent free to all public school teachers, estimated to number some 600,000. Its usefulness as a vehicle linking the central administration to the vast and far-flung network of schools was immediately evident. For that reason, it was one of the CPI initiatives that managed to survive after the declaration of peace. After the CPI was shut down, it was placed under the jurisdiction of the Department of the Interior. The biweekly had been conceived as a tool for use during the wartime state of emergency. As Creel pointed out, "we foresaw a time when, perhaps, if the war with its burdens and losses continued, the national morale would need the support of a message that went without fail into every home. For this purpose there was no other agency so effective, so sure, as the public schools with their twenty millions of pupils."[57]

The periodical for schools told inspiring stories of the war, described the efforts of the Red Cross, the Americanization being carried on by students among immigrants, the campaigns for national loans, ways of reducing food waste, and so on. The last five or six pages contained specific sections for rural schools, elementary, junior high, and high school classes. The teachers were advised to conduct programs intended to encourage the growth of patriotic sentiments among the students. The objective was to make "every school pupil a messenger for Uncle Sam." A number of special editions focused on promoting the Four Minute Men organization for students, the *Junior Four Minute Men*. In general, the teacher would teach one aspect of the war to the class, using the bulletin as a textbook. The students would then write a theme on the subject, and the best papers, selected by the teacher or the school principal, were then read by the students either in class or, more frequently, in full-fledged speaking competitions in front of all the students and their parents and relatives.[58]

Teachers proved to be very receptive to the government's appeal. Creel recalled the letters that immediately began pouring in from teachers in far-off and isolated areas: "The national government," he commented, "had reached out and placed a hand on their shoulder to encourage them and to ask for their aid and support. They saw a new vision and a new, vitalizing mission."[59] The NSS hoped above all to draw rural America into the national dialogue, and it became a permanent tool for nationalizing the outlying masses of America.[60]

In the context of the division that focused on women's role in the wartime emergency, the CPI operated a correspondence bureau that answered thousands of letters sent by women from every corner of the United States. Many government offices and members of Congress would forward to the CPI letters they received from women, entrusting to that agency the task of responding. And so, the Women's War-Work Division, aside from its task as a clearinghouse for communication among writers, photographers, advertising people, journalists, directors of volunteer organizations, and members of the government keen to incentivize and promote women's contribution to the war effort, also became a major force for the support of morale among American women.

According to estimates from the time, the bureau answered some 50,000 letters. They came from women in every walk of life, in every part of the United States. Some letters came from upper-class women asking for information and material for their cultural and philanthropic enterprises. Other letters came from young women eager to volunteer. And many were letters written by mothers, wives, and fiancées of men at war, mostly from the country, who were struggling to deal with the new conditions that the war had imposed on them. The answers attempted to respond to the most direct requests and often sought to put the writer in touch with aid groups or women's work agencies capable of involving them and helping them in a more stable and lasting way.[61]

This CPI initiative differed from those efforts mentioned earlier because it did more than just spread messages from the leadership to the outlying population by attempting to provide meaningful answers to problems posed by anonymous individuals. The message in this case therefore ran in both directions—from the outskirts to the highest levels and then from the highest levels back to the outlying areas. In its answers, the CPI wanted to produce an echo of its work by involving local efforts. Through this correspondence service, the CPI could have its finger on the pulse of public opinion; this was especially important for the most remote regions. In this case as well, what is most striking is the modernity of the initiative, which in the future would develop into the letters pages of mass periodicals and radio and television programs.

The CPI initiatives, several examples of which we have examined, created a network of mass communications in the territory of the United States that was of vital necessity to the government, especially during the war years. In order to ensure that Wilson's words received mass distribution and to urge his fellow citizens to new heights of patriotic devotion, Creel neglected none of the existing networks of communication while also creating new networks. Journalists, photographers, directors, and writers, movie-house impresarios and advertising professionals of every kind, religious, teachers, social workers, and even boy scouts were used in the most expansive propaganda campaign that the world had ever seen.

As we will see in the following chapters, the Domestic Section of the CPI was soon joined by a Foreign Section, whose objective was to promote the image of America and Wilson's policies around the world, in enemy countries, neutral countries, and especially, in Allied countries. The sphere of activity eventually extended to the entire planet, and it reveals the same conviction of being in the right and the same enthusiasm for spreading the new Wilsonian gospel that was at work within the United States:

> We fought indifference and disaffection in the United States and we fought falsehood abroad. . . . We sought the verdict of mankind by truth telling. We did not call it "propaganda," for that word, in German hands, had come to be associated with lies and corruption. Our work was educational and informative only, for we had such confidence in our case as to feel that only fair presentation of its facts was needed.[62]

What emerges forcefully from these undertakings is the vitality and modernity of American society at the turn of the century.

Italian society of those same years was radically different from U.S. society. The first element that stands out is how primitive the political management of the war by the Italian liberal class was. As a whole, at least until Caporetto, that class failed to understand the importance of the ideological involvement of the masses, both civilian and military. The propaganda remained rudimentary, while coercion and repression were the chief methods for working on the lower classes. But in those same years, Italian society was rapidly being transformed into a mass society. This fact led to the genuine fascination that the Italians developed toward the end of the war for leaders and slogans from outside Italy—for Wilson and Lenin and for the corresponding myths of America and Soviet Russia. In this process, on both sides of the Atlantic, the petit bourgeoisie acquired new roles in the areas of propaganda and mass politics. Especially in the realm of emerging dynamics and aspects such as these, the comparative study of historical development in more than one country helps to cast light on the more profound shifts of societies. One of the chief shifts consisted of the changing relations between leaders and the masses, and Wilson was assuredly a forerunner of those changes.

— 4 —

Propaganda in Uniform

Propaganda was the prevailing characteristic of American operations in Italy during the last year of the war. The propaganda was a product of the joint input of both Italian and American politicians, and there was a broad-ranging cooperation in this field, despite the fact that their reciprocal political mistrust and disagreements had never been fully resolved. The emergency that followed Caporetto and the specter of social revolution drove them to act in a timely manner, postponing for some calmer future date the solution of their political disagreements. Propaganda, therefore, was the only field in which the two "allies-by-accident"[1] actually joined forces in an effective and successful effort.

In this chapter, we are chiefly interested in showing that the rise of Wilson's influence and reputation in Italy was the product not only of the effective watchwords that he launched from America, but also of the modern, fine-grained, and wide-ranging propaganda campaign that the American president ordered throughout Italian territory, pursued with an extremely realistic approach and lavish resources. This was one of the first mass campaigns to which the Italians had been exposed; it was also one of the most efficient ever staged. Three American organizations were the chief protagonists of the campaign: the American Red Cross (ARC), the Young Men's Christian Association (YMCA), and the Italian office of the Committee on Public Information (CPI). These three organizations flooded Italy's relatively backward society with an array of propaganda media developed in a wealthier and, more importantly, a decidedly mass-oriented society.

The effect of American propaganda on the Italian masses was greatly facilitated by the existing myth of America that had developed in previous decades in conjunction with the massive emigration of Italian peasants to the New World. The prior existence of the myth of America explained the messianic expectations of the Italian popular masses with respect to the United States' entry into the war. Antonio Gramsci noted:

> For the lower classes in Italy, for patriarchal peasants and factory workers untrained in the class struggle because not earning wages from large-scale industry, Wilson is the living symbol of America, wealth, the opportunities of hard work and fortune that America represented to the spirit of the Italian people, specifically individuals who had already emigrated once or who saw emigration as the answer to their very specific problems. The intervention of the United States in the war was incredibly effective in bolstering morale, shaken by gloom and fear in the wake of Caporetto, unbelievable to those who had never lived among the peasants and could not recall the seriousness, the messianic hope that future emigrant devoted to refuting all objections raised to his plans, repeating insistently a single answer: "La Merica is still Merica." [Illiterate Italians heard "L'America" as "La Merica," and "Merica" became shorthand for a certain peasant vision of the United States—*translator's note.*][2]

Everywhere, the Americans working in Italy had the impression that they were planting seeds in quite fertile soil.[3]

This impression allowed Wilson to come to the aid of his Italian ally in the aftermath of Caporetto without being obliged to compromise himself excessively with the questionable aims of Italy's governing class. Thus understood, the American action was aimed more at the masses than at the political or military leadership. It was designed to create a direct link between the Italian people and the American president, in correspondence with a basic orientation of Wilsonian policy. This was both a strength and a weakness in Wilson: it gave his image an element of charisma on the world stage that had been previously unknown, yet it also drastically restricted his capacity for dialogue, as became evident after the cessation of hostilities, first in his relations with the Allies, especially with Italy, and later in his interactions with the United States Congress.

Aid as Propaganda

The khaki uniform of the U.S. army with its broad-brimmed hat became popular in Italy not so much because of the presence of fighting troops, but because of the pervasive aid and propaganda activity carried out in the immediate aftermath of the defeat at Caporetto by two American humanitarian organizations, the American Red Cross and the Young Men's Christian Association. It was no accident that the personnel of both organizations wore the official uniform of the U.S. army: they were an integral part of the U.S. war effort, and they saw themselves as such. It struck them as natural to bring to the demoralized Italian troops and civilian population not only material assistance, but also the American political message, which combined the image of a wealthy, generous, and invincible America with Wilson's democratic ideals. In a short time, ARC and the YMCA became a symbol of the mythical America and its concern for the common man. It is difficult to overestimate the propagandistic impact of these two humanitarian organizations on the humbler classes of the Italian population.

The first organization to arrive in Italy was the American Red Cross. Beginning in early November 1917, it started operating as an emergency aid organization for refugees from the territories that had been invaded, as well as in supplying military hospitals, and so on.[4] This allowed Prime Minister Orlando, from the first speech that he delivered to the Italian parliament in the wake of Caporetto on 12 December 1917 onward, to link the work of the American Red Cross in Italy with the very recent U.S. declaration of war against the Austro-Hungarian Empire.[5] From that day on, it became a constant refrain to present this humanitarian organization as the vanguard of the American army, but it was an army that never arrived.[6]

The Permanent Commission of the ARC, under the command of Colonel Perkins, arrived in Rome on 20 December 1917 and set up operations in a seven-story building in the Via Sardegna, immediately establishing three separate departments: Civil Affairs, Military Affairs, and Medical Affairs.[7] Its relief programs extended over the entire territory of Italy. When the Armistice was signed, the American staff numbered 949, while roughly a thousand Italians were working for the organization. The no-nonsense, friendly working style of its officers and their vigorous appearance in spotless uniforms made a very positive impression. They seemed to spread an aura of immense efficiency, bottomless resources, and a can-do attitude, capable of completing almost any project successfully. For a long time, they remained almost the only visible example to the Italians of what the U.S. ally was capable of doing. For many observers, their appearance on the Italian horizon following the disaster of Caporetto was the event that, more than any other, succeeded in restoring Italian morale.[8]

One image frequently associated with the work of the American Red Cross in Italy during the Great War is that of the ambulances operating at the front, described by Hemingway in *A Farewell to Arms*, the popular novel based on the American writer's actual experiences in Italy as a Red Cross worker in the summer of 1918.[9] The popularity of the ambulance service was also in part due to the fact that the cream of American youth enlisted in it. Not only was knowing how to drive a car in those years almost exclusively limited to the children of well-to-do families, but also a poetic aura surrounded the ambulance driver, a new heroic figure who combined in his work courage, altruism, and adventure. The ambulance service, initially dubbed the American Field Service (AFS), began to operate on a volunteer basis even before America entered the war. Since their country was neutral, many volunteers were forced to leave for Europe secretly. The first organizers of the AFS were Herman Harjes, A. Piatt Andrew, and Richard Norton, all three well-to-do young men, who canvassed the campuses of the leading universities in search of recruits. After America declared war, the ambulance service was absorbed into the American Red Cross. It attracted students from American universities in numbers that seemed to correlate directly to the prestige of the universities: Harvard sent 325 volunteers, Yale 187, Princeton 181, Cornell 105, and so on.[10] The first seventeen vehicles were donated with funds raised at Yale and Harvard. At a certain point, the exodus became so massive that the president of Harvard, A. Lawrence Lowell, issued a circular letter urging students to continue their studies without interruption.[11] Therefore, aside from Hemingway's participation, which had "its consequences for American literature," the ambulance service functioned as an "emotional apprenticeship" for such future talents as John Dos Passos, E. E. Cummings, Julian Green, Malcolm Cowley, Donald Moffat, Sidney Fairbanks, Jack Lawson, and others, many of whom commemorated their experiences in their writings.[12] The "literary" allure that emanated from this wave of youthful American volunteers on the battlefields of Europe was even sensed by Henry James, who wrote a pamphlet in their honor that was sold for propaganda purposes in London at the symbolic price of one penny.[13] This aspect of the involvement of the young offspring of the American wealthy classes in the Italian war, midwife to emotions, initiations, and artistic inspiration, summons to mind the relations of American intellectuals with Italy in the decades prior to the war.

The American Red Cross's commitment in Italy intensified over the course of 1918. Already, by mid-January, three ambulance sections of the

ARC began to operate on the Italian front; they were joined by two more in the months of April and June, for a total of 104 ambulances, 25 auxiliary vehicles, and 135 men.[14] At the end of July, another contingent landed in Genoa, with 30 sections, for a total of 360 ambulances, 48 auxiliary vehicles, 77 officers, and 1,641 enlisted men.[15]

At the front, aside from transporting the wounded, the ARC also organized and operated twenty-two canteens that provided food, aid, and entertainment to the soldiers. These canteens were located in the immediate vicinity of the front lines, and they generally featured a large hall with tables and chairs, a kitchen, and an open space equipped with games and sports. The canteens served coffee, milk, hot soup in the winter, cold drinks in the summer, cigarettes, candy, and stationery to write letters home. It was estimated that roughly one million soldiers made use of these services each month.[16] These Americans, with "shaven faces, khaki uniforms, and big round hats"[17] delivered beverages, food, and cigarettes on a regular basis to the trenches or distributed them to troops on the move. Henry Villard, who served as an ambulance driver, recalled the work that the ARC did at the front:

> The *posto di ristoro* . . . was a focal point for the propagation of the faith, faith that the Yanks were coming, faith in the invincibility of the United States, faith in the unwavering friendship of Americans. As we were constantly reminded, the whole point of the Red Cross operation was to bolster Italian morale and keep our wavering ally in the war. . . . The Red Cross officer in charge of a *cucina* had to combine the attributes of a propagandist, a scoutmaster, a Y.M.C.A. director, and father-confessor; he had to be equally at home with the officers and infantrymen who rallied around him. He had to be tactful and versatile, too, and like the ambulance drivers, cool and courageous under fire.[18]

It was during the course of one of these distributions in the trenches that Hemingway sustained leg wounds from a grenade that exploded at about a yard's distance; the grenade killed a soldier who happened to be between Hemingway and the point of explosion. It was also during trench duty that the only death of a member of the American auxiliary services in Italy took place. Lieutenant Edward McKey was killed by a bomb while engaged in conversation with two Italian officers.

In the main train stations of the Italian peninsula, the ARC organized an efficient system of hostels and canteens for soldiers, known as military rest houses *(posti di conforto militari)*. In these facilities, which were either free of charge or charged a nominal fee, soldiers being transferred could enjoy hospitality, food or beverages, cigarettes, chocolate, and the inevitable propaganda postcards and stationery. The estimates of the average monthly number of troops passing through the main rest houses offer an idea of the impact of the work by the American Red Cross on the mass of Italian soldiers: Genoa (500,000 soldiers per month), Ancona (100,000), Naples (90,000), Piacenza (30,000–40,000), Milan (15,000), Palermo (12,000), Villa San Giovanni (11,000), Terra Nova, and, beginning in late July 1918, also Vicenza (50,000).[19]

And yet direct relief to the soldiers was only one small part of the ARC's activities in Italy. The Department of Military Affairs, which was responsible for the sectors in question, absorbed only slightly more than 10 percent of the $115 million spent between November 1917 and June 1918. Nearly 65 percent of the total, however, was used by the Department of Civil Affairs on civilian aid—that is, relief to the refugees fleeing territories that had been invaded, payments to the families of soldiers, care for children (orphanages, schools, nurseries), the operation of canteens, cafeterias, and *ouvroirs* (workshops) for civilian populations.[20]

The work of the American Red Cross was carried out in the north as well as the south and on the islands, in major cities as well as in the countryside and small provincial towns. Italy was broken down into sixteen districts, and each district was placed under the jurisdiction of a delegate of the American Red Cross. Beginning in November 1917, the American consuls stationed in a number of major cities were involved in the ARC's aid work; among them were the consuls of Venice, Florence, Milan, Genoa, Livorno (Leghorn), Turin, Catania, Palermo, and Naples. A complex system was organized, including means of transport and about sixty warehouses, whereby aid could be distributed in detail to hospitals, refugees, orphans, and needy families. The distribution of food and supplies was accompanied by speeches and offerings of American propaganda material, which the Red Cross employees always had in great supply. These employees believed that it was their duty to bring to every corner of Italy, even the most isolated country village, both material aid and reports on America's vast program of war readiness and a new political credo, in the form of the words of President Wilson.

The ARC did not limit its activities to treating the soldier's wounds; instead, its primary goal was to heal the "wounds to the soul" of the Italians— that is, the demoralization and opposition to the war that was spreading among soldiers and civilians, undermining the resistance of the Italian army and rendering it easy prey to enemy, pacifist, or Soviet propaganda.[21] With extreme clarity, the American humanitarian organization in Italy targeted its campaign from the very beginning at a reinforcement of the so-called Fronte Interno, or "home front"—that is to say, that alliance of public and private forces that was fighting to mobilize all the reiuctant components of Italian society to support the war not at the front but within Italy. It had redoubled its activities following the recent disaster at Caporetto, in part because many observers (including many Americans) had seen that defeat as a product principally of a collapse of morale. Given the wealth of resources employed, the efficacy of the forms of intervention selected, and, the inherent attraction of Wilson's message, the ARC campaign was one of the most successful initiatives among the many undertaken in the aftermath of Caporetto. "The Red Cross is doing a great work here," Ambassador Page wrote Wilson in January 1918, "and it has, as far as it goes, undoubtedly, an excellent effect as propaganda."[22]

The ARC's action fit perfectly into the welter of local and national patriotic initiatives (committees, charitable institutions, organizations providing relief and moral support, etc.) that characterized the final year of war in Italy. A veritable army of the petty bourgeoisie mobilized in support of the war and therein found a new and gratifying social role. The American humanitarian organization was always careful to balance the two aspects of its action—material aid and "moral" aid, relief, and propaganda. Even the ambulances, before being sent to the front, were paraded through the towns and cities and presented as the vanguard of the powerful U.S. army, soon to be present on the Italian front as well. The American writer Dos Passos, a Red Cross ambulance driver in Italy, recalled with distaste in his memoirs the "ornamental" role that the numerous parades forced him into:

The Italians were trying to boost public morale which had hit bottom after their smashing defeat at Caporetto. A great deal was made of our entrance into Ventimiglia. The newspapers tried to give the impression that our little Section I was the vanguard of a great American army. We were greeted by crowds and flagwaving and singing schoolchildren. People pitched flowers and oranges into the ambulances. . . . They [two Red Cross majors] rubbed me the wrong way by declaring in a fit of winey candor that we were at the Italian front only as a propaganda gesture to help keep the Italians in the war. I knew that well enough. . . . What I liked to think I was doing was dragging the poor wounded wops out from under fire, not jollying them into dying in a war that didn't concern them.[23]

To obtain a more complete idea of how the ARC operated in Italy, let us examine a typical method of intervention: cash contributions on behalf of the poor families of deserving soldiers. The first campaign of this kind of relief was organized in April 1918 in order to commemorate the first anniversary of the U.S. entry into the war. During this campaign, 7,051 villages, towns, and cities were visited, and a total of 6.4 million lire was distributed. About 290,000 families received this form of relief.[24] A telegram sent in this period to the Ministry of the Interior in Rome by a Carabiniere officer in a small town in the south (Avigliano, in the province of Potenza) offers a vivid description of the welcome the local population gave to the American Red Cross:

> Today 10 am at the initiative of this deputy mayor huge procession with music flags civilian military and church authorities representatives from local associations all marched to the gates of the town to welcome members of the American Red Cross who arrived here from Potenza stop amidst enthusiastic applause and cheers the procession arrived at town hall where the ARC committee handed over 12,000 Lire to distribute to the poor families of soldiers in combat. Speeches were delivered invoking victory of the Italian-American brotherhood after which the delegation was accompanied once again to the edge of town, again to applause and cheers, to the tune of the American national anthem stop.[25]

The enthusiastic descriptions sent to Rome by the prefects of many Italian cities and towns reflected the staging of similar mass events in various Italian regions.[26] Accounts provided by Americans confirmed both the wholehearted support of the local authorities and the unflagging enthusiasm of the crowds.[27]

The success of the April campaign encouraged the ARC to institute a permanent program of cash awards to be paid to needy families of soldiers at the front who had distinguished themselves by outstanding discipline and fighting spirit. At first, the Italian military leadership was asked to provide lists of the most deserving soldiers. This gave officers an effective tool with which to apply pressure on and promulgate propaganda among the enlisted men. The awards, at first for a sum of 50 lire in June 1918 and later raised to 75 and 100 lire, were paid directly to the families of soldiers, chosen especially because they were located in the most remote and far-flung corners of Italy. A partially preprinted postcard was given to the families along with the award, so that they could then send the postcard with news of the payment to their loved one at the front. In the summer of 1918, with this method, the families of some 3,600 soldiers were given cash awards each month: "the delivery of the thousands of cash awards . . . in all the villages of Italy [served] to demonstrate the attentive relief provided by the ARC and the Italian government to the families of those drafted into war."[28] In addition to the payments made through the Comando Supremo, as we have seen, the American Red Cross also arranged to distribute payments of its own. As shown in Table 1, this form of aid accounted for the largest share of overall spending by the American humanitarian agency in Italy. As Prezzolini recalled:

> The Comando Supremo provided funds so that individual commanders at all levels could, personally, send subsidies to the families of needy soldiers who had behaved well, thus creating a personal bond of gratitude between the commander and enlisted man. This personal bond was reinforced by correspondence between officers and soldiers. When the soldier was on leave, the superior officer would write him a postcard or a letter, reminding him of his duties. . . . The American Red Cross assisted in this effort with thousands of monthly subsidies.[29]

Both at the front and in Italy, the American Red Cross enjoyed complete cooperation from the military leadership, from the state bureaucracy—both central and local—and from the various local leading citizens. This was further evidence that in 1918 broad sectors of the Italian governing class, out of conviction or opportunism, had subscribed to the American message. Everywhere they turned, the Americans working with the Red Cross encountered clear evidence of the bond that Italian mass emigration in the preceding decades had created between the United States and poorer and more remote areas of the Italian peninsula. In those areas, their presence helped to reinforce the mythical image of America, land of plenty and liberty, as described in the stories told by the emigrants. In some cases, the celebrations held for the arrival of the American Red Cross took on religious overtones. For instance, in Nuoro, according to Bakewell's colorful description, the distribution of

Table 1. Total expenditures of the American Red Cross Commission to Italy, November 1917–June 30, 1919 (in lire)

Civil affairs	74,332,817	(64.71%)
Military affairs	11,719,570	(10.20%)
Medical affairs	15,187,618	(13.22%)
Administrative bureau	8,854,823	(7.71%)
Tuberculosis division	3,486,067	(3.03%)
Restricted funds and miscellaneous	1,299,182	(1.13%)
Total	114,880,066	100%

Breakdown of the Expenses of the Three Chief Departments

1. Department of Civil Affairs

Administration	1.33%
Relief of refugees	33.11%
Canteen service	9.93%
Children's work	17.27%
Relief of Italian soldiers' families	22.14%
Ouvroir Department	15.91%
Other funds and miscellaneous	0.31%
Total	100%

2. Department of Military Affairs

Administration	1.70%
Italian soldiers at front	24.20%
Ambulance service	33.65%
Canteens and rest houses	36.59%
American soldiers at the front	3.86%
Total	100%

3. Department of Medical Affairs

Administration	1.67%
Surgical dressings service	7.83%
Hospital service	90.02%
Nurses' Home, Milan	0.48%

Source: C. M. Bakewell, *The Story of the American Red Cross in Italy* (New York, 1920), appendix I, pp. 209–10.

aid by the delegates of the American Red Cross had to be interrupted long enough to allow the local population to stage a religious procession held in their honor. The main feature of that procession was a large image of the Virgin Mary, and in her hand there fluttered a flag with the Stars and Stripes.[30]

The American forms of propaganda stood out against the Italian army's traditional, widely disliked techniques for the education of soldiers, especially before Caporetto: pompous lectures delivered by smart little teachers avoiding combat, or "by lawyers who drive up from Italy by car, and know nothing [about the war]," pamphlets and posters sent out to an army with a high rate of illiteracy, boring and often incomprehensible speeches delivered by career officers to troops forced to stand in ranks for hours and listen.[31] Even the free life insurance policy, which was one of the most important measures ordered by Minister Nitti on behalf of the fighting men, nonetheless clashed with the peasant mind-set of the foot soldier and his relatives, many of whom, in indignation or despair, interpreted the life insurance policy as an omen of impending doom or as shameful blood money paid in exchange for the soldiers' lives.[32]

Caporetto, in any case, led to a radical shift as well in the internal army propaganda and, in more general terms, the treatment of enlisted men. The *Servizio P* was created; this was an office in charge of propaganda, aid, and monitoring and surveillance of the army. This office attempted, for the first time, to establish a closer link with the infantry, employing new attitudes and techniques, and "to care for, lead, safeguard, and educate the enlisted population."[33] The *Servizio P* was the creation of reserve officers and was in clear opposition to the mentality of career officers. "It was the creation of educators and of men who had previously been leaders of men." It was the work of such intellectuals as Giuseppe Lombardo Radice and Gioacchino Volpe, who wanted to change the way officers at all levels communicated with soldiers, reducing the coercion and increasing the persuasion.[34] The delicate and difficult duties that fall to an *ufficiale P,* noted General Pennella, commander of the Italian Second Army, "demand the soul of a convinced apostle."[35] They did their best to educate officers to speak to enlisted men. In this connection, there were the famous *spunti di conversazione,* or conversational gambits—pamphlets that were widely distributed throughout the army.[36] These leaflets consisted of brief, simple discussions of topics that might be of interest to soldiers: food, the American intervention, life insurance, and the like. It was "suggested" to the noncommissioned officers working most closely with the enlisted men about what and how to talk to simple foot-soldiers. In that way, the propaganda would be more likely to appear as spontaneous and casual conversation. The *Ufficiali P* (or "P" Officers) also attempted to improve the material conditions of the soldiers' lives—rations, rest, leaves, hygiene, family aid—by listening to their complaints, amusing them with entertainment, and offering them spiritual comfort.

America joined this effort of ideological apostleship by the *Servizio P* in one of two ways. First, it offered the cooperation of organizations already present in Italy—the Red Cross, the YMCA, and the CPI—whose activity was moving in that direction. Second, it provided content for the new propaganda effort. Wilson and, more importantly, America dominated the pamphlets, posters, lectures, trench-distributed newspapers, and topics of conversation:

> Our allies perform miracles. We thought the Americans were a people of merchants, obsessed with earning money, and instead we discover that they are a people of knights in shining armor: they have gone to war with no other ambitions than to uphold Right and the Law, with no hatred other than for the new tyrants of the world, and not satisfied with generous offerings of the gold from their treasuries, they are now shedding their own radiant blood in the fields of France. They fight, and win. . . . If the Americans, far away, untroubled, living in tranquility on the far shore of the Ocean, felt the need to come here and fight on behalf of an Idea, what should we Italians do, since we are fighting not only for ideals, but also for our independence and for our future lives? To fight alongside America in this war represents for millions of Italians, who have gone to America in search of work and prosperity, an immense rehabilitation. Ask the people who live there, ask the letters that our fellow Italian immigrants write us from there, what opinion they had of Italy before the war and what opinion they have now. We were the Chinese of the world, but now the name of Italian is a title of glory.[37]

The Italian infantryman might well have been susceptible to this sort of approach. It is possible to sense the effort made by the governing class, then steeped in an elitist and highly rhetorical culture, to employ language that would be easily understandable and persuasive to the fighting masses.

Another example that shows the Italian high command's interest in directing the attention of the soldiers to the American intervention was the competition that Gioacchino Volpe announced in July and August 1918 among the soldiers of the Italian Eighth Army who had spent time living in the United States. A cash prize would be awarded to the most noteworthy essays that answered the following questions: "What constitutes the greatness of America? Why were Americans unwilling to submit to German arrogance?" A hundred or so soldiers responded, with essays that offer a concrete image of America among Italian soldiers:

The United States is a country of endless, fertile, productive land, countless mines, ports bursting with merchandise, astounding elevated railroads, and other such things: and all of this is fed and propelled by the great stream of migration that flows, trustingly, toward the United States. . . . America is the land not only where people work hard, but where work and workers are valued and respected. . . . America is . . . also the homeland of liberty. . . . We southern peasants were very happy to discover America. Americans are truly democratic. . . . The United States is capable of amazing things. . . . The Central Powers are destined for defeat, because America can exert a formidable effort. . . . With its high sense of justice, . . . the U.S. will fight at our sides, until the day of victory.[38]

However popular they might have been, the Americans of the Red Cross and the YMCA did not have a peer relationship with the mass of soldiers and the Italian population. There was an element of missionary work about their actions that placed them on a superior plane. There were many visible signals of their superior status. For example, all the members of the ARC and YMCA assigned to the Italian army, including enlisted men and noncommissioned officers, were treated as officers and could make use of mess halls and transportation reserved for Italian officers. The monthly pay they received from the American government, equivalent to 500 lire for ordinary soldiers and 750 lire for officers—even if that money had to pay for room and board as well—was not of the same order of magnitude as the pay received by Italian soldiers. The Italian salaries amounted to a few dozen lire per month for those soldiers who were married and with dependent children or other relatives.[39] Between January and July 1918, a very high percentage (50 out of 135) of the drivers for the first contingent of American ambulances at the front received decorations for valor. As Robert Lewis shows, this avalanche of medals was apparently awarded "commonly if not casually," not so much for actual heroic deeds, but rather for the simple fact that the drivers were Americans.[40]

Both Wilson and his representatives in Italy served as vehicles for a new image of a more democratic governing class, at least in the sense that the new image tried to win the consensus of the masses and was therefore more concerned with their living conditions and ways of thinking. Hence, the use of propaganda was far preferable to repression. In comparison with the attraction of Wilson's appeals and the concrete deeds of the humanitarian organizations that he sent to Italy, the limitations of the Italian governing class, still locked in a hidebound, nineteenth-century elitism, became especially glaring.

The Young Men's Christian Association

The YMCA (known as the Opera di Fratellanza Universale—Institution for Universal Brotherhood—in Italy) was an integral part of the American army in Europe. As soon as the United States went to war, the secretary general, John R. Mott, volunteered the full services of the YMCA to the government and took on the task of providing material and spiritual aid as well as entertainment to the soldiers sent to the western front. With this goal in mind, more than 2,000 *foyers* (soldiers' homes) were created in France. The YMCA volunteers, who also wore the uniform of the American army, openly carried out political propaganda: what better way to raise the morale of the soldiers than to spread reports of American technological and military superiority and the moral superiority of the American president's message?

The YMCA arrived in Italy in January 1918, under the command of John S. Nollen. It established its headquarters in Bologna, where the headquarters of the Intendenza Generale (General Superintendency) of the Italian army was already located. In contrast with the ARC, the YMCA's activities focused on the soldiers at the front, in the hospitals, in the rest camps, and in the military schools. The association was subdivided into various regional offices. Before the armistice there were offices in the areas of the Third, Fourth, Sixth, Seventh, Eighth, and Ninth Italian armies, as well as in Rome, Venice, Bologna, Milan, Turin, Florence, Ravenna, Faenza, Imola, Ferrara, Lugo, Modena, Parma, Pistoia, Treviglio, Cento, and Porretta. After the armistice, regional offices were also set up in Trento (Trent), Trieste, Belluno, Udine, Vicenza, and Brescia, as well as in Naples, Palermo, Genoa, and La Spezia, where Italian American troops that had served in the Italian army were being repatriated. Later, the red triangle of the YMCA also followed Italian troops to Tripoli, to Albania, and to Durrës (Italian Durazzo). The objective was to keep up morale among the troops through a careful blend of aid and propaganda. As an appointment book that the association distributed to the soldiers put it:

> As long as President Wilson and his son-in-law, Doctor Sayre, an officer of
> the Association, have been involved in promoting the welfare of the Italian

army and people, it has made efforts to bring assistance of every sort. . . .
The purpose of the Association is now and has always been the three-fold
task of building a healthy body, mind, and spirit. It hopes to be a helping
friend to every soldier.[41]

All the headquarters, generally established in a villa that had been requisitioned and made available by the military authorities, had a storehouse of
material and a group of administrative officers and soldiers responsible for
each department—entertainment, education, physical exercise, and so
on—and each was given an appropriate number of motor vehicles. These
offices regularly supplied materials and services for aid and recreation to
the hospitals and *case del soldato* (soldiers' homes) within its jurisdiction.
At the end of the war, 800 case del soldato were being served, and one
quarter of them, as we will see, were being run directly by the American
organization.[42]

Caporetto had eliminated any misgivings the Italian Comando
Supremo (chiefs of staff) might have had about the YMCA's activities[43]
and brought a new understanding of the importance of moral aid to the
soldiers at a time when a great number of the soldiers' homes, organized
before Caporetto by the personal efforts of a military chaplain, Don Minozzi,[44] had fallen into enemy hands. The YMCA astonished the Italians
with the lavish array of resources it made available.[45] The organization also
had considerable knowledge of propaganda and an ability to capture the
soldiers' imaginations, which was precisely what the new military leadership desired. The shock of Caporetto had also forced the more recalcitrant
fringes of the Italian governing class to acknowledge the American myth
and resources. In July 1918 Don Minozzi, pushed aside by the new aid
group, observed with profound annoyance that everyone was now saying
the same things:

> No one but America can save the world, America which alone is truly
> great, austere, generous, pure, and brilliant, devoted exclusively to the
> highest ideals of humanity, land of freedom *par excellence*. . . . It was a
> prostitution of Italy, which was eagerly and hastily selling herself to the
> wealthiest buyer in her eagerness to serve.[46]

During 1918, the YMCA created and directly managed a network of
some 200 case del soldato, both permanent and mobile, and also generously
funded and supplied the case del soldato run by the Italians. At the front, it

also organized refreshment stands at points where the greatest number of troops passed through, as well as at the main railroad stations and yards. Behind the lines, YMCA personnel regularly paid visits to hospitals and military convalescent homes, refugee camps, boot camps and rest areas for enlisted men, officer schools, and prisoner-of-war camps. In the fall of 1918, the association employed 270 Americans. Since each of those Americans had at least six Italians reporting to them, the total number of YMCA personnel in Italy was around 1,800 men. With continuous and urgent demands for help from Italian military commanders, this personnel was insufficient, but the YMCA's work was amplified by the full collaboration offered by the Italian military structure.[47] After the armistice and the subsequent demobilization, the YMCA's workload only increased, at least until the spring of 1919.

The YMCA secretary in khaki became a familiar figure to the Italian soldiers:

> Every day, one or another of our platoons sees the American, who teaches calisthenics and sports: one or another of our detachments is visited by a small troupe of soldier-actors, who provide their fellow soldiers, under the supervision of the American, with a few hours of entertainment; one or another of our hospitals is visited by the American, who hands out little presents or amuses the convalescents with a little music. And learned professors teach the English language to officers and soldiers, who take courses in the subject: and the conference rooms of the various centers are equipped with gramophones and letterhead stationery of the Fratellanza [Italian name of the YMCA—*translator*]; and the train carrying our fellow soldiers, liberated from prisoner-of-war camps, found along its route, at the trunk station, amidst the shadows, the chill, the fog, an American delegate handing out postcards, cigarettes, victuals. . . . This, gentlemen, is the true greatness of fine hearts.[48]

The YMCA casa del soldato became a symbol of the work that the American humanitarian organization was doing among the Italian soldiers. It might be housed in any type of building, from wooden huts in mountainous areas or structures shipped directly from the United States in prefabricated sections all the way up to a country villa or a city hotel requisitioned by the Italian military authorities. In general, the Casa del Soldato flew both Italian and American flags, crossed next to the red triangle that was the symbol of the YMCA. The interior of the homes was made cozy with decorations, posters, and furnishings, some of which were contributed by soldiers. The homes were equipped with record players, records, books, magazines, guitars and mandolins, desks and stationery, board games, and sometimes a piano and a movie theater. Outside, there were generally fields for volleyball, lawn bowling (bocce), basketball, and the like. Hundreds of soldiers came through every day; in many areas, this was the only place the Italian infantry could obtain rest and recreation.

The YMCA representative in charge of the casa del soldato would generously distribute coffee, crackers, chocolate, cigarettes, stationery, postcards, pens, and pencils. The troops must have been struck by the contrast between the attitude of the Italian military leaderships and that of the Americans. Don Minozzi, for instance, remembered the hostility of many Italian officers to providing the soldiers with aid. He quoted the director of the Italian soldiers' homes at the front, Major Vernetti, in July 1918:

> Stationery, why give them any more, they even have too much. The Commissariat supplies the soldiers, giving them three postcards a month, with postage, and half a pencil: what more do they want? Why should they write so much? Soldiers have other things to do. . . . We need to stop stuffing them will all these luxuries. War is war. And everyone has to wage war.[49]

It was estimated that each month the YMCA distributed to the soldiers about a million envelopes and sheets of writing paper, 800,000 postcards, a million cigarettes, and almost 300,000 pens and pencils (see Table 2). It also organized lectures, sports matches, showings of movies, concerts, theatrical productions, and schools to provide basic literacy for the enlisted men and to teach the officers the English language.

The movies, a new mass medium that attracted people from every walk of life and social class, played an important role. A small army of 350 projectionists, with more than 300 movie projectors, 40 of which produced their own electric power for open-air projections, traveled throughout northern Italy, projecting some 500 movies, some of which were made in New York and Paris, while some were produced in Italy. In the period between January 1918 and the spring of 1919, it is estimated that more than 19 million people watched films projected by the YMCA, a far greater number than the 11 million who attended a YMCA theatrical performance.

Table 2. Material distributed to Italian troops by the YMCA (January 1918–March 1919)

Stationery	15,000,000
Postcards	12,000,000
Penholders	1,080,000
Pencils	2,160,000
Pens	2,160,000
Bottles of ink	30,000
Magazines	307,000
Books	75,000
Guitars	1,800
Mandolins	1,800
Harmonicas and ocarinas	500
Phonograph players	900
Phonograph records	1,800
Phonograph needles	1,500,000
Bocce games	750
Bowling	450
Ring-toss games	450
Ping-pong	375
Rubber balls	750
Soccer balls	24,930
Volleyball balls	2,250
Basketballs	1,500
Cage-balls	110
Cigarettes	15,000,000
Packets of chocolate	50,000
Boxes of candy	500,000
Boxes of crackers	500,000
Board games (checkers, bingo, etc.)	1,800
Entertainment Division	
Entertainers hired	250
Concerts held	15,960
Spectators	11,289,225
Pianos purchased	95
Pianos rented	85
Movie Division	
Projectors	275
Projectors with generator	40

(continued)

Table 2 *(continued)*

Series of movies in circulation	500
Staff working in the division	350
Shows	22,035
Transportation Division	
YMCA trucks and automobiles	125
Italian trucks and automobiles	75

Source: YMCA, *L'opera dell' YMCA presso l'esercito italiano* (Rome, 1919), pp. 61–62, Fondo della Biblioteca Museo ed Archivio del Risorgimento, now in the Biblioteca di Storia Moderna e Contemporanea in Rome.

In the home setting, the propaganda was self-evident. It took the form of the abundance of goods distributed free of charge and the concern shown for the welfare of enlisted men. The myth of America, a land of limitless resources available to anyone who was willing to earn them through hard work, and the myth of Wilson, the democratic president who spoke to the common man, both emerged strengthened.

The soldiers responded gratefully to the work of the YMCA. The memoirs of several of the American YMCA representatives at the Italian front are filled with references to the expressions of wild enthusiasm with which their work was greeted. The YMCA representatives were aware that this was due only in part to their organizations charitable activities: behind these activities loomed the image of America, rendered even more mythical following the harsh experience of the trenches. For that reason, in tense situations or just before an offensive, the Italian commanders would ask the American secretaries to go personally into the trenches to talk to the soldiers and to distribute material for their personal comfort.[50]

Even though the association's propaganda efforts were concentrated in the zone around the front, they also reached central and southern Italy and the Italian islands. For instance, Constantine Panunzio, an Italian American who was serving in the YMCA and who was later recruited by the CPI, traveled for a month through the most remote and depressed areas of Sicily; everywhere he went he encountered cheering crowds crying "hooray for America."[51] As a pamphlet published by the Italian YMCA stated:

The field of propaganda for civilization is unquestionably one in which our secretaries, who speak fluent Italian, sow good seeds for an abundant harvest. The people of every class, and especially the untutored or doubtful people in the far flung districts of the countryside, are anxious to hear the messages of their foreign brothers in arms on whose assistance to the common cause they have very vague ideas. From our mouths, the truth sounds nobler and more persuasive.[52]

And that was how the Italians began to play basketball, to fall in love with American movies, to consume chewing gum.[53]

Soldiers as Propaganda

General John J. Pershing, supreme commander of the American Expeditionary Force (AEF) in Europe, concentrated the American army on the French front. He believed that U.S. forces should not be scattered across numerous points along the front; instead, he thought they should be concentrated on a single area and placed under the command of American officers. That belief, of course, mirrored the opinions and orders of Washington, which never responded adequately to the increasingly pressing demands that troops be sent to the Italian front. These demands arrived both from Americans in Italy (for instance, Ambassador Page, the commissioner for propaganda Charles Merriam, the U.S. consuls in Venice and Milan, and Fiorello La Guardia) and from nearly all the Italian politicians and military figures (Orlando, Sonnino, Nitti, and Diaz).[54] In both military and political terms, Italy was the "step-sister" of the Allied nations, receiving financial aid and material supplies, as well as being the object of both humanitarian initiatives and propaganda campaigns, but never receiving American soldiers. More than any other contribution, receiving American troops would have demonstrated unity of intent between the two allies; it would also have done more than anything else to lift Italian morale.

The only exception to this approach was the deployment of an American regiment, the 332nd "Ohio" Infantry Regiment, sent to Italy in the summer of 1918; a great uproar arose over its arrival and deployment to the Italian front. The regiment was sent to Italy primarily for propaganda purposes: to show the Italians that the Americans were arriving and that this regiment was just the vanguard of the powerful American army that would soon arrive on the Italian front. From the beginning, this was clear to the American soldiers being sent to Italy; they knew that they were a "propaganda regiment," likely to see more parade grounds than trenches.[55]

The regiment was under the command of Colonel William Wallace[56] and was made up of three battalions of roughly 1,000 men each. It arrived in Italy on 27 July 1918 and was given enthusiastic welcomes in Turin, Milan, Verona, and all the small towns it passed through on its way to Villafranca. There a solemn welcoming ceremony was held on 1 August. Orlando attempted, unsuccessfully, to move the ceremony to Verona because "popular excitement would certainly be expressed with greater warmth" in a large city, and it was important to ensure that "the ceremony attracted as much attention as possible."[57] For the occasion, the king, along with Orlando, Diaz, and Ambassador Page, reviewed the American troops; at the same time, the supreme commander issued an order of the day to the Italian army, written in both Italian and English, announcing the arrival of American troops in Italy. "The great Nation, which has come to the battle field in the name of Humanity and Right, . . . —it read—has today sent her troops also to our front as a solemn and proud sanction of the brotherly solidarity which she has already affirmed in other ways."[58] Ambassador Page recalled the great expectations that the Italians had been fostering; greeting the American soldiers, he reminded them that "[n]ever has any people looked to another with more friendliness and eager expectation than the Italians look today to us Americans. They have just celebrated throughout Italy 'The Fourth of July' as if it had been their own National holiday."[59]

The arrival of the Americans was immediately exploited by the army's *Uffici P,* which competed in singing the praises of these "crusaders" for their courage and military training. "On the front of the Eleventh Italian Army Corps, American units are about be deployed"—a communiqué issued by the head office of the *Sezioni P* announced. "This is the finest flower of the youth from across the Atlantic Ocean, bursting with vigor and daring, magnificent in their strength and enthusiasm; they have come among us to bring, with their example of perfect faith, the resources of the most advanced military techniques."

At the end of the summer of 1918, the trench newspapers and documents concerning the morale of the troops made increasingly frequent mention of America and the Americans. A *spunto di conversazione* leaflet for the soldiers, for instance, stated:

The appearance of Americans on our battle lines, and no longer merely as militia for the Red Cross or as founders of Case del Soldato ("soldiers' homes"), but now as full-fledged combatants, is always a subject of special interest to our soldiers: and it can provide officers with subjects for conversation for quite a while. And it truly constitutes the most magnificent and decisive factor in 1917–18.[60]

The "Propaganda Regiment" was held behind the lines for nearly the whole time it spent in Italy. Only for a brief period was the Second Battalion sent to occupy a secondary area on the front. American soldiers were not there to fight but to raise Italian morale through their presence alone. They were sheltered from the dangers of war and were instead used as invaluable propaganda tools; they were made as visible as possible among civilians and soldiers. It was truly an ironic twist of fate that during a drill behind the lines, a bomb exploded, killing an officer and four American soldiers and wounding dozens more. Normally, their days went by with too little excitement. One soldier in this regiment wrote that many of his fellow soldiers were afraid that the war would be over before their regiment even saw the front. None of them could understand why the Italian front seemed so quiet.[61]

Generally, American soldiers were transported from place to place by truck or on foot in order "to show Italy to the regiment and the regiment to Italy." For a period they even were obliged to change uniforms several times a day to create the impression that there were many more of them! As Sergeant Joseph Lettau wrote around the beginning of October 1918:

> The work of the day consisted of long, vigorous hikes with full mobile equipment worn. . . . It was at this time that the changing of clothes was adopted in order to create a false impression as to the number of Americans in Italy. Upon going out in the morning, overcoats and helmets were worn and upon returning in the afternoon by a different route, the overcoats and helmets were out of sight and raincoats and caps were worn. The next day, perhaps, the change would be to leather jerkins. The object was attained, for later, the Austrian prisoners reported that they had been under the impression that there were several divisions of Americans in Italy.

With or without the assistance of the YMCA, the regiment band provided much appreciated shows of American music. The Italians, it became clear, were very fond of jazz, ragtime, and traditional American songs.[62]

For the first few days of the battle of Vittorio Veneto, the American regiment was held in reserve, but on 28 October it was assigned to the Italian

Tenth Army, which had been ordered to break through the enemy front and lead the advance of the Italian army. It was not until the last day of the war for Italy, 3 November, that part of the regiment was engaged in active combat against an enemy that had asked not to fight because reports had already arrived that the armistice had been signed. This action was sufficient to earn the American regiment a special mention in the report on the battle of Vittorio Veneto. Or at least, on 2 January 1919, perhaps in consideration of President Wilson's imminent arrival in Italy, Diaz suggested that the commission that was preparing the report might make special mention of the American regiment's contribution. The Ohio regiment's role continued to be one of propaganda, even after the war had ended.[63]

Captain Fiorello La Guardia

Fiorello La Guardia is one of the best-known Italian Americans. Adolf Berle, a close associate of Franklin Roosevelt, considered the two most famous names of his generation to be Franklin D. Roosevelt and Fiorello La Guardia.[64] La Guardia's fame is tied especially to the years 1933–1945, during which he served three consecutive terms as New York City's energetic mayor, using every means at his disposal to fight the city's problems in the difficult years of the Great Depression and the Second World War. He created modern New York, and his years in office have been described as "twelve years of the best reform government in American municipal history."[65] Although La Guardia had always been a member of the Republican Party, through his exemplary work in New York City, he clearly was a key ally of Roosevelt's New Deal.[66]

The years of the First World War correspond to the early phase of La Guardia's political career. On 2 April 1917, when Wilson appeared before Congress to ask for a declaration of war against Germany, La Guardia was a freshman member of the House of Representatives. To general astonishment—not least the leaders of his own party—he had managed to win a seat in a heavily populated New York congressional district that traditionally voted Democratic. He was also the first Italian American elected to Congress. Throughout his long political career, he never felt at ease in either the political social world of Washington, the halls of the Capitol, or even among his party's high leadership. He remained a perennial outsider to the traditional political machine, loyal to his "insurgent" spirit and to his very personal political style. That style may have led to the mistrust of the higher political echelon, but it helped him garner an exceptional popularity among the immigrant masses.[67]

One little-known aspect of La Guardia's political career is the year he spent in Italy toward the end of the Great War. He was one of the Americans who spent the longest time in Italy and who was deeply involved in joint military, political, and propaganda activities. He arrived in Italy during the first half of October 1917, before Caporetto, and stayed until October of the following year, when the war was drawing to a close. His official duty was to run the aviation training camp in Foggia, a joint Italian and U.S. initiative for the training of American pilots. La Guardia carried out this task with his customary energy and highly personal interpretation of orders and ranks. His unique style won him the unquestioning loyalty of his subordinates and the constant annoyance of his immediate superiors. Alongside this duty, he was also assigned to perform more political tasks. Thus, he served as a liaison between Rome and Washington, as well as between Italian and American and Inter-Allied headquarters in Paris. In addition, he worked on a wide-ranging campaign of propaganda in the difficult post-Caporetto conditions, traveling the length and breadth of the Italian peninsula and delivering heartfelt speeches in his quaint Italian to large crowds.

La Guardia was a second-generation Italian American, but he was an outsider with respect to Italian immigration. His family possessed a certain degree of culture and achievement. Fiorello spent his childhood in small frontier towns in South Dakota and Arizona, where his father, a music teacher, had accepted a position as bandmaster in the U.S. army. The frontier made a deep impression on Fiorello's personality and his vision of life. He saw himself as a man of the West, honest, straightforward, self-confident—a man of character. He spent his years as a young man in Trieste and Fiume; he worked for U.S. consulates first in Budapest and later in Fiume. This was a period of intense exploration for him, as he studied European languages and international law and immigration law, subjects that would prove useful to him later in life. When he returned to the United States, he moved to New York, where he obtained a law degree at great personal sacrifice.[68]

At the age of thirty La Guardia had accumulated varied life experiences that allowed him to satisfy his intense personal desire to attain a degree of distinction, to win power and reputation, and, at the same time, to defend the less advantaged, the inevitable victims of the abuse and exploitation he had witnessed repeatedly on both sides of the Atlantic. With his magnetic personality, he attracted the loyalty of the masses of immigrants in the crowded tenements of New York: his skills as a speaker were a product of the sincerity that his audience sensed in his words, but they were also linked to his theatrical gifts, which allowed him to dominate center stage. He also spoke the languages of the immigrants: Italian, Yiddish, Hungarian, Serbo-Croatian, and German. He understood their problems, and he intended to solve them. These gifts led to his election to the House of Representatives in 1916.

In the middle of the summer of 1917, when Congress adjourned after passing the main measures providing for national mobilization, La Guardia enlisted in the Army Aviation Section of the Army signal corps and, just before shipping out to Europe, was promoted to captain. He chose the aviation section because of his personal interest in aviation. He flew as a hobby, piloting aircraft that a friend of his, Giuseppe Bellanca, built alone in a garage near his home. These were the pioneering years of aviation: La Guardia's experience piloting home-made aircraft (consider, for instance, that the pilot's seat consisted of a Vienna straw-seat chair tied to the fuselage and that the slightest breeze interfered with proper control of the plane), though limited, was still greater than what most would-be pilots could claim at the time.[69] The Aviation Section was happy to recruit an officer with flying experience, especially one who spoke Italian. He was assigned to the Aviation Training Field (Campo di Addestramento Aeronautico) in Foggia, which, by a twist of fate, had been his father's birthplace.

Fiorello La Guardia was one of a very few congressmen who felt a duty to volunteer for the war. Many factors must have contributed to his decision. Since he had urged people who had voted for him to go to war, it was in his nature to feel that he had a moral obligation to do the right thing and volunteer himself. Another aspect of his personality was his desire to personally measure himself against the challenges of warfare in a theater of war. He must also have wanted to prove that Italian Americans were full-fledged citizens no less patriotic than Americans whose people had come over a long time before his. Finally, he must have given some consideration to the advantages that serving in the war would mean for him in his later political career in terms of experience, contacts, and reputations.

La Guardia's versatile and intense activity in Italy indeed garnered publicity for him back in the United States that he would have been unlikely to have gotten by staying in Congress, an isolated representative of the Republican Party. Articles began to appear in high-circulation publications praising the personality and deeds of this "congressman-aviator." The *New York Times,* for instance, wrote: "President Wilson and the United States could not have chosen a better representative in Italy than this brave soldier," or "La Guardia could not perform a nobler work than the one he is at present conducting, whereby he is serving his two countries." A feature article in the *Literary Digest* described the close collaboration that La Guardia and the famous violinist Albert Spalding (who was also sent to the training camp in Foggia) had developed, depicting it as a magnificent example of the blending of the races in America. A photograph of the short, stout, dark-complexioned La Guardia standing next to the slender, fair-haired, aristocratic violinist helped to illustrate the idea. The article went on to describe how Spalding had quickly become La Guardia's right-hand man in his extensive travels throughout Italy, as La Guardia covered the peninsula in his efforts to persuade the Italians—with astonishing candor—to redouble their commitment to the war effort, or in meetings with Italy's King Victor Emmanuel III and General Diaz. What emerged was an image of a congressman working hard at the highest levels of the war operation in Italy.[70]

This growing public notice must have come as a welcome development to the newly elected politician who had proven skillful in the art of capturing votes and winning positive publicity. In this area, he did not tread lightly; he even employed damaging personal attacks against his adversaries. Once he won public office, however, La Guardia demanded such total and painstaking honesty from himself and his colleagues that he became a legend. In Berle's words, he had a "tempestuous, passionate honesty."[71] With this pairing of opposite qualities (what Mann calls the two aspects of Dr. Jekyll and Mr. Hyde of La Guardia's political personality), he achieved something that no other Italian American had done before him—winning election to the United States Congress and later obtaining a unique position in the American political realm.[72]

In Italy, La Guardia's activity fell into one of three main categories: his work in the field of aviation; his political and bureaucratic activity in the various supervisory agencies and bodies with which he was working in Rome and Paris; and his intense engagement in the area of wartime propaganda.

La Guardia's activity in the aviation sector included his work as the director of the training camp at Foggia and his concerted efforts to improve his flying skills and attain his dream of taking part in combat flying missions at the front. Despite his best efforts, he never succeeded in being appointed lead pilot; he always flew as copilot or bombardier. He did take his pilot's license, but his attempted solo flight at aviation school ended in disaster. Strong winds made him lose control of the plane, driving it out of the training area. When he attempted an emergency landing, the aircraft overturned, and he suffered a painful hip injury. "I can't take the buzzard off, and I can't land him," he seems to have confided to a subordinate, "but I CAN FLY the son of a gun!" He took part in combat missions on the Italian front as copilot as part of a crew that included the very stiff Major Piero Negrotto, who looked aristocratically upon the world through his monocle, and the ace of Italian aviation, Captain "Fred" Zoppoloni. In one incident, after bombing Austrian positions, they were intercepted by enemy aircraft and would probably have been shot down if English aircraft had not come to their aid.[73]

La Guardia's dual role as officer and politician also brought him duties and contacts that were well outside the boundaries of the military world. He began to travel frequently to Rome and Paris as a representative of the joint Army and Navy Airship Board. Beginning in the spring, he was virtually the chief of American aviation in Italy. During his stays in Rome, La Guardia met a great number of Italian politicians, and he established close friendships with many of them. In particular, he became a close friend of Francesco Nitti, then minister of the treasury and the chief leader of the non-Socialist left. Through Nitti (among others), he established contacts with the Italian military and civilian leadership. At the front La Guardia had extended meetings with General Diaz and the king, who entrusted him with messages for American headquarters in Paris. Diaz expressed his concern and apprehension for the failure to send American troops to the Italian front, while the king confided his fear that Italy's decision to ally itself with the Triple Entente had not been understood and that this might result in a costly isolation of Italy from its allies. During one of his stays at the front, La Guardia was invited to meet Gabriele D'Annunzio as well. But the poet apparently was not very impressed with the informal and ironic manners of this quaint Italian-American politician. La Guardia is said to have pointed out that the two men had a great deal in common: "You are in the Air Service, so am I. . . . You make speeches; I make speeches too. The people don't understand your Italian, but they pretend they do. They don't understand me either, but they ask what I am trying to say." La Guardia added that D'Annunzio, always deadly serious about himself, was not at all amused by these observations, but that the king found them very funny when La Guardia told him about the meeting. La Guardia's autobiography portrays the king as an amiable and witty personality. Once, for instance, when La Guardia confronted him with a problem associated with how the port of Genoa operated, the king supposedly exclaimed: "But you should take that up with Signor Nitti in Rome. You see, I am not the President of a republic. I am only a king. I do have many powers."[74] According to rumors, La Guardia was sufficiently close to the king to call him "Manny."[75]

La Guardia had managed to insert himself into the highest Italian political and military spheres (he was also awarded the Croce di Guerra) and could have been used as a mediator between the two countries, which remained politically and culturally aloof from each other. In a confidential report that he wrote on congressional letterhead stationery for the American headquarters in Paris in December 1917, La Guardia mentioned various confidential conversations he had had with both Nitti and Eugenio Chiesa, commissioner of the Italian government for aviation, and concluded by saying: "My personal acquaintance here and my standing as a member of the House of course can be utilized in any way you deem advisable to bring about closer relations and obtaining such concessions as may be conducive to our common interest." His invitation to make use of Nitti was left unanswered. In the same report, La Guardia described Nitti as "the Man of the Hour in Italy."[76]

In his exuberance, La Guardia took part in some questionable enterprises. Once he went to Spain with false documents and succeeded in obtaining supplies of steel and other raw materials for Italy from that neutral country.[77] On another occasion he got in touch with Hungarian exiles who planned to start a revolution in their homeland. A proposal that he conveyed through Ambassador Page to pursue this initiative received a stern rejection from Wilson, who reiterated his determination to keep foreign relations on a morally impeccable plane. Wilson concluded by observing to his secretary of state that "too many irresponsible 'agents' are at large, and they are apt to do a great deal of harm." Accordingly, on 5 January 1918, Lansing informed Ambassador Page that he was turning down La Guardia's plan.[78] In this and in other cases (Crosby, Gino Speranza, Ambassador Page himself), Wilson discouraged any initiatives that were not conducted by his narrow circle of personal emissaries.

Aside from the military and diplomatic arenas, wartime propaganda was the realm in which La Guardia made the best use of his volcanic energy and his skill as a speaker. As we have seen, he was one of the few Americans who arrived in Italy before Caporetto; thus, he was one of the few people that the

American ambassador, Thomas Nelson Page, could use for a campaign of speeches designed to boost Italian morale and encourage resistance in the immediate aftermath of the catastrophic defeat. In his autobiography La Guardia recalls the cautious way in which Page entrusted him with his first mission. La Guardia would be sent to make a speech in Genoa, at the Palazzo della Borsa (the stock exchange). If the speech was poorly received, the embassy would refuse to acknowledge him as an official speaker, but if the reception was positive, he would be sent on other speaking engagements in the largest Italian cities. The Italians warmed immediately to this peculiar orator, who was occasionally incomprehensible because of his carefree blend of proper Italian with Apulian (Pugliese) dialect and with the Italian American pidgin of New York's Little Italy. After the audience's initial bewilderment, they were soon drawn in by La Guardia's passion, profound conviction, and transparent sincerity, as well as his theatrical way of communicating his feelings to the crowd. Silvio Crespi, who took part with him in the fourth of July celebrations in Florence, was stunned by the "astonishingly impetuous" way in which La Guardia addressed the Italian public.[79] In reality, La Guardia was the very model of the well-integrated, successful, and democratic Italian American that was especially popular in Italy at the time. "La Guardia is more popular here than if he were an Italian deputy," exclaimed one member of Orlando's cabinet. "I love him like a brother. He combines in his own person American strength and Latin geniality. In fact, forming a link between the two races." His propaganda campaign was very effective.[80]

La Guardia's propaganda activity, which began even before American humanitarian and propaganda organizations arrived in Italy, continued under the sponsorship of the CPI, which was constantly on the hunt for good American speakers who knew Italian. Evidence of how useful La Guardia's words and spirit were at that juncture in Italy is provided by how frequently the various patriotic committees printed and distributed his speeches. Unquestionably, La Guardia's speeches, delivered in a simple and direct style, along with his passionate convictions, contrasted favorably with the obscure and pompous speeches delivered by Italian orators. The Comitato Lombardo of the Unione Generale Insegnanti, one of the most important institutions of the so-called Fronte Interno ("domestic front"), published in pamphlet form the speech that La Guardia delivered on 3 February 1918 at the Teatro della Scala (La Scala) in Milan in order to "offer it for the reading enjoyment and consideration of soldiers, laborers and factory workers, women, students, all those who have not had the good fortune to hear the sincere, acute, and captivating words of this valorous American congressman," "a vigorous man of action, a typical product of a young and powerful race," who delivered "a magnificent speech that moved the audience to enthusiastic applause."[81]

La Guardia's words must have been startling compared with the empty, pompous language of Italian orators of the period, stuffed with classical metaphors and Latin mottos. As we have seen, the shock of Caporetto prompted a number of the more enlightened intellectuals to rethink the way they spoke to the soldiers and to the common people, in an attempt to become more effective and comprehensible.[82]

Another speech, which La Guardia delivered in Bologna (again printed and distributed in pamphlet form by the Unione Generale Insegnanti) sought to encourage Italians to support the war effort. It shows how critical, if not outright brutal, La Guardia's words could be. He scolded the Italians for eating too much, working too little, and using American funds for purposes other than those intended:

> Final victory depends upon your resistance. Now that we are here, let us speak with what may seem like brutal frankness, and let us tell you that there is no point in talking about your past glory, we must have done once and for good with this glory! . . . Your factories need to work more. You have magnificent factories, immense factories: I have seen some very major ones, but I also saw that they are closed on Sundays. . . . We cannot take this or that man out of military service, to avoid combat, if there is another one who works better in his place. I am talking to women especially, and I say to them: 'Don't let the cowards avoid combat." . . . And another important thing. We must try to limit the food supplies because, if you allow me to say it: You eat too much! This should be rejected. Food is not well disciplined. . . . And now that we are feeding the nations of the Triple Entente it is right to say this to you. To say that what you are doing is too little! Then it behooves me to say again that if we lend you money we give you that money to spend it all for the war effort and not to steal it or to build buildings with it! . . . These are all the little things that if you eliminate them, they will help you to win the war! Your first duty is not to act against the Fatherland! You have no choice: either you win this war and preserve your place among Nations . . . or you will become the gardeners of Germany![83]

Beginning in the spring of 1918, the name of La Guardia appeared regularly in the lists of orators of the CPI's Division of Speakers. Yet, La Guardia's histrionic and folksy style, despite his popularity, was not exactly what the leadership of the CPI was looking for. In their view, he was not the kind of speaker who should represent America. In a secret report to Washington, the director of the CPI in Italy spoke of La Guardia in critical terms:

We are much handicapped by the lack of competent men to speak for America. This task is much more personal than any other and these men give a direct impression of America not obtained in any other way. For that reason it is essential to have men who will make good "samples" of America. At present our personnel is not strong enough for this purpose. Neither La Guardia nor Cotillo, both of whom have their excellent points are sufficiently representative of the best that is our country; and I am afraid that they will make the wrong or more accurately not the very best impression. . . . The fine, deep, permanent democratic impression that should be made is still lacking and I don't see how we can produce it with the staff we now have.

We suspect that what the chiefs of the CPI in Italy really wanted were blonde, cautious, distinguished speakers in the Anglo-Saxon mold, the only ones who could truly represent America with their personal appearance.[84]

Aside from Ambassador Page, who was the first to run the risk of involving La Guardia in American propaganda, the only American who sensed the potential of the newly elected congressman beneath his rough exterior was Gino Speranza: Captain La Guardia, he wrote in his diary, "he is certainly a character, with solidity, I believe, behind his unconvincing appearance." Shortly before, he had called him "a mighty live wire."[85]

— 5 —

The Arrival of the
Professional Propagandists

Although the propaganda campaign analyzed in the preceding chapter is surprising in its breadth and incisiveness, it was not until the spring of 1918 that Wilson's propaganda project attained its full scope. In April 1918, the Committee on Public Information (CPI) opened an office in Rome. Initially, it established operations within the American embassy, pressing into service as its first core group of workers a team of embassy employees who had already begun to implement American propaganda in Italy, under the direction of the United Press journalist John Hearley. Ambassador Page, who had always been keenly aware of the need to build bridges between these two countries, which culturally were so different and so profoundly ignorant of one another, had decided, on his own initiative, to establish an embryonic center for propaganda alongside the political intelligence office created immediately after the American intervention. Soon the CPI broke away from the embassy and opened offices of its own at Via del Tritone 142, in the heart of the Italian capital.

The Italian Bureau was part of a larger organization of offices and agents that extended across Europe, Central and South America, and Asia. While the Domestic Section aimed to win over American public opinion in support of the war and Wilson, the Foreign Section, which began operations in October 1917, extended its field of operations around the world. In Creel's own words, this was a "fight for world opinion," launched to win the entire human race over to the ideals of the United States and the American president.[1]

With this end in mind, the Foreign Section organized an international network of agents and supplied them with a constant flow of information, articles, and propaganda material. Until February 1918, George Creel oversaw this activity personally; he was succeeded by Will Irwin until 4 July of the same year and thereafter by Edgar Sisson and Harry Rickey. In Europe, branch offices were opened in Allied and neutral nations, such as England, France, Italy, Spain, Switzerland, Holland, Sweden, Denmark, and Russia. In America, the Foreign Section structure included primarily three operative units: (1) the Telegraphic Service, run by Walter Rogers, which sent out daily dispatches, by cable or wireless, to the foreign press; (2) the Foreign Press Bureau, often known as the Poole Service after the name of its director, the writer Ernest Poole, who developed and sent via diplomatic pouch feature articles about daily life in America and at the front; and (3) the Foreign Film Division, which organized the selection and distribution of American films overseas. An agreement with American overseas film distributors allowed the CPI to select commercial films to be distributed and to require anyone who showed the movies to present with them shorter films prepared by the CPI. In addition to the Poole Service, which soon became a key overseas feature of the CPI, there was a Pictorial Service, which distributed photographic material of all kinds—ranging from posters and postcards to photographs for the press or for exhibitions, all the way down to little American flags and boutonnieres—to thirty-five countries on a weekly basis. All of these services required the presence of CPI representatives in foreign countries; these representatives were responsible for effective local distribution of the material. In seventeen countries, the CPI had its own commissioners and offices; in countries that had no official representative, some twenty diplomatic or consular representatives and a dozen ordinary American citizens living abroad served as the CPI's agents.[2]

Creel was understandably proud of the gigantic organization that he had assembled in just a few months and that was now trumpeting the American social and political model, along with the words of the charismatic American president, around the world. "From being the most misunderstood nation in the world, America became the most popular," while Wilson now had a worldwide stage. Pamphlets containing his speeches, translated into many different languages, enjoyed circulation well into the millions. In the *Complete Report,* written in 1919, Creel's pride in his work and his total devotion to Wilson can be seen in a phrase in which he suddenly addresses the president directly: "I am proud to tell you, sir, that your declarations had the force of armies."[3]

Charles E. Merriam was put in charge of the Italian office. Merriam, a brilliant and ambitious professor of political science at the University of

Chicago, attempted to enter politics after the war, when he ran unsuccessfully for mayor of Chicago; later he founded the study of behaviorism in political science. On 29 March 1918, he landed in Europe. He had prepared by reading a few books on Italy and the Italian language on the ship coming over, and he carried with him letters of introduction from George Creel, which allowed him to gather information and advice in London and Paris before arriving in Italy.[4]

Like so many intellectuals involved in the Wilsonian crusade for world democracy, Merriam was a progressive Republican, and he never seems to have felt any conflict in terms of political loyalties. In this connection, a suggestion that he sent to Washington in the summer of 1918 is particularly illuminating. At the height of the Italian propaganda campaign, when he was insistently requesting prestigious American speakers: "It would of course be preeminently desirable to have President Wilson himself! As I stated in a previous report he would receive an ovation in Italy. . . . After the President, the presence of Colonel Roosevelt particularly in Italy would be of incalculable value and would go a long way toward stiffening the morale of the entire country."[5] Merriam did not seem to have the slightest notion of the bitter political differences, to say nothing of the personal hatred, that divided Wilson and Theodore Roosevelt, which made his idea naïve, to say the least.

Aside from this momentary slipup, Merriam was anything but naïve; indeed, he was cunning, capable, and tireless. In a short time, his title as "high commissioner of public information for Italy," his personal style as a special envoy from the federal government and the White House, along with the abundant resources made available to him, made a profound impression on the Italian leadership, providing him with access to the top political and military figures. He frequented Nitti and enjoyed private meetings with Orlando, Sonnino, Bissolati, the king, and General Diaz. The enthusiasm he aroused is documented by a letter from the Comando Supremo to Orlando in August 1918:

> Merriam expressed his gratitude and satisfaction with the meetings that he had with His Majesty the King and His Excellency General Diaz. . . . His power truly seems to be considerable. He appears to have brought with him trusted colleagues, who are scattered throughout Italy, to monitor the attitudes of the population and to gather information of all sorts (political, economical, financial, etc.). He has often asked that messages that would be useful to President Wilson be communicated to him directly.[6]

Aside from the high leadership, Merriam perhaps had greater hopes of reaching and influencing the Italian masses and bringing the new American credo to the farthest corners of the Italian peninsula. In order to achieve this objective, he organized a wide-ranging propaganda campaign. In contrast with the relief organizations analyzed earlier, for Merriam propaganda was a full-time occupation. In order to do his job well, he had to conduct a thorough and careful analysis of Italy's political situation, both at the highest levels and in the various classes and the most diverse regions of Italy. He did so with noteworthy energy and determination in the six months that he spent in Italy.[7]

In Italy, as in other European countries,[8] the CPI commissioner's work ran on a collision course with the work of the American embassy, invading the ambassador's traditional areas of exclusive jurisdiction. An irremediable disagreement developed between Merriam and Page as well, despite their virtual agreement on the war and the situation in Italy; the clash culminated in Merriam's return to the United States at the beginning of October 1918 and, after that, with the subordination of the CPI to the embassy, in a shift in status that was facilitated by the impending general demobilization. The clash was not a product of any arrogance or misguided intentions of the CPI overseas staff; rather, the problem lay in an objective overlapping of responsibilities created by the way that Wilson organized his diplomatic services. Under Wilson, along with a continuous undercutting of the traditional diplomatic channels, parallel structures and personnel were empowered. In some cases, like the CPI, these personnel were official; but more frequently, like Colonel House and the Inquiry, they were unofficial or answerable directly to the president. As we will see, this duplication of structures and muddling of roles did nothing to facilitate a dialogue between countries that were just emerging from centuries of reciprocal cultural distance and mistrust, countries that had differing political languages and structures.[9]

Merriam poached qualified staff from other American agencies already operating in Italy and established information exchange and collaboration with others. Inside the embassy, he managed to obtain the services of Gino Speranza, the chief of the political intelligence office. From the leadership of the American Red Cross and the YMCA he obtained advice and assistance, especially for the work to be done in the provinces. The American consuls in the main Italian cities provided extensive cooperation. From the circles of the American journalists working in Rome he recruited John Hearley and Edward Strutt of United Press [as United Press International was then known—*translator*], John Bass and Edgar Mowrer of the *Chicago Daily News*, and Arthur Benington of the *New York World*. From the American Aviation Section in Italy he drew Fiorello La Guardia, Arthur Spalding, Kingsley Moses, and Walter Wanger. He also obtained the full cooperation of Italy's civilian and military authorities. The office's monthly budget, which had to cover local expenses, though not the material and staff sent from Washington, amounted to $10,000 and was raised to 15,000 toward the end of the summer of 1918.[10]

With an enthusiastic and well-prepared staff and with plenty of propaganda material, the CPI launched a program of "mass education in Italy."[11] Its objectives were not limited to the immediate necessity of responding to the crisis of Caporetto and therefore of lifting Italian morale by publicizing the decisive contribution of American help to the Allied cause. The CPI also intended to influence the way people thought and to spread Wilsonian ideals. The Italian campaign was an example of that fusion of domestic and international goals characteristic of the New Diplomacy: the goal was not only to improve Italy's ability to wage war, but also to shift the domestic political climate in favor of America and Wilson. If the goal of making Wilson and his country popular was amply attained, influencing the domestic political situation in a lasting manner was not. Wilson's popularity vanished like a soap bubble when the peace negotiations turned thorny. Misunderstandings and hostility again reigned. No domestic political force of Wilsonian inspiration could serve to interpret between the different languages and mediate the conflict in aspirations. This does not mean that Wilson's widespread popularity, though short-lived, was not intense while it lasted. This phenomenon raises many questions about the paths Italy might have traveled at that moment of great change if that popularity had only been exploited more constructively.

The CPI's Propaganda Work in Italy

The employees of the Rome office, about fifty people in all, were divided into four departments: the News, Photographic, Speakers, and Cinema departments.

The News Department, directed by John Hearley (who also served as Merriam's replacement when he was away), distributed news reports that it received on a daily basis by telegraph from the CPI offices in New York and

Paris. (The Paris office was a clearinghouse for continental Europe and also gathered and edited the news that arrived from the French front.) the department also distributed feature articles from the Poole Service, which came by mail from New York on a weekly basis. Through the Agenzia Stefani, which at the time was the largest press agency in Italy, hundreds of newspapers received "American" news every day. According to Creel, they published at least half the American news, thus demonstrating both the new interest that had developed for America and the skill of the CPI journalists and volunteers who worked tirelessly back in the homeland to "fabricate" the kind of news needed to meet the growing foreign demand. The department also assembled its news in a daily bulletin that it distributed to some 200 selected individuals in the fields of journalism, government, and academia. Aside from the material that was sent to all countries, a dozen articles about farming and life in the American countryside were sent to Italy every week for use by the provincial papers.[12]

The Photographic Department, under Byron M. Nester, distributed huge volumes of propaganda material. The statistics provided in the final report of the Rome office indicate the distribution of over 4.5 million postcards, 360,000 pamphlets on the American contribution to the war, 326,000 extracts of President Wilson's speeches 200,000 small American flags, 70,000 posters of the president, 66,000 American war posters, 155,000 badges and ribbons with Italian and American colors [red, white, and green and red, white, and blue—*translator's note*], plus 33,000 pieces of sheet music, with the American national anthem and other popular songs. Nearly 3,000 exhibitions were organized with American photographic material, while approximately 16,000 small towns and villages received distributions of material from this department alone.[13]

The weekly reports on the work done in this sector showed the astonishment of the employees themselves at the "enormous" demand for their material. In his continual requests for supplies from Washington, Merriam felt the need to provide an explanation:

The appetite for our post cards and pictures seems to increase in proportion to the distribution. The two million cards asked for are already allotted, and we are piled high with requests in many directions. Therefore I have wired asking for five million additional. The demand may seem large but I beg to remind you that there is a very large correspondence carried on between the soldiers and their families entirely by means of cards, and they have the postcard habit on a huge scale. The cards are excellent prop-aganda as they pass through many hands, and it is very desirable for us to meet this demand. There is also a great demand for pictures of all kinds il-lustrative of American life and war activity. There is a very special and in-cessant demand for pictures of the president, and we shall be very glad to have the million cards bearing a tribute to Italy, which you have promised us. The picture side of our work is extremely important and should be vig-orously supported. Probably the field for picture propaganda is greater in Italy than anywhere else; the Italians have a great fondness for pictures, and they do great good particularly in the southern part of the country where [there] is a large percentage of illiteracy and where propaganda lit-erature is entirely useless.[14]

The following week, Merriam added: "Probably you will think that I am endeavoring to cover Italy *literally* with these cards."[15] A month later, in connection with the American flags, he observed:

There is an immense demand for flags and the American colors all over Italy and it is impossible to obtain them here. . . . There is an almost pa-thetic desire on the part of many Italians to possess one of our flags, and it is this demand we wished to meet. On the 4th of July we were swamped with requests for our flags.[16]

Another widely requested item was large-format framed photographs of scenes of American life, American fighting men, or portraits of Wilson for display in shop windows or other locations where large volumes of people were likely to pass, such as train stations, urban public transportation vehi-cles, or company canteens or cafeterias, theaters, and hotels. In this connec-tion, for instance, Merriam made an agreement with the Singer sewing machine company, which promised to display CPI photographs in the roughly 400 stores that Singer owned in Italy.[17]

In the National Archives in Washington are preserved the register books of the distribution of propaganda material carried out by the Rome office in the 11 June 1918–14 January 1919 period. The descriptions of the distribu-tion are very detailed, and they show that, with the exception of the massive donations of many tens of thousands of postcards made, especially initially, to the YMCA, the American Red Cross, the American consuls in Venice, Turin, Livorno, Genoa, Florence, Palermo, Naples, and Milan, and a number of Italian Army Corps, the distribution of all propaganda articles took place separately in small quantities (for instance, 200–500 postcards or 200 pamphlets or 500 badges). The distribution was through a very fine-grained network that made use of its own agents, the mayors and prefects of towns, as well as Italian volunteers and civil resistance organizations. Most of the latter type of distribution covered mainly central and southern Italy, while the north was more frequently covered by American consuls, the army, and the YMCA, which had its headquarters in Bologna.[18]

In early September 1918, the director of this sector sent an alarming message:

> This Department can no longer run on its present scale. On Saturday alone demands were received for photo displays from 21 cities, nine Army Corps, and the Italian Propaganda Office. Reports from U.S. Consuls say these displays give splendid results. . . . A bi-weekly illustrated paper can be used to great advantage beginning with 1,000,000 copies per issue. The supply of pamphlets and boutonnieres is wholly inadequate. On these lines this department will need a large increase in staff and room.[19]

The Cinema Department

As we have seen, Americans had already become moviegoers, and American-made movies were viewed around the world. With the war, this powerful mass medium was exploited intensively, both in America and elsewhere, where movies had the added power of novelty. Cinema had the power to rivet the attention of broad swathes of the population impervious to other means of communication. As Creel put it, the three fundamental weapons in the CPI's battle to win over public opinion were "the Written Word, the Spoken Word, and the Motion Picture."[20]

At first, the CPI distributed only documentaries made by army directors; later, it also produced its own full-length feature films, the best known being *Pershing's Crusaders, America's Answer,* and *Under Four Flags;* these films were widely seen. For the production of this sort of commercial film, England, France, and Italy were invited to form partnerships with the CPI.

As we have seen, the American Film Division had made agreements with the leading American movie exporters, whereby foreign distributors or individual movie theaters that refused to show American propaganda films would not be allowed to show commercial films. This gave the CPI a powerful way of controlling the movie markets of foreign countries. In neutral and hostile countries, in Creel's words, "Charlie Chaplin and Mary Pickford led *Pershing's Crusaders* and *America's Answer* into the enemy's territory and smashed another Hindenburg line." In Allied countries like Italy, American movies were assured of extensive publicity because the opening showing of each movie became a local occasion attended by public authorities.[21]

In Italy, the CPI's Foreign Picture Service shipped 420 films, with a total length of about 120,000 meters.[22] The distribution of American movies reached its high point in the summer months of 1918. In a carefully compiled record book for the period between July and October 1918, the office distributed roughly sixty American newsreels and about fifty documentaries on American cities and countryside, on U.S. economic activities, on preparations for war at home, and on collaboration with Allies at the front (there was even a documentary on American troops on the Italian front).[23] In order to make the best use of available material, in the area around Rome it was decided to show the movies in about twenty Roman movie houses during the weekend, while showings were organized in the small towns around Rome during the weekdays. Unquestionably, the CPI especially covered Rome and surrounding areas though it also shipped many films to cities and towns in both northern and southern Italy.[24]

The Department of Speakers

The duties assigned to the Department of Speakers, which was directed by Rudolph Altrocchi and Kingsley Moses, were more complex than those of other departments. The reason was that it was necessary not only to distribute the material sent out from American headquarters, but also to program the work of speakers throughout Italy—that is, plan their itinerary, make travel and speaking arrangements, provide the speakers continuously with new information for use in their speeches—as well as distribute propaganda material, and monitor the effectiveness of their work as much as possible. More than that, the office had to decide which zones of Italy most needed propaganda and was required to carry on an in-depth analysis of the political situation and mind-set of the civilian populations in the various regions of Italy. The speakers were asked to describe in their reports the impressions and information they had gathered on their trips; they were also expected to establish contacts with leading local figures, who would then become points of reference and sources of information for the office. In this activity, then, propaganda always went hand in hand with political intelligence-gathering.

In order to carry out the office's first duty—the organizing itineraries for the speakers, obtaining travel permits from the central Italian and American authorities, and publicizing their arrival as well as organizing the audiences—the office, in collaboration with the Opere Federate (volunteer organizations for civilian propaganda) and the "publicity" office of the American Red Cross in Rome, developed a list of Italians who were both interested in America and influential in their communities. By the beginning of August 1918, that list contained about 1,500 names and addresses.[25] A list of Italian towns with more than 10,000 residents was also compiled; it contained the names of 539 places. Constant contacts were maintained with the mayors and leading citizens of these towns and cities, in part through the delivery of a weekly newsletter prepared by the office.

At its busiest moments, the department had about a dozen speakers traveling around Italy. Some of them, such as Rudolph Altrocchi of the University of Chicago and Arthur Benington of the *New York World,* worked for the Italian CPI for nearly the entire duration of its operations. Others who had come from America, such as the New York state assemblyman, Salvatore Cotillo, or American Socialists, were in Italy only to make a propaganda tour, though in some cases they stayed for months. Other Americans who were in Italy during this period, such as Fiorello La Guardia or Constantine Panunzio, offered their services on numerous occasions. In addition, Italian volunteers supported the work of the American speakers; among them were Oreste Poggiolini and the social worker Guglielmina Ronconi and her students, Mary Orsolini and Adalgisa Persico; these women delivered short talks especially to groups of women and children in factories or in schools, usually after the showing of an American movie. The department estimated that in just three months, from July to September 1918, it had reached a total audience of about 5 million people. Altrocchi offered the following recommendations to all the speakers:

> From my experience in talking to all sorts of Italian publics I draw the conclusion that the following things are necessary and impressive: First of all vehement sincerity . . . ; then overwhelming, serene sureness of victory; a few staggering facts; a touch of humor; and in form, short, colorful, dignified but striking phrases, utterly deprived of flowery rhetoric. This style of oratory is so new to the Italians that they are captured by it and remember our message.[26]

With rare exceptions (which we will cover later), American speakers received enthusiastic receptions everywhere they appeared. The passage that follows, selected out of many in the same tone, derives from a report sent by Cotillo's secretary during their tour of southern Italy, with stops in Naples and surrounding areas, Calabria, Puglia, and Sicily, between mid-July and mid-August 1918. The following description refers to the visit to Avellino:

> The manner in which the senator was received there was far beyond our expectations. We were met at the station by all the authorities. The town was bedecked with American and Italian flags. . . . The whole population turned out to cheer us on our way to the hotel. The following day the senator was given a luncheon by the city authorities at which several stirring speeches were made of Italy's great affection for America, and her reliance on America's cooperation. The senator made a short address which brought forth great cheers for America and Wilson. *Wilson has certainly taken the Italian people by storm. Every place we visit we find that his name is worshipped.* We have met hundreds of people who are more conversant with Wilson's speeches than I am. One man told us that he has re-read Wilson's speeches more than twenty times. . . . Beyond a doubt, the hearts of those people beat for America.[27]

The organizers focused on rural areas, where large reservoirs of ill-concealed opposition to the war could be found. Benington became an expert on the Marche and Umbria, while Altrocchi focused on Tuscany. Others, such as Henry C. Sartorio and Agostino D'Isernia, traveled in the northern regions, while Cotillo and Panunzio spent months traveling around the south. Socialist-inspired defeatism was a problem especially in the central and northern regions, according to the CPI agents. Even if reports from these areas were filled with descriptions of popular enthusiasm for America and Wilson, they also noted "difficult" areas, such as, Osimo in the Marche, Prato, San Gimignano, Colle Val d'Elsa, Pontedera in Tuscany, Terni in Umbria, Turin, and surrounding cities, where the public appeared to be hostile, at least at first, and slow to warm to images of victory and the decisive American aid.[28] These places had not produced massive emigration, and therefore the American myth lacked deep roots there; the appeal of anarchists and especially pacifist Socialists was especially strong in these areas.

American speakers soon acquired considerable familiarity with the areas they toured and with the prevailing mind-set among the peasants. A report from Arthur Benington[29] offers an excellent demonstration. In this report, one can almost hear the peasants talking: clearly, it is an analysis based on direct experience and frequent and significant contacts with the population of the Italian countryside. The report begins with the observation that the rural masses are mostly ignorant of the war and its ideological motivations. It goes on to point out how difficult it is to reach the peasants, because they are scattered throughout the territory and tend to be hard at work in the fields, especially during that part of the year (summer of 1918). The report then describes their views of the war:

> The *contadini* [peasants]—especially the women—talk in the following strain: "This is a war of the *Signori* (gentlefolk). They have all signed a paper to keep the war going as long as possible, because they make money out of it. Only one thing matters to us—to end the war as soon as possible. We do not care how it ends; it is no affair of ours; we shall not suffer from any terms that are made. It does not matter to us if the *Signori* who own the farms lose them; it means only that other *Signori* will take possession of them and we shall divide the produce with the latter instead of the former. As we have to divide the produce anyhow it doesn't matter with whom we divide it. We would just as soon divide with Germans or Austrians as with Italians. It is the *contadini* who supply men for the army and it is our grain and meat and oil that is taken to feed the army. It is our women and old men who have to work to keep the war going; and all we care about is to have the war end and to get our husbands and sons and brothers back home again."

Benington interpreted this situation as evidence of the absolute need for an intense propaganda campaign by the Americans. He also suggested the most suitable means of propaganda for conducting such a campaign:

> It is impossible to exaggerate the importance of propaganda work among the *contadini*. . . . To meet this problem most effectively I suggest that several large camions [*sic*] be equipped with moving picture apparatus, and that films specially prepared for the simple country folk be shown at the small towns, on Sundays and on feast days and during the week, the coming film being announced about a week beforehand by a poster stuck up at the nearest post-office. The pictures should be selected carefully. If the operator or chauffeur could give a brief talk in Italian, so much the better. But these people are deeply impressed by moving pictures, and few of them have seen even those of their own war.[30]

Aside from the peasants, the CPI speakers focused on factory workers and laborers, another social class that was hostile to the war and dominated by the Socialist Party. Benington, for instance, spoke with considerable satisfaction of the work he had done among the factory workers in Terni, the largest industrial center in central Italy. At the beginning of August 1918, he wrote:

> I consider my meeting at Terni the greatest success of any in my tour of Umbria as it included a greater number of hearers and they [were] of just the class that, after the *contadini* [written in Italian], are most in need of stimulation. And the response [I] got from that sea of faces was sympathetic and intelligent.[31]

In a report he wrote after the armistice, Benington urged the continuation of American propaganda in Italy so that, with the power of Wilson's message, it would be possible to combat the growing strength of the extreme Socialist fringe groups in the Italian countryside and industrial areas:

> The great mass of the Italian people is now enthusiastic about America, about everything American, and especially about President Wilson. . . . Conditions in Italy, however, had not yet reached a stage which will permit the U.S. to give up its propaganda work safely. . . . The principal objective from now on is stimulating the people to resist the dangerous Socialist propaganda that is actively at work among them.[32]

From this point of view, the CPI was given great help by the mission of the American Socialist interventionists, led by John Spargo, president of the Social Democratic League of America, and including Charles E. Russell and A. M. Simons, who visited Italy in August and September 1918. In contrast with the mission of Samuel Gompers (a union leader who was disliked in Italy in part because of his open hostility to Italian immigration)—which was widely acknowledged to have been unsuccessful in terms of mass propaganda[33]—Spargo and his comrades, with their vision of the war and of the importance a victory of Wilsonian democracy had for the future of Socialism around the world, managed to generate excitement and enthusiasm among the Italian Socialists. Their words were exactly what was needed to win the Italian Socialists over to Wilsonian ideals: Merriam immediately realized the enormous importance of the cooperation of the American Socialists for his work and asked whether he could keep Spargo in Italy at least until the end of November. The CPI archives contain a typewritten outline, with handwritten corrections, of a speech by Russell, which helps us understand the arguments that the Socialists of the American mission used to arouse the sympathies of the Italian Socialists:

> This war is the final conflict between two great ideas, two hostile conceptions of life, society, and government. On one side is the autocratic idea in which people are ruled by inherited right and have no share in the government that rules them. On the side is the democratic idea in which the people have through the ballot and through their elected representatives complete power over their government. . . . This democratic principle has been won slowly in this world by centuries of fighting and struggle. It is the most precious possession of all free peoples. It is what marks the difference between them and subject races like the Germans. It's also the very life of Socialism. With it alone we can have any hope to build the cooperative republic. With it alone we can hope to bring about the industrial democracy that is so dear to us. Socialism could no more exist without democracy than we could have life in a vacuum. What is really at stake, therefore, in this war is the life of Socialism. . . . Instead of being true, as you have been told sometimes, that this is a war in which the workers have no concern, the truth is you have more concern than all the capitalists on earth. Because . . . rich men always have a sufficient defense in their wealth. The working man has no defense except in democracy.[34]

Bissolati lavished praise on their speeches and encouraged them to continue their work in Italy. That work was also perfectly in line with the CPI approach. Creel commented from America, with reference to an article by Spargo that had just been published by the *New York Tribune:* "More clearly than anything that has yet been written this summary presents my views and the policy that I desire to have pursued." The CPI's positions, perhaps to a greater degree than Wilson's, were solidly anchored to a line of democratic reformism.[35]

The department, with the help of reports from the speakers and secret information from various sources, and through a careful reading of the press as well as increasingly numerous contacts with influential Italians living in the provinces, could boast that it had organized an intelligence network sufficient to allow it to determine which areas of Italy most needed its propaganda: "Tuscany is more affected by *disfattismo* than any other province in Italy—except perhaps Piedmont (which is the home of Giolitti)," as Arthur Benington summarized the situation in one of his reports.[36] From this basic work for the Italian territory, combined with his personal contacts with the Italian leadership and with other Americans involved in intelligence in Italy (first and foremost, Gino Speranza, but also the journalists Edgar Mowrer and John Hearley and the embassy secretary Norval Richardson), Merriam developed the component elements for a sophisticated analysis of the Italian political situation, which he sent back to Washington. This analysis came to the attention not only of Creel, but also of House and Wilson.[37]

"Political Intelligence" and Parallel Diplomacy

The CPI's political analysis was based on the belief, widely shared by Americans in Italy, that the collapse of Caporetto had been a sort of military strike, a product of enemy propaganda, along with the pacifistic propaganda being spread by the Vatican, the followers of Giolitti, and the Socialists.[38] The soldiers, discouraged and demoralized, had simply refused to fight. This attitude of rejection of the war, the product of a widespread ignorance of the ideals underlying the fight on the Allied side and lack of belief in ultimate victory, was prevalent among the civilian population as well. For that reason, one of the chief goals of the CPI agents was to distribute among the populace reports on the vast war footing of mobilization in the United States and of American democratic ideals, of which "they were largely uninformed, and in general were highly skeptical."[39]

Far more seriously, Caporetto had brought to the surface a larger Italian social and political crisis and had uncovered the fragility of its political ordering. Both Merriam and Speranza considered the Italian governing class as a holdover from an antidemocratic and clientelistic past. Giolitti, in particular, was considered to be a cynical and corrupt politico, skilled at political maneuvering with opportunistic alliances and the exchange of personal favors. He was a figure reminiscent of American city bosses, who had been the targets of moralistic Progressive reformism. Obtaining the declaration of war in May 1915, Speranza pointed out, had required a national groundswell of new political forces in defiance of the political establishment, which favored neutrality. But government was still just as remote from the governed, and became, ever further removed as the war went on. Caporetto revealed the seriousness of the situation and demonstrated that it could even develop along the same lines as what was happening in Russia. The Italian situation could be described as the coexistence of two nations on the same territory: the people, the "real Italy," which was alien to the institutions and decisions of the governing class, the "legal or official Italy."

This distinction between the "real Italy" and "official Italy" became the fulcrum of the American analysis of the Italian situation. According to that analysis, Italy's social, economic, and political institutions mirrored neither the wishes nor the interests of most of the population. While "official Italy" was antidemocratic, imperialistic, antithetical to Wilsonian principles, and often corrupt, "real Italy" was liberal, instinctively democratic, and profoundly in sympathy with Wilsonian principles. The distinction was not along class lines because the separation cut transversely through the upper classes and the labor movement. It was more accurately a separation between the old regime, represented by Giolitti, Sonnino, and Salandra along with the leadership of the Socialist Party, and the emerging progressive forces, represented by interventionists, dissident Socialists, and some members of the trade union movement. These progressive forces were not yet completely organized, but they were deeply rooted in unexpressed popular aspirations; if they triumphed, they would establish a democratic and pro-American regime in Italy.[40]

This distinction between a "real" Italy and an "official" (or "legal," the terminology first preferred) Italy was hardly a new concept in Italian political analysis. It had been forged in the final decades of the nineteenth century by Stefano Jacini (1827–1891), a perceptive liberal politician who had participated in building the unified Italian state, while maintaining a capacity for critical observation of the characteristics and bottlenecks of the process of unification.[41] It was a distinction conceived to focus on one of the chief problems in Italy—that is, the gap between the liberal ruling class and the unwashed masses of the Italian population. The new state was unable to involve the masses in Italian public life: this was one of the first problems to be confronted. As Massimo D'Azeglio said in his renowned quip: "We have made Italy; now we must make Italians.[42]

American political observers in Italy thus found already rooted in the domestic political debate the distinction between "the two Italies." They reinterpreted it, however, through Wilsonian thought: the distinction between governments and peoples was one of the bridgeheads of Wilsonian foreign policy. Initially drawn up for Germany at the time of the declaration of war, when Wilson stated that the United States had no quarrel with the German people and was fighting only against the autocratic German government, this distinction was ultimately extended to all countries that were led by nondemocratic governments. It culminated in the establishment of the idea that this was a "peoples' war" against a narrow group of selfishly ambitious governments, which possessed large armies but lacked popular support.[43] American observers who emphasized the gap in Italy between the people and the government were merely applying a Wilsonian principle that characteristically linked American foreign policy to the domestic affairs of the country in question. It would seem natural to apply this distinction to enemy nations but not to an Allied nation. Instead, this vision reflected exactly the profound mistrust that characterized relations between Italy and the United States during the war years.

For these reasons, even though he was working closely with the Italian political and military leadership, Merriam was always careful not to identify the United States with the world of Italian officialdom. In particular, he emphasized that, while "official" Italy paid only lip service to Wilsonian principles, the "real" Italy was sincerely attracted by American ideals. The incredible popularity of the American president showed that he was the true spokesman for the unspoken ideals of the common people. From that basis, the logical conclusion was to urge Wilson to seek direct contact with the Italian people by reaching out to them, bypassing the current leadership, in order to build a just and lasting peace in Europe. This approach, which would ultimately lead to the fiasco of Wilson's appeal on Fiume, was present in many of the CPI's reports in Italy:

> The European governments are willing to take America's men, her money, her munitions, her food, her moral support through the preaching democracy and universal peace; but in the end at the peace settlement they expect to have their way. They are willing to allow us to talk democracy as a war measure, but they intend to have "no such nonsense" in the finish. . . . However, . . . the president could make peace terms on his own basis, that is, on a democratic basis, but . . . he would have to go over the heads of the governments' representatives and appeal to their people. . . . In this sense America bears a tremendous load of responsibility. . . . America stands not only for democracy but for all the unrealized ideals of many of the European peoples; and they must not be disillusioned.[44]

Even if these concepts constituted the leitmotiv of the CPI's reports, Merriam's analysis did not stop here. The separation between government and people could be overcome by establishing an American-style democratic regime in Italy. The process would have to begin with the real Italy, which would elevate to power a new governing class, different from the imperialistic and antidemocratic class that had governed the country up to that point.

It was along the same conceptual lines that Gino Speranza, an Italian American journalist who lived in Rome from 1915, pushed his analysis. As chief of the "intelligence office" of the American embassy in Rome, for more than two years he sent weekly reports first to Washington and later to Paris on the evolution of the Italian political, military, and economic situation. In those reports there emerged a noteworthy understanding of conditions in Italy. Their analysis could have proved invaluable for providing a window into an understanding of America's distant Mediterranean ally, an understanding that went beyond what was available from books, as well as an examination of Italian public opinion and the views of the leading national political figures. These reports never reached either Wilson or House, nor did they reach Wilson's experts who were studying Italy in the context of the Inquiry, the organization of experts that we will soon examine.[45] Instead, those reports were systematically buried in the archives of the State Department, which, as we will see, remained sidelined from the construction of Wilson's foreign policy.

Merriam and Speranza worked together on an analysis of the Italian political situation, despite the friction that soon developed between the Italian section of the CPI and the American embassy in Rome. Merriam probably relied on Speranza's deeper and more penetrating understanding of Italian political affairs. Their analysis went so far as to theorize the possibility of forming a "Labor Party" in Italy that could bring together all the forces and politicians who were most likely to align with Wilsonian ideals. In other words, they were advocating the formation of a political force that could become a genuine national Italian interlocutor for Wilson's foreign policy. Speranza believed that this liberal-democratic movement was in full development in the last year of the war, even though uncertainties remained concerning the final outcome, especially because of the unknown factor of returning veterans and their political orientations. This new political force could incorporate reform Socialists, democratic interventionists, labor union organizations, along with the great mass of the Italian populace, which was considered "liberal" by nature, historical tradition, and basic "common sense."[46]

It was harder to predict who could lead this new political force. The reports from Merriam and Speranza evaluated the various leaders of the period, submitting detailed portraits to Washington. Bissolati was considered a capable and honest politician, but too old and lacking a sufficient following.

The CPI reports devoted extensive space and interest to Turati: they described his awkward position within the Italian Socialist Party, where he was continually attacked by the maximalists; his influence in the Socialist parliamentary group and in Italy; his devotion to Wilsonian ideals; and his tendency to collaborate with the government, at least as far as the demobilization phase and the postwar years were concerned. The hypothesis was advanced that he could *passare il Rubicone* ("cross the Rubicon") and break away from the intransigent wing of the Socialist Party.[47]

Extensive space was also devoted to Nitti, then the minister of finance, who made no secret of his desire to become prime minister in a broad-based popular government: he was generally judged in negative terms, however. Only Page and La Guardia considered him to be "the Man of the Hour in Italy."[48] They praised the political objectives of the man who would become head of the Italian government after the collapse of the Orlando coalition; the press often referred to Nitti as "l'Americano."[49] The other Americans described him as a camouflaged version of Giolitti, an opportunist expert in the tactics of delay and alliance, a classic example of an Italian without a strong moral sense but skilled at palace intrigues. This judgment was similar to Lansing and Wilson's assessment of Nitti, stemming from the hostility of the Italian ambassador Macchi di Cellere and extending back to Nitti's visit to the United States in the spring of 1917 when he was a member of the official Italian mission.[50] The CPI even took under consideration the lively personality of the emerging agitator Benito Mussolini: he was described as a broad-minded man but better suited to short-term political battles than to the tasks of organization and future political strategy.[51]

Basically, Merriam and Speranza deplored the absence in Italy of leaders with a sufficient following among the masses and a broad-ranging vision of the forces then at play on the domestic and international levels. This kind of democratic leadership was especially needed in Italy at this crucial moment: the Italians want a "great leader," Speranza wrote. Such a leadership would persuade them to accept reasonable solutions to thorny international problems, including the Adriatic question.[52]

It was precisely the absence of persuasive leaders capable of replacing an unpopular government that forced even those observers, such as Merriam, who had developed a complex and accurate view of the Italian situation, to fall back into the prevailing attitude among Americans of going no further than the ecstatic exaltation of Wilson's leadership, with an emphasis on his growing appeal to the Italian masses. Unfortunately, it was only a short step from the idea of emphasizing the Italians' enthusiasm for Wilson and the unpopularity of their government to the idea of urging the American president to bypass that government and address the Italians directly, with the goal of establishing a lasting peace in Europe. Quite a few took precisely that step, to such a degree that Wilson's Fiume appeal made in April 1919 appears to be the objective of a vast front of American opinion rather than the isolated act of a moralizing president who had lost touch with reality, as it has so often been described. Instead, it seems to have been the culmination of a process in which many components of the American culture of that time we have already analyzed converged: nationalism, prejudices, missionary spirit of Progressive origin, ignorance, and difficulties with intercultural communications. These elements were accentuated by the glaring shortcomings of the Italian governing class, by the stark aspects of the war, and by the social situation in Italy, as well as by the power of one of the first mass political myths in contemporary history.

The prevailing attitude of American political observers in Italy can be even more easily seen through their personal letters. Let us examine, for instance, a letter written by John Hearley, after he had replaced Merriam as director of the Italian office of the CPI and was awaiting Wilson's arrival in Italy. After describing "the unpopular stench called government in Italy," he added: "Wilson could so easily capture the whole situation for himself and do it in a perfectly legitimate and natural way. Come down and play moral politics to the crowded and expectant galleries."[53]

Even Ambassador Page—who had done his best, both out of personal conviction and out of duty, to improve communications between Italy and the United States throughout the war years—fell prey to this general moralizing atmosphere. Just a few days before Wilson's appeal to the Italians, Page wrote to Colonel House commenting on the growing hostility of public opinion to Wilson's position on the Fiume question:

> One of these days the truth will be known and these people who are being led to believe that we are trying to deprive them of something for which their sons have fought and died and they themselves have suffered and endured will know the truth. . . . I feel, on the other hand, that he [the president] may have to appeal to the people, and then leave it to Time to let them recognize anew who has at heart their true interests.[54]

Similarly, Ray Stannard Baker, a Progressive journalist who had been sent to Italy by House in September and December 1918 to report on the Italian situation, concluded one of his reports on the labor movement with the following observations:

> No people in the world are more devoted followers of a leader, when once they have accepted him utterly, as they have Mr. Wilson, than the Italians, and none are more sensitive. These [labor] groups will follow him to the end while . . . the nationalist and imperialist groups, while they now give him lip service, do not really believe in the principles he has laid down. . . . As Massingham says in the last number of *The Nation:* "Mr. Wilson may have to come out and appeal to the scores of millions who accept his leadership against the Trusts and the Cabinets who reject it.[55]

Wilson held Baker in such high esteem that a short while later Baker was appointed the first officer for press relations in the context of the American delegation in Paris, and after that, Wilson's official biographer. Wilson read Baker's reports from Italy in which, after various meetings with members of the union movement and political left wing in Milan, Turin, Florence, and Rome, Baker enthusiastically described the Italian labor movement's devotion to Wilson. Baker, too, adopted the stance so prevalent among his fellow Americans who often urged Wilson to set himself up as the true defender of the Italian masses.

Obviously, Wilson could not become the leader of the Italian people, and consequently the Italian people themselves violently rejected the effort he made in that direction. The failure to identify a domestic political force to support with determination a force that could become the interlocutor in Italy of Wilson's larger program and the grateful heir of a portion of Wilson's appeal to the Italian masses was the Achilles' heel of the American political strategy concerning Italy. Unfortunately, neither Wilson nor his main collaborators had any interest in this aspect. As far as Italy was concerned, the American president remained obstinately attached to the simplistic distinction between the Italians and their unpopular government. Unquestionably, this Manichaean attitude hindered Wilson in his quest for a constructive endgame with Italy, much as his unwillingness to place his trust decisively in the Socialists was a stumbling block. Another problem was his tendency to overestimate his own skills at direct leadership of the masses, not in America alone but around the world. The very success of the American propaganda campaign in Italy, the continual reports from his delegates and envoys concerning the Italians enthusiasm for Wilson and his words, the almost religious devotion that he himself experienced during his trip to Italy, immediately prior to the peace conference—none of these factors encouraged him to pursue a policy of dialogue with the Italian leaders, whether members of the governing coalition or the opposition.

Wilson's Popularity in Italy in 1918

The vast extent of the "Wilsonianism" phenomenon in Italy became unexpectedly evident on the fourth of July 1918, when, for the first and last time in Italian history, massive celebrations were held throughout the length and breadth of the Italian peninsula in honor of the anniversary of the American nation's independence. Everywhere, popular participation far outstripped the organizers' expectations and plans. The Italian press described the phenomenon in a chorus singing in unison the praises of Wilson and America. Celebrations were held in all the leading Italian cities, such as Rome, Milan, Florence, Naples, Palermo, Bologna, Turin, and Genoa, and a myriad of celebratory demonstrations were also held in such provincial towns as Campobasso, Ascoli Piceno, Sassari, Teramo, Siracusa, Reggio Calabria, Caltanissetta, Lecce, Brescia, Forlì, Livorno, Catania, Catanzaro, Perugia, Messina, Verona, Siena, Rovigo, Arezzo, Benevento, Caserta, and Grosseto.

At the same time, the provincial secretaries of the Opere Federate were sending in reports on the celebrations held in smaller towns, from Cefalù to Fiesole and from Nola to Marino.[56] In reference to Florence, Silvio Crespi noted that "the whole city and its province are in jubilation in honor of the American Republic."[57]

On 5 July, in most Italian newspapers, news of the celebrations the day before was reported in large front-page headlines, often topping the page. Among those papers were *Il Corriere della Sera, La Tribuna,* Genoa's *Il Secolo XIX, Il Popolo d'Italia, Il Giornale d'Italia, Il Mattino* in Naples, and *La Domenica del Corriere,* as well as many local dailies, including Sassari's *La Nuova Sardegna, Il Giornale di Sicilia* in Palermo, *L'Ordine* in Ancona, and Genoa's *Il Piccolo* and *Il Cittadino.* All the reports published descriptions of "feverish crowds," "immense demonstrations," "vast masses of people," huge numbers of American flags, ribbons, and cockades, portraits of President Wilson, and articles praising the colossal American contribution to the war effort and President Wilson's principles.

Enthusiastic descriptions of the Italian popular mobilization for the fourth of July celebration, as well as the play it was being given in the press, can also be found in dispatches sent from CPI's Rome offices to headquarters in Washington:

> Celebrations were held in all the large cities of Italy and in many of the small ones and in every instance so far as I have been able to learn all have been a tremendous success. Without entering into discussion of minor details it is safe to conclude that there never has been anything to equal the celebration of the fourth of July in Italy from the point of view of international demonstration. The enthusiasm, the cordiality, and fundamental sympathy shown in these meetings—judging from the reports—were remarkable, amazing almost. Many of our people and many of the Italians as well seem to have been profoundly touched by the evidence beyond any question of the sincerity of the Italian friendship for America.[58]

These phenomena were only partly spontaneous. Behind them had been an intense preparatory activity carried out by the CPI, which considered the vast national echo of the celebrations to have been one of its most spectacular successes. The preparations extended to the point of inviting the renowned poet and soldier Gabriele D'Annunzio to write a poem in honor of American involvement in the war. D'Annunzio wrote and sent the CPI a poem he had written on those themes.[59]

During the summer of 1918, Wilson and America began to occupy an increasing space in the trench newspapers and the propaganda of the Italian army's *Uffici P.* The propaganda office of the Comando Supremo even expressed concern because, in the imagination of the soldiers, the American intervention was acquiring "outsized proportions."[60] The popularity of Wilson and America was becoming evident at the front in other ways as well: according to a concerned article published in the Turin newspaper, *La Stampa,* a survey conducted in Italy's southern regions revealed that the great majority of the soldiers home on leave said that they planned to emigrate to America as soon as the war was over. These were the same peasants who called Wilson "the modern saint."[61]

From the summer of 1918 on, Wilson's popularity among the Italian masses was such an evident phenomenon that, when the young American undersecretary of the navy, Franklin Delano Roosevelt, then visiting Rome, asked Merriam who was the most influential politician in Italy, Merriam replied promptly and proudly, "President Wilson."[62] Everyone who was working for the CPI in Italy was struck by the popularity of the Wilson myth, and, in their reports to Washington, they described their astonishment at the Italian populace's enthusiasm. Hearley, for instance, wrote to Creel in October 1918:

> One thing stands out clear and certain here. President Wilson has not merely caught the ear of the Italian masses but has touched its soul. . . . The President's poster picture inscribed with the Italian words "for the rights of the peoples" is framed and hangs in countless simple homes throughout Italy, and this office is in constant receipt of requests for more and more of them. The people have a spiritual faith in the President, and they promise, should he fail them or the world, a disappointment that would be as fundamentally and pathetically tragic as the loss of a life-long and necessary religion.[63]

Many other American observers borrowed images and words from religion to describe the attitude of the Italian people toward America and Wilson. Harvey Carroll, the American consul in Venice, for instance, wrote: "Indeed Italy sees in America a kind of embodiment of Divine Providence,"[64] while Arthur Bliss Lane, private secretary to Ambassador Page, noted: "At that time Wilson was revered as though he had a divine quality."[65] In November 1918, Ambassador Page wrote:

> At present he [Mr. Wilson] is respected and feared by the public men and adored by the people of Italy. His pictures are everywhere. . . . The feeling about him among the people is expressed in a story I heard of one old woman the other evening who said she had heard that over in America there was a great saint who was making the peace for us. "Che bell [*sic*] Santo quel grande Santo Americano!"[66]

One of the most evocative descriptions of Wilson's exceptional popularity in Italy comes from the memoirs of an eyewitness, Norval Richardson, the first secretary of the American embassy in Rome. Thinking back, he proposed that in no other country on earth had President Wilson attained the same exalted heights of popularity that he enjoyed in Italy at the end of 1918: Richardson added:

> [I]t was a short-lived popularity—it disappeared almost entirely a few weeks after the Peace Conference had been in session—but it was tremendous while it existed. At that time you could not go anywhere in Rome without finding a life-sized portrait of President Wilson . . . a religious significance quickly developed about his name.

Richardson also recalled that an Italian friend had taken him to a military barracks to see a little improvised shrine, with burning candles, erected by the enlisted men at the foot of a large poster of Wilson. Later, he reported another significant testimonial, using the words that a Sicilian had said to him during a conversation about Wilson:

> I think of him as something remote, set apart from the rest of us, not a man of actual flesh and blood, but some one with only a mind and a voice that rings across the world from some far-distant Olympus. Do you know, I am almost afraid to see him. I am afraid he will be just like the rest of us.[67]

Wilson's trip to Italy during the first week in January 1919, a few days before the opening of the peace conference, proved the crowning touch to America's propaganda work in Italy, and it made clear to the world the unparalleled popularity that the American president had attained among the Italians. Wilson, accompanied by his wife and staff including George Creel, visited Rome, Milan, Turin, and Genoa. Aside from the imposing official welcoming ceremonies, observers were struck by the constant involvement of the populace, especially the long lines of exultant, profoundly moved common people along either side of the streets or tracks where the presidential car or train passed by.

As we will see, Rome enveloped Wilson in an intense round of official obligations, and he was unable to speak to the public as he had hoped. The American president and his colleagues concluded that there had been an intentional effort to prevent a scene of popular acclaim of Wilson, and decided once again that all dialogue with the Italian leadership was impossible.[68]

Therefore, the very success of the American propaganda campaign in Italy—a campaign that found a fertile cultural terrain and yielded unhoped-for results—ultimately reinforced Wilson's rejection of any attempt to establish a dialogue with the top Italian political leadership. Never again would the Americans perceive such a clear distinction between the good Italian populace and its bad, nonrepresentative government.

— 6 —

Wilson's Diplomacy toward Italy

In the preceding chapters we have seen how Wilson, in part through the extraordinary success of the propaganda campaign, acquired a popularity and an authority in Italy never before enjoyed by a non-Italian leader. But as we will now see, this endowment was squandered at the decisive moment of the peace negotiations. Among the many elements that had a negative influence on the dialogue between the two nations was the labyrinthine structure of Wilsonian diplomacy, which ran along parallel tracks: an official track, run by Secretary of State Lansing, and a semiofficial track, under the supervision of House and, in part, Creel, involving individuals and agencies directly tied to the president. Even when the Italian leaders belatedly and clumsily attempted to get in touch with the American president, it was not easy for them to find a way of reaching him. An analysis of Wilson's attitude toward the Treaty of London shows that from the moment America entered the war as an ally of Italy, he was not interested in any dialogue with the Italian government.

The clash between Wilson and Orlando in Paris particularly concerned the territories to the north and east of the Italian national frontiers, ceded to Italy by the countries of the Triple Entente as compensation for joining the war on their side. As we have seen, in the Treaty of London the Allies had awarded Italy not only "Italia Irredenta," that is, the provinces of Trento and Trieste, but also certain areas of the Tirolo (Tyrol), Istria, and the Dalmatian coast, inhabited by populations that were non-Italian by language, descent, and cultural tradition. Moreover, Italy had obtained a protectorate over part of Albania, a naval base in Vlorë (or Valona)—an important asset for control of the Adriatic—as well as recognition of Italian occupation of the Dodecanese and of its rights in the future division of Asian Turkey and the African colonies.[1]

The United States refused to recognize the many reciprocal promises of territorial and colonial expansion among the Allies that were contained in the secret treaties negotiated prior to their entry into the war. As we have seen, there were about ten or so of these treaties, and they affected the entire planet, with the sole exception of the American continent.[2] It was chiefly an awareness of how the methods and goals of American foreign policy differed from those of the Allies that led Wilson to make a distinction with regard to the U.S. position in the context of the front opposing the Central Powers. The United States was thus an "Associated Power," never an official ally, of the western bloc nations. Once he had thus defined America's anomalous position in the war, Wilson no longer cared to discuss the content of the secret treaties with the other allies. He always made a great show of studiously ignoring those treaties, in part because he did not wish to threaten Allied unity while the war was still being fought and because he believed that his country's negotiating position, as well as his personal influence and popularity, would be reinforced during the months of American fighting, until they ultimately almost automatically overlapped with the Allied strategies.

In the context of the ideological conflict separating the Allies from the liberal United States, the disagreement between Italy and America gradually took on special intensity. Little by little, Italian foreign policy became symbolic of the reprehensible "old diplomacy" and European imperialistic politics. Once Italy had been pigeonholed into this uncomfortable role in the context of the deeply moralistic and ideological sphere of American politics, dialogue became less and less feasible. The final result was that in Paris the United States worked out various compromises with France, Great Britain, and Japan[3] but remained especially intransigent with Italy. Ultimately, any agreement proved impossible. Italian public opinion, even the most liberal wing of Italian public opinion, saw this approach as a clear case of anti-Italian discrimination. France and England's hostile attitude toward an ally to whom they had promised "too much" when it joined the war, without ultimately receiving all the help for which they had hoped, was a factor in the American refusal to negotiate with Italy. In turn, the absence of a direct Italian American dialogue offered greater opportunities for Italy's critics in various Allied capitals to express their views and only made Sonnino's foreign policy more rigid. Thus, the United States' entry into the war not only led to the well-known feud between Italy and America, but also intensified Italy's isolation in Europe.

Wilson repeatedly denied that he had ever been aware of the Allies' secret treaties before his arrival in Paris for the peace conference. In August 1919, for instance, in his testimony to the American Senate, when asked whether he had had knowledge of the various secret treaties prior to the peace conference, with express reference to the Treaty of London, Wilson answered: "No, sir, I can confidently answer that 'No' in regard to myself."[4]

Wilson's statements cannot, however, be reconciled with the documentation and accounts now available to us. Analysis of these documents shows that Wilson was familiar with the pact in question from the time of its signature: news of its conclusion arrived with the same dispatch that informed him of the sinking of the *Lusitania*, a dispatch that he most certainly read. His sources of information were not Italian, since the Italian authorities were complicit and actively involved in promoting a state of secrecy regarding the existence and contents of the pact. The sources were primarily English and, as we will see, were strongly critical of the pact's provisions and Italian foreign policy generally.

The year 1917, especially the period between the United States' entry into the war and the drafting of the Fourteen Points, was a year of crucial importance to the development of American policy on Italy. If Wilson's position toward Italy was still quite vague in the first months of 1917, by the time he announced the Fourteen Points, that position was already completely defined. After that time, the attitude toward Italian ambitions remained generally stable. Beginning in 1918, there was not much point to discussing how aware America was of the Treaty of London, since it had practically become public knowledge. In November 1917, the Bolsheviks published the secret Allied treaties, and between the end of 1917 and the first few months of 1918 a number of English and American newspapers reported the contents of those agreements.[5] However, Wilson continued to deny that he had become aware of their contents even then.

The Treaty of London, was probably the first Allied secret treaty known to Wilson and his administration. Moreover, the American government probably knew more about this treaty than any other during the war and, given the series of debates that ensued, both during and after the peace conference. In August 1919, Robert Lansing, who had been appointed secretary of state in June 1915, stated the following in his Senate testimony: "I was more familiar with the London agreement, that affected the Italian boundaries, than any other."[6]

The official mission of Lord Balfour, the British minister for foreign affairs, to the United States immediately after the Americans declared war, was of decisive importance to the American understanding of the Treaty of London. According to many available sources, during that mission Balfour apparently discussed in detail the future arrangement of Europe with House, Wilson, and Lansing and informed them of the contents of a number of secret treaties, including the treaty with Italy.[7] In all likelihood, however, Balfour did not mention the existing agreements for the division of the German colonies in Africa; nor did he speak about agreements with the Japanese concerning Shantung and the Pacific islands, agreements that were of particular interest to Great Britain.[8] References to the Treaty of London were frequent. The British minister was highly critical of the inter-Allied treaties negotiated by his predecessor, Lord Grey. Great Britain had been obliged to sign the treaties in order to obtain the help of its lesser allies in a very difficult phase of the conflict and now felt obliged to honor them.[9]

There seems to be no doubt that Balfour also informed Wilson of the treaties discussed with House. Two days later, in Wilson and Balfour's confidential conversation, in House's presence, House noted: "The ground we covered was exactly the same as Balfour and I had covered in our conference Saturday."[10] Balfour confided to his biographer in 1928 in connection with his conversations with Wilson in April 1917: "I was bound to tell him. But it was a very delicate business, for of course [the treaties] *were* secret. The way I got over it was to tell him about them *as* a secret,—as man to man. I told him personally."[11] On 4 March 1918, Balfour told the House of Commons, in response to a specific question from a member of parliament: "The honorable member may rest assured that the President Wilson is kept fully informed by the Allies."[12]

When Balfour informed the American leadership of the Treaty of London, therefore, he had repeatedly emphasized both his own rejection of the objectives of Italian foreign policy that it contained and the sense of obligation that Great Britain nonetheless continued to feel to respect the commitments it had made in a crucial phase of the war.[13] This attitude remained the basic stance of the European Allies toward Italy until the Paris negotiations and led the United States to oppose the Italians' unjust and exorbitant demands: the Americans alone, free of any prior commitments, could do so.

In this light, Sonnino's mistrust and concern over the potentially unfavorable repercussions for Italy of the French and English missions in America appear fully justified. On 16 April 1917, he concluded a letter to the Italian ambassador to Washington with this statement: "For Italy control of the Adriatic is a life-or-death question."[14] The words of the Italian minister for foreign affairs eloquently express his awareness of the growing international hostility surrounding his political approach, as well as his apprehension concerning the consequences of the entry into war of a partner so unlikely to recognize the Allies' commitments to his country.

Wilson,[15] House,[16] and Lansing[17] were all convinced until the end of the war that holding an in-depth discussion of final war aims while the war was underway would only shatter the solidarity of the Allied nations, at a time when victory demanded the greatest possible cohesiveness. Thus, they chose to put off any discussions until the peace negotiations "because by that time they [the Allies] will, among other things, be financially in our hands."[18]

This attitude, known as the doctrine of postponement, betrayed an inadequate understanding of the complexity of the European war, the national antagonisms, and the spread of nationalistic and irrational attitudes that ran through the Old World societies and that had done so much to fuel the outbreak of war. This doctrine was based on excessive trust in the decisive influence that economic factors and Wilson's international prestige would exert at the negotiating table at the peace conference. In that period, the intertwining of the objectives, behaviors, and institutional ties between the American political and financial worlds was still in its beginning stages; it would develop in the decades that followed, especially as a result of the crash of 1929. In 1918–1920, the American financial world was far more independent of the political world, and in its international actions it basically respected private criteria of foreign investment, which the political leadership had only the scantiest power to influence. Wilson, therefore, had none of the negotiating power in Paris that the American administration would have after the Second World War, when it controlled the conditions that would allow it to launch an aid plan on the scale of the Marshall Plan.[19]

For the American president, the doctrine of postponement also concealed a tendency to place undue emphasis on ideological warfare and focused on his personality and his capacity for world leadership to the neglect of other tools available to the United States in the military, economic, and diplomatic realms. As a logical consequence, during the war Wilson's energy was directed basically toward winning for himself the charismatic role of messenger of peace, with only the scantiest consideration for how this hegemonic role, once attained, could be managed in concrete terms. This factor, together with the systematic underuse of diplomacy, also led to only superficial attention to the more complex European political panorama and especially to overlooking the less powerful allies. Thus, over the course of 1917–1918, Wilson and his administration almost never used the fundamental power with respect to Italy that the United States had acquired in the management of the war, and determined to do so only once the war was over. If we stop to consider the phase of social crisis (the riots in Turin in August), political crisis (the fall of the Boselli cabinet), military crisis (Caporetto), and economic crisis that shook Italy throughout the second half of 1917, and if we also think of the many voices that called for change in Italian foreign policy (Bissolati, Albertini, Salvemini, Nitti, Malagodi, and, more in general, the forces that had coalesced around the Rome Congress in the spring of 1918), we may safely venture the hypothesis that during 1918, or at least until November of that year, there were far better conditions for an Italian American compromise than would be present in later months.

The doctrine of postponement, on the other hand, was dictated primarily by the belief that it would be impossible to reach an agreement on the secret treaties, not so much with Great Britain and France as with the minor allies, including Italy. House recalled in 1928: "England and France might have come to a quick decision, but, of necessity, they would have had first to reach an agreement with Japan, Italy, and Russia. Could any satisfactory agreement have been reached with them? I doubt it."[20] The belief that it would be impossible to establish a constructive dialogue with the Italian political authorities stayed with Wilson and his colleagues throughout the period of actual warfare. As a result, instead of being discussed and considered, the Italian problem was frequently overlooked and pushed to the side. In drawing up the Fourteen Points, for instance, according to House's own account, the point regarding Italy was never the subject of any discussion between him and the president.[21]

As we have seen, many American advisers and experts tended to reinforce Wilson's belief regarding Italy, emphasizing as well the fact that the territorial designs were shared by only a minuscule nationalist political faction, headed by Sonnino. Thus, Wilson came to firmly believe that over time he could take the place of that faction as the guiding hand of Italian public opinion. This belief engendered a basic attitude not unlike the one that developed toward the German Empire; it was based on a challenge to the highest circles of leadership and, at the same time, the establishment of an open and direct dialogue with national public opinion. In this connection, Wilson would later confide to Oscar Crosby on 5 July 1918: "I know that Europe is still governed by the same reactionary forces which controlled this country until a few years ago. But I am satisfied that if necessary I can reach the peoples of Europe over the heads of their Rulers."[22]

The fiasco of Wilson's appeal to the Italian people in April 1919 showed the degree to which this attitude was mistaken.

In Italy's case, the doctrine of postponement therefore concealed the belief that any direct approach to the Italian leadership would simply be useless, both because the reciprocal political positions—theirs and those of the United States—were considered to be too distant to be bridged and because it was thought that with time, as a result of the growing popularity and power of the Wilsonian program, American watchwords would take the place of the imperialistic programs of a weak and isolated government, both domestically and internationally. Additional pressure in this direction came from the increasingly numerous and enthusiastic reports that were pouring in from American agents, who described Wilson's growing popularity in Italy during 1918. This explanation alone accounts for the American president's insistence on avoiding any confrontation with the Italian government, even in the months that separated the cessation of hostilities from the formal start of the peace conference. By that time, the doctrine of postponement had already lost whatever justification it might earlier have had.

On the American domestic political stage, many saw Wilson's decision to postpone the solution of his disagreements with the Allies until the peace conference as a serious error in judgment. According to these critics' point of view, Wilson should have demanded an agreement on the war aims prior to American intervention. It was easy to level these criticisms in 1919, when the fundamental role the United States had played in the war was already clear and the disappointing outcome of Versailles was known. These criticisms would have been far more difficult to perceive in 1917, when the situation was completely different. In 1917, it was impossible to say with any certainty just how important the American contribution to the war effort would ultimately prove to be, and many were confident that it would continue to be negligible for a long time to come. Moreover, the tensions between Germany and America, which became increasingly acute following the sinking of the *Lusitania*, were independently pushing the United States toward intervention.

In 1919–1920, understanding the consequences of failing to establish a prior agreement with the Allies on the common war aims became one of the chief targets for attacks on Wilsonian foreign policy. According to Walter Lippmann, "This omission vitiated everything else, but it was compounded by the fact that we had no diplomatic service capable of diagnosing Europe, that we never negotiated but simply enunciated, that what diplomatic service we had was insulated from the President, who worked by intimation from Colonel House, who had his own irresponsible diplomatic service."[23]

The Rise and Fall of House

Edward Mandell House, known by his honorary title of Colonel, was Wilson's closest friend and adviser for almost his entire presidency.[24] Wilson himself had said: "Mr. House is my second personality. He is my independent self. His thoughts and mine are one. If I were in his place I would do just as he suggested. . . . If any one thinks he is reflecting my opinion by whatever action he takes, they are welcome to the conclusion."[25] Given that until the end of the war House never held any official positions, he played a unique role in President Wilson's political machine, a role that struck and astonished both American and foreign observers. Legends grew up around this "backwoods politician," this "Silent Partner" of Wilson's cabinet.[26] In reality, as events later proved, the close collaboration between the two men could function only as long as one condition held: the Colonel's nonofficial position and his modest and submissive attitude. When House began to behave in a more decisive and independent manner during the peace negotiations, the differences of opinion between the two politicians began to surface, and their friendship and collaboration came to a sudden end.

During the war years, foreign policy became House's chief area of interest. Both within and outside of the national borders, he came to be seen as the main point of access to the remote Democratic president, as well as his most authoritative spokesman. Each year, beginning in January 1914, House would travel to Europe as Wilson's personal envoy and establish confidential relations with European statesmen, politicians, and intellectuals. Throughout the war, he regularly received secret reports from American ambassadors in the Old World. As the chief of the Inquiry, the organization of experts charged with preparing the American peace program, he helped to choose both the staff and strategies for the peace negotiations. Finally, in Paris, he was second only to Wilson in terms of stature and influence in the context of the American delegation. In conclusion, both during the war and in its immediate aftermath, House's role increasingly became that of a of "super-ambassador," if not quite the status of a full-fledged, if unofficial, secretary of state.[27] In foreign affairs, at least war-related foreign affairs, House became "the second most powerful man in the land."[28]

Despite the many studies that have been devoted to House, he remains a controversial figure. Was he truly "the best diplomatic brain that America has yet produced," as an English diplomat and historian claimed at the time[29] (and as his monumental diary later led others to believe), or was he a superficial individual, a schemer who was too quick to compromise, as other historians insist?[30] Was he "the Talleyrand from Texas" or, to be more precise, "one who would pass in Texas for a Talleyrand," as one French writer of the time sarcastically suggested?[31] Was he straightforward in his relations with Wilson, or was he devious and unreliable?

An analysis of House's role in Italian American relations can help to answer these questions. In Paris, first in the armistice negotiations and later in the peace negotiations, he became one of the leading figures in Italian American dealings. His involvement did nothing, however, to help resolve the intricate welter of complex attitudes and growing disagreements between the two countries. To the contrary, an examination of his behavior leads us to the conclusion that his role as intermediary was misleading to both Wilson and the Italians.

In more general terms, an analysis of House's role in Italian American relations can help us better understand the cultural background that made the dialogue between the two countries so difficult. While the disagreement that erupted in Paris between Wilson and the Italian representatives, Orlando and Sonnino, has been studied extensively, the same cannot be said for the events preceding, and the secondary actors in, this historical drama. But this background often reveals the cultural oppositions and prevailing mind-sets to a much greater degree than do the actions of the principal characters involved.

Until the end of the war, House shared President Wilson's indifference toward political dialogue with Italy. House's attention was focused on relations with Great Britain, France, or Germany rather than with the lesser powers of the Allied front. As we have seen, this was not only because of Italy's relatively minor importance, but also because House was convinced that a constructive dialogue with Italy was impossible. House's diary reflects this attitude. He makes few references to Italy during the course of the war. He includes a few sarcastic allusions to how reactionary Sonnino's policies were, but gives no serious consideration to efforts designed to reconcile the war aims of the two countries. Nor did the Colonel ever think it necessary to go to Italy during any of his numerous missions to Europe as Wilson's personal representative.

In the final phase of the war, House's influence over Wilson reached its peak. The unofficial network of individuals, institutions, and contacts that House had constructed around himself became a de facto alternative to the structure of the State Department. House was one of the leading figures in that world of unofficial personalities and more or less improvised diplomats, which contributed to creating the Wilsonian foreign policy. He gradually became the pivotal figure in the American war policy and peace program. As noted earlier, many considered him to be the only direct channel for reaching Wilson. As Walter Lippmann observed with some irony in Paris, House's role was that of "the Human Intercessor, the Comforter, the Virgin Mary"[32] for the high-flying president, so distant from ordinary mortals.[33]

Although the Colonel became Wilson's chief channel for conveying the views of Europe's most important leaders, especially those of Great Britain, he remained almost completely inaccessible to the Italians. The two phenomena were not entirely unrelated. In 1917–1918, both within the ranks of the Foreign Office (at the time headed by Lord Balfour) and among the English opinion leaders of the democratic area, there was growing hostility to Sonnino's obsessive political focus on the Treaty of London (for instance, from the influential editorialist of the *London Times,* Henry Wickham Steed, and the expert publicist for the "New Europe," Robert W. Seton-Watson, who also worked for the Foreign Office in that period). House's close ties with the English political universe steeped him in Britain's growing intolerance and rejection of Italian foreign policy.

It was at the opening of the peace conference that House's diplomatic career reached its high point. He was not only one of the five American plenipotentiaries, but the only one, aside from Wilson himself, who was involved in the most sensitive questions and was constantly kept informed of the progress of the most secret negotiations. When Wilson was absent, House acted as his substitute. House, even more than Wilson, was on a confidential basis with European statesmen, who valued House's style and placed full confidence in him. Moreover, several Inquiry experts and several of his family members occupied key positions in the ranks of the American delegation.

Yet, it was precisely this official and openly prestigious position within the American delegation that sowed the seeds of House's demise. House was now no longer the president's personal adviser, working safely in the shadows; instead he was a high official, working openly alongside his chief. Once he emerged from behind the scenes and assumed the role of a leading protagonist, he immediately revealed the differences between him and Wilson, in terms of both diplomatic method and substance. The essential character-istic of House's personality—notably his amiable and conciliatory attitude, which had been so useful to Wilson in previous years—now became the source of friction with the president and with other American negotiators. By this point, House had overestimated his own skills as a diplomat.[34] He was now more determined in his views, and he took center stage without managing to conceal how much he was enjoying the cheers of the crowd. Wilson ultimately decided that House's behavior was undermining his plans. He did not like the facile manner in which House accepted compro-mises, his new assertion of independence, and his friendly relationships with European leaders, which often gave Wilson the feeling that he was be-ing kept out of the loop. Between March and April 1919, their long friend-ship came to an end.[35]

Paradoxically, the Italian leaders, who had had no interactions with House when he was the influential adviser of the American president, in-creasingly relied on him during the phase in which he was gradually losing his influence. The more House lost power, the more the Italians came to consider him as the sole possible "savior of Italy."[36] As Henry White, one of the American plenipotentiaries, observed, the Italians had been "grievously misled . . . [by House's] tendency to compromise and by the assurances of friendship and sympathy, of a general nature at least if not actually with their particular views."[37]

Thus, as we will see in greater detail in the next chapter, the Italians, un-aware that House's influence was declining, continued to use him as their go-between in Paris for their negotiations with the president. During the entire conference, they saw House as the sole American delegate capable of listening to their arguments sympathetically, and, as the situation worsened, they increasingly relied on his intermediation. As Secretary of State Lansing recalled in his memoirs:

> It was not until the latter part of March, 1919, that these statesmen [Or-lando and Sonnino] began to suspect that they had been misinformed and that the influence of their American friends was not as powerful with Mr. Wilson as they had been led to believe. It was an unpleasant awakening. They were placed in a difficult position. Too late to calm the inflamed temper of the Italian people the Italian leaders at Paris had no alternative but to press their demands with greater vigor since the failure to obtain Fiume meant almost inevitable disaster to the Orlando Ministry.[38]

Throughout Italian American relations during the war, Italy never managed to find reliable channels of communication with President Wilson. For a long time, on both sides, no effort was made to find potential points of agreement. All the same, when the Italians finally decided to do so, they always worked through the wrong people: officials at the State Department, Ambassador di Cellere or Ambassador Page, the counselor Oscar Crosby, Captain La Guardia, or else, in the end, the person who may have created the largest number of misunderstandings—Colonel Edward Mandell House.

The Creation of the Inquiry and the Fourteen Points

The Inquiry was an advisory organization in the field of foreign policy, created personally by Wilson in September 1917, a few months after the United States went to war. Its chief task was to contribute studies and data gathering for use in the formulation of the American peace program during the country's critical transition from its traditional isolationist stance to its more recent international involvement. Its members were intellectuals who came largely from America's leading universities. Wilson, himself, an outsider in the American political world but a highly respected member of academia, preferred to turn to the academic world for consultants on formulating of his foreign policy. In that sense, the Inquiry can be considered a new approach which Wilson brought to the conduct of foreign affairs. One of its founding members later called it a "strange experiment in the mobilization of the political and social sciences to help in shaping the outlines of the new world structure which had to be built out of the ruins of the war."[39]

At the peak of its importance, the Inquiry grew to include some 130 experts, most of them university professors. It investigated political, economic, ethnic, and strategic issues concerning the countries involved in the war, assembling and analyzing an enormous mass of data in the more than 2,000 reports that it produced. One of its first major contributions was made in drafting the Fourteen Points, when many of the concepts recommended by Inquiry experts were incorporated into Wilson's programmatic manifesto. Aside from the sheer volume of studies, the importance of the Inquiry lay primarily in the education and background of the experts who accompanied Wilson to Paris as technical advisers, who were frequently called upon to advise him, and who in some commissions actually served as negotiators.

This unusual organization, set at the confluence of the political and intellectual worlds, offers us a significant sampling of the orientations of that vast and composite ideological front that, in the war years and the war's immediate aftermath, identified itself with the New Diplomacy. A study of the Inquiry is especially interesting because, during the war years, other indicators of American public opinion were particularly unyielding of information. In the press, for instance, the joint effects of the control exerted by the CPI and the self-censorship adopted "patriotically" by publishers as a group ensured that reporting or editorializing that was critical of or hostile to the Allies or the war effort simply did not make it into print. In contrast, in the case of the Inquiry, the very nature of its institutional duties and autonomous standing with respect to the official structure allowed it considerable freedom of expression.

From the papers of the Inquiry, therefore, we can trace the development of the Wilson administration's attitude toward Italy over the year and a half that preceded the explosion of the Adriatic question at the Paris peace conference. When analyzing the many reports on Italy, we are struck by the seriousness and detail of the studies that undergirded Wilson's laconic statements about that country; at the same time, we observe the excessive emphasis on the technical aspects of the boundaries by experts who were culturally very distant from the intricate and incandescent welter of European nationalisms. Thus, the work of the experts, though very careful in terms of scholarship, wound up providing justification for Wilson's intransigence and worsening the problems of intercultural communication between Italy and the United States.

From the point of view of the Inquiry, the peace conference marked the culmination of fourteen months of intense preparation. For those who believe, therefore, that the complexity of inter-Allied relations in that period, and in particular, the worsening Italian difficulties at the Paris peace conference cannot be understood merely through an analysis of the personalities of the members of the Council of Four,[40] an exploration of the work done by the Inquiry offers many interesting nuggets. The history of the Inquiry is intertwined with the history of the American intelligentsia, which at the time was presented unceremoniously with the duties, responsibilities, and dangers that intervention in the European war entailed. Participation in the war, opened vast new international horizons, but it also reawakened old isolationist tendencies, along with the complex and ambivalent set of feelings that the American nation harbored toward the Old World. Europe was clearly where America's deepest roots lay, but the nation rejected the social and political model of the Old World, the product of thousands of years of history. American intervention could thus be viewed both as an idealistic American contribution to the defense of western democratic civilization and as a new European pitfall, designed to lure the United States out of its lofty and majestic isolation and drag it into the dangerous maelstrom of power politics.

The Inquiry was organized, assembled, and financed outside of official diplomatic structures. House was put in charge of it, and its members generally came from circles unconnected to the complex world of international diplomatic relations. This led Walter Hines Page, the American ambassador in London, to speak with irony but also concern about the "amateur touch" of the foreign policy developed in Washington.[41] With the expansion of the Inquiry and the progressive development of House's role as an international mediator, an unofficial diplomatic structure came into being, which was parallel to the official structure and in some ways alternative to it.

During the summer of 1917, Wilson's awareness of the profound difference between American and Allied political objectives had been bolstered by the events surrounding the response to the August papal note denouncing the "useless slaughter." In drafting his response, the American president felt obliged to be somewhat vague lest he offend the Allies: "I have not thought it wise to say more or to be more specific," he confided to House, "because it might provoke dissenting voices from France or Italy if I should,—if I should say, for example, that their territorial claims did not interest us."[42] It was Wilson's awareness of the divergence of American political objectives from European aims that had led him to plan the establishment of the Inquiry.[43]

Wilson intended that the Inquiry should not only gather documents and data, carrying out studies in preparation for the American peace program, but also identify pressure suitable to induce recalcitrant Allies to accept the American point of view. The Inquiry therefore had a technical task but also political duties. In his formulation of these duties, the American president appeared to be far more of a "realist" than is usually thought. Aside from the official statements and declarations of the belligerent states, then, the Inquiry was also asked to investigate the political positions expressed by minority opposition parties and those social groups in the various European countries that could become internal supporters of U.S. policy. Where Italy was concerned, however, both in the work done by the Inquiry and, in general, in the large American position, both before and during the peace conference, precisely this political effort to seek out alliances and opportunities for compromise was lacking. In the absence of such work, a number of "scientific" studies, a tendency toward moralizing, and a Manichaean view of matters took center stage.

At the beginning of its working existence, the Inquiry, through the work of three members of its Executive Committee—Sidney Mezes, Walter Lippmann, and David Hunter Miller—exerted considerable influence on the drafting of the Fourteen Points. These three members provided a report, in two successive versions (dated 22 December 1917 and 2 January 1918), that influenced the content and sometimes the very wording of the points concerning European territorial disputes.[44] Lippmann recalled his contributions in the following words: "The method we used in working on these [territorial points] was to take the secret treaties, analyze the parts which were tolerable, and separate the parts which were tolerable from those which we regarded as intolerable, and develop an American position which conceded as much to the Allies as it could but took away the poison in each case. Each point is constructed for that purpose. It was all keyed upon the secret treaties." With regard to Italy, Lippmann recalled: "The sensitive spot was Italy. We shaved down the Italian claims to the indisputable Italian territory, which meant that they were not to have Trentino, the Austrian part, and they were not to have Fiume."[45]

House recorded in his diary that Wilson gave careful study to the recommendations of the experts, especially those concerning territorial disputes. One purpose of the American president's message was to urge the Allies to amend their war aims in a more liberal direction—that is, they should restrict their territorial gains to those zones that were indisputably part of their nation. This was especially true for Italy: "The President was especially disturbed by the Treaty of London and the arrangements made for the partition of the Turkish Empire. Mr. Wilson was aware of the extent to which Great Britain and France were committed to Italy by the Treaty of London. It was important to make plain that the United States was pledged to principles that conflicted directly with that treaty in so far as it assigned foreign nationalities to Italian sovereignty."[46]

The Fourteen Points had made no reference to Allied secret treaties. In particular, the ninth point, regarding Italy, does not refer to the Treaty of London. Wilson preferred to limit himself to a statement of principle, without going into the merits of the individual Italian ambitions, when he stated: "A readjustment of the frontiers of Italy should be effected along clearly recognizable lines of nationality." If, however, we consider the two Inquiry reports that House and Wilson used in drafting the American document (on one copy of the first report, we can still see Wilson's handwritten notes),[47] we see that the examination of and judgment on Italian territorial ambitions is extremely detailed. We can therefore conclude that, even if they did not have the exact text of the Treaty of London, the Inquiry experts were perfectly informed as to its content.

The first Inquiry report was delivered to House, who discussed it with the president on Christmas Day 1917. The report acknowledged Italy's "right" to rectify its frontiers "on the basis of a just balance of defensive and nationalist considerations," and it optimistically noted: "It is our belief that the application of this plank will meet the just demands of Italy, without yielding to those larger ambitions along the eastern shore of the Adriatic for which we can find no substantial justification."[48] Wilson noted in the margin of the Inquiry report: "That is the readjustment of the frontiers of Italy along clearly recognized lines of nationality." This comment became the content of the ninth of the Fourteen Points, concerning Italy.

The smallness of the territorial gains proposed by the Inquiry and contained in the Fourteen Points had to be offset by other compensations in terms of prestige and/or economic or colonial acquisitions. Otherwise, the American peace proposal left unresolved the basic political problem faced by the Italian government of how to offer a justification to their people for those long years of war waged for results that could have been substantially obtained without going to war. Speaking of the reactions to the Fourteen Points in the Italian army, Ambassador Page reported that soldiers were asking: "What are we fighting for if Trent and Trieste are not to be Italy's?"[49] In a series of letters and telegrams, Page became a spokesman for Italy's bewilderment and disappointment over Wilson's message, and Page found a sympathetic audience in Lansing.[50] Wilson, however, despite the entreaties of his secretary of state, did nothing to alleviate or discuss Italy's perplexed confusion, save to convey to the Italian ambassador a bland and generic mention of the problem-solving function of the League of Nations, which would ensure the security of the Adriatic zone.[51] In reality, this stance only called into question the very wisdom of the Italian government's decision to join the war on the Allied side. Without developing any alternative justification for the long and painful Italian war effort, American policy was casting discredit on the liberal governing class and stoking the fires of domestic social and political conflict. The seriousness of the consequences, therefore, helps explains first the intractable response of the Italian government, and in time the response of the broader Italian public.

After its contribution to the drafting of the Fourteen Points, the product of a still embryonic structure, the advisory organization created by the American president grew rapidly. Its makeup and organization were basically the work of a founding core group, a quintet consisting of Sidney Mezes (director), Walter Lippmann (secretary), David Hunter Miller (treasurer), Isaiah Bowman (geographer), and James Shotwell (historian). The offices of the Inquiry were established in New York, first in a number of rooms at the New York Public Library and later in a larger building made available by the American Geographical Society.

Mezes, president of the College of the City of New York and a professor of the philosophy of religion, was appointed director of the Inquiry—despite his lack of expertise—exclusively because as a relative of House he was judged to be reliable. Mezes remained director for the entire time of the Inquiry's existence, even though in the actual management of this Wilsonian organization he was gradually replaced by the more capable, competent, and strong-willed Bowman. David Hunter Miller, a New York lawyer who had recently joined the State Department, was also recruited to work for the Inquiry through his personal ties to the Colonel. He brought with him, and in particular he developed within the context of the Inquiry, an impressive international legal expertise that proved extremely useful when the time came to draft the peace treaty.[52] Isaiah Bowman, a respected geographer and the director of the American Geographical Society, was appointed executive officer by House in August 1918; this virtually stripped Mezes of any real authority.[53] The dual leadership of the group of American experts was maintained in Paris, too. Formally, Mezes was in charge, but in reality, Bowman was the chief. James Shotwell was the historian of the Inquiry, not only in the sense that he was an academic historian, but also because through his subsequent writings he provided an invaluable account of the people he met and the events to which he was an eyewitness in the context of the Inquiry.

Walter Lippmann,[54] the popular editorialist of *The New Republic,* exerted a dominant influence over the organization in its early stages and during the first phase of the Inquiry's activities. Lippmann had left journalism several months before to work in the Wilson administration, first as assistant to Secretary of War Newton Baker (June–October 1917) and, later, at

House's invitation but at Wilson's explicit behest,[55] as the secretary of the Inquiry (October 1917–June 1918). Not yet thirty years old, Lippmann was already one of the most influential political commentators in America. From then until the end of 1918, his contribution to the construction of Wilson's foreign policy was considerable, as a journalist, as secretary of the Inquiry, as Wilson's interpreter, and in general, as an "idea-man."

Lippmann's support of Wilson's foreign policy lasted just over two years. During 1918, Wilson proved less and less willing to listen to the journalist's suggestions, until he finally openly rejected Lippmann's positions in the summer of that year.[56] In addition, as early as the beginning of 1919, Lippmann began to doubt the effectiveness of Wilson's foreign policy and to form negative opinions on the results of the peace conference. In this rethinking he was following an arc common to many radical U.S. intellectuals.[57]

Lippmann's working style, based more on political instinct than on research, his ostentatious awareness of his influence over Wilson, along with his serious organizational shortcomings and inability to work with other experts, soon alienated the other members of the Executive Committee of the Inquiry.[58] The conflict became especially bitter with Bowman, who was more capable as an executive. This drove Lippmann to quit the Inquiry at the beginning of the summer of 1918; he took a position in Europe as a captain in military intelligence. During the summer of 1918 and later, in Paris, when he attempted to reestablish contact with the men of the Inquiry, as well as with President Wilson, his efforts were greeted with silence and indifference. When he left the Inquiry, a precious body of skills and expertise at political analysis was lost, and this was reflected in the attitude toward Italy.

As is evident even from this first glance at its founding members, the areas of interest of the Inquiry's central nucleus were extremely diversified. None of them, had to do specifically with the art of international diplomacy or the territories that were likely to be the object of the peace negotiations. In that period, it was difficult to find in the United States historians, economists, political scientists, or even geographers, who had anything more than an elementary understanding of the languages and issues of central and southeastern Europe, Africa, or Asia. In American universities, in particular, up to that point a provincial attitude of disinterest toward the world outside of North America had largely prevailed; this was a reflection in cultural terms of the country's political isolationism.[59]

Overall, more than sixty reports discussed Italian problems, and roughly forty of those reports were devoted exclusively to Italy. During 1918, given the increasingly evident disintegration of the Hapsburg Empire and the growing success of the Slavic independence movements, the experts shifted their attention to the Adriatic side of Italy's borders. That area, in contrast with Trentino, was increasingly being colored with the vivid hues of propaganda, ultimately becoming a symbol of the ideological conflict between old and new diplomacy. Thus, there gradually spread among the experts an attitude of increasing openness toward concessions along Italy's northeastern border, in consideration of primarily strategic and economic factors. At the same time, views on the Adriatic question became more and more rigid. The sole exception was a gradual recognition that the Italian character of Trieste should play as important a role in decision making as the fact that it had also long been the port city of the Austrian and Slavic hinterland.

While understanding of Italian problems was in short supply within the Inquiry, the dimensions of the Italian question, as it burst into being in Paris, were generally underestimated. A single member, young and not particularly expert, was officially assigned to study Italy. The studies on Italy, numerous though they were, did little more than analyze almost exclusively the problems of the frontiers. Those studies were assigned to different individuals and divisions, without adequate coordination.

William Lunt, in his early thirties, was a professor of English History at Cornell University and Haverford College, and he was the only expert assigned to the study of Italy within the context of the Inquiry. In this capacity, he was also asked to join the American delegation to the Paris peace conference. He had been selected because of his familiarity, imperfect though it was, with the Italian language and Italian history, which he had acquired during his studies in the Vatican libraries on relations between the Holy See and England during the Middle Ages. Like many other "experts," he had been chosen more for his presumed research skills than for any real knowledge of the material in question.[60]

Lunt produced only one report, voluminous though it was, on Trentino, *The Italian Tyrol.* In this report, he analyzed the linguistic and ethnic makeup of the population in minute detail, village by village.[61] Since this sole report was delivered to the Inquiry in November 1918, after the conclusion of the armistice, it is clear that Lunt studied only Trentino-Alto Adige, and not the areas in Istria and Dalmatia that were the subject of disputes with the future Yugoslavian state, or any more general political

problems.[62] On the whole, therefore, he seems to have remained impris-
oned by the initial approach of the Inquiry, which had focused principally
on this border area between Italy and Austria. It was only beginning in the
spring of 1918 that the success of the burgeoning Yugoslavian movement
and the Americans' growing acceptance of the idea of dismembering the
Hapsburg Empire brought the Adriatic question into the spotlight. Thus,
because he focused on an area of diminished interest both inside and outside of the Inquiry in 1918, and because Wilson conceded that area to Italy
at the very outset of the peace negotiations, Lunt does not seem to have
played an influential role in constructing American policy on Italy.

More influential were those experts who studied Italy in conjunction
with the chief area of study. In examining the Inquiry documents on Italy,
one is astonished by the large number of experts and sections that studied
Italy. Among those writing reports on Italy, aside from Lunt, were Austin
Evans and Louis Gray of the General Research Division, Douglas Johnson
and Ellen Semple of the Maps-Cartography Division, Robert Kerner,
Charles Seymour, and Clive Day of the Central European Division, James
Shotwell and Preston Slosson of the Diplomatic History Division, George
Louis Beer of the Colonial Division, as well as Mason Tyler and Walter
Lippmann.

Therefore, we cannot say that the Inquiry neglected Italy in its work. But
what does emerge is, on the one hand, a scattering of the studies among numerous individuals and divisions and, on the other hand, an excessive focus
on technical problems concerning the frontiers. In other words, there was a
glaring absence of any overall vision of the Italian domestic and international political situation, seen as a context in which to place the country's
territorial claims. This necessarily led to an insufficient development of the
American negotiating position—that is, to the means of pressure and dialogue that the United States could use in its relations with the Italian ally,
means to which Wilson had referred when first planning for the creation of
the Inquiry.

Especially lacking was any clear understanding of the level of emotions
that surrounded the Italian territorial claims. Often, for instance, emphasis
was placed on the validity of the boundaries that Austria supposedly conceded to Italy in the spring of 1915 in exchange for Italian neutrality.[63] Even
though the Inquiry studies were based on accurate ethnic, strategic, or economic considerations, therefore, they led to politically unacceptable conclusions. In particular, the liberal Italian governing class—which had pushed a

nation with prevalently pacifistic sentiments into war—could not accept such a negotiating position because it implied that Italian intervention had been pointless and was therefore tantamount to recognizing the failure of that government's overall political approach.

Marginalizing the State Department and the Two Embassies

Wilson underused the State Department throughout his presidency. Of course, the long tradition of American isolationism meant that the State Department was not up to the task that went with the new United States role following intervention. A radical reorganization and expansion of the department would have been needed. But the American president preferred to leave the State Department as it was and to delegate crucial aspects of his administration's international activity to persons and agencies that answered directly to the president. He entrusted the State Department only with the management of strictly routine duties. For that, purpose, the supervision of Robert Lansing, secretary of state beginning in June 1915, was quite sufficient. Wilson had very little respect for Lansing's legalistic approach. With his customary sarcastic style, Lippmann wrote in September 1919:

> The State Department was incredibly unprepared and incredibly complacent about it. . . . Extraordinary as it sounds, it is nevertheless true, that American entrance into the war produced no radical change in the Department. We had decided to abandon "isolation," but the State Department remained almost as isolated from Europe as it ever was. No administrative collapse in any department was so complete as the collapse of the State Department. . . . Mr. Wilson acted through other agencies, informed himself from other sources, and acted independently.[64]

Lansing was a political realist, profoundly unsuited to sharing the idealism of Wilson's international vision or to appreciating the charismatic appeal of his public position. His personal notes are filled with criticisms of Wilson's infatuation with words and of Wilson's fondness for coining slogans without any appreciation for how "loaded with dynamite" and dangerous to future negotiations those slogans could be (such as the policy of self-determination for peoples). Even the Fourteen Points met with skepticism from Lansing. In particular, he could see the point of the Italian demand for ports on the Dalmatian coast and in Albania for defensive purposes:

Of course it [this Italian demand] loses much of its force if the President's idea of an international guaranty of political and territorial integrity prevails and is effective. It seems to me that unless all doubt as to the efficacy of the proposed guaranty is dispelled, the question will have to be solved.[65]

Lansing's realism brought him closer to the approach of Sonnino and Orlando, but it placed him very far from his inspired president.

It is understandable, then, that Wilson would employ Lansing only to handle everyday issues that arose in international relations, while jealously concentrating under his own control and in the hands of his trusted collaborators the management of his overall international program. Wilson would never have entrusted to Lansing projects that demanded a major ideational effort. This was precisely what Wilson meant when he profoundly offended Lansing in Paris, asking in a resentful and impolite tone about a draft treaty that Lansing had asked two lawyers to draw up: "Who authorized them to do this? I don't want lawyers drafting this treaty." Lansing, himself a lawyer, felt personally attacked by Wilson's words and retreated into a defensive attitude that he maintained for the rest of the peace conference. Following this episode, relations between Lansing and Wilson, which had never warmed to anything more than a chilly formality, became increasingly hostile on both sides.[66]

While George Creel and his newly founded CPI were enthusiastically spreading American propaganda overseas, the Inquiry was in New York quietly preparing the studies necessary for developing an American negotiating position. Both the CPI and the Inquiry had only the most infrequent and distant relations with the diplomatic structure, a situation that was destined to create friction, misunderstanding, and waste of energy. Nearly all the commissioners whom the CPI sent to Europe, for instance, clashed with career diplomats, while the professors working for the Inquiry, even though they were experts in their respective fields of research, were nothing better than apprentices in the minefields of diplomatic relations in wartime.[67]

The work of the two ambassadors did nothing to lessen the communications problems between Italy and the United States: if Vincenzo Macchi di Cellere was incompetent but influential in Italy, Thomas Nelson Page was more competent but without influence in the United States. Neither of the two succeeded in attracting the attention and influencing Wilson or the powerful Colonel House.

Ambassador di Cellere, an old-school diplomat loyal to Sonnino, never grasped the modernity of the Wilsonian political message. In the various descriptions of the American president that he sent to Rome, he variously described Wilson as an overambitious politician, concealing his desire to become the arbiter of the peace agreement behind a curtain of noble principles, or—heaping ridicule upon him—as an incorrigible utopian who dreamed of encouraging world peace and security, not through defensible frontiers and a balance of power, but through a new supranational organization.[68]

During the period of Italian and American co-belligerency, di Cellere did not meet with the American president as often as his French and English counterparts did. What is worse, in his infrequent conversations at the White House, he failed to understand Wilson's basic attitude toward Italy and overestimated his own powers of persuasion. For instance, his first reaction to the Fourteen Points was positive: to Wilson's great astonishment, he went so far as to call on the president to thank him for his words about Italy.[69] Later, di Cellere interpreted simple acts of courtesy on Wilson's part—such as the American celebrations for the anniversary of Italy's entry into the war, his participation in the reception held at the Italian embassy for the signing of the armistice, or the invitation extended to him and his European colleagues to travel with him on the ship that would be taking him to Europe for the peace negotiations—as signs of the president's sympathy for Italian ambitions. Di Cellere never suspected how deeply the president was opposed to Italian territorial expansions or how intrinsic that opposition was to the program that Wilson was putting forward for peace in Europe. Di Cellere's last dispatches from Washington were therefore a genuine distillate of misunderstandings. In most of them, the Italian ambassador repeated the same concept over and over: "Wilson is on Italy's side and wants to support her."[70]

Di Cellere could have limited the scale of this diplomatic failure if he had had greater access to the well-informed and influential Colonel House, whose amiability and openness to conversation differed sharply from the president's chilly reserve. Instead, however, right up until the last days of the war, di Cellere failed to recognize that the path to Wilson ran through House and not through the higher echelons of the State Department. It is hard to understand why the Italian ambassador did so little to establish and cultivate ties with House, since as early as 1915 he had grasped the extent of the Colonel's influence on the president and had sent Sonnino a critical but accurate description of the close collaboration between the two men.[71] Shyness, negligence, or mere incompetence are the only explanations for his inevitably unsuccessful behavior.

The result of all this was that the Italian minister for foreign affairs was receiving misleading information from his ambassador in Washington. Especially during the last months of the war and the first days of peace, Sonnino was repeatedly reassured about Wilson's favorable attitude toward Italy and Wilson's intentions to help Italy in the face of the European Allies' unfriendly intentions. Since House did nothing to make clear Wilson's opposition to Italy's territorial ambitions during the armistice negotiations, Italy developed its program for the peace conference based on the groundswell of national and nationalistic enthusiasm over the unexpected victory of Vittorio Veneto, without any clear understanding of American opposition to its plans. The first meeting with Wilson in Paris in mid-December 1918 was probably a bit of a cold shower for Orlando and Sonnino. But by then it was too late to easily introduce radical changes into the Italian peace program. Any such changes, which would necessarily entail giving up clauses in the Treaty of London, could only be envisioned in conjunction with the formulation of international compensation in Italy's favor.

In contrast with di Cellere, ambassador Thomas Nelson Page proved to be a good source of information. Grateful to the Colonel, who had helped him obtain his position as ambassador,[72] Page kept House constantly informed of developments in the Italian situation. His reports were surprisingly accurate for a more or less improvised diplomat. Nonetheless, Page's "travails" in Rome to keep the American embassy in tune with events never won much attention from House, who shared Wilson's scorn for almost the entire American diplomatic corps overseas.[73]

Page's observations were perhaps influential only at the beginning of the war. In April 1915, he traveled to Nice to meet with House, who was on one of his first peace missions to Europe in the capacity of Wilson's personal envoy. On that occasion, Page described to him "the intricacies of Italian politics" and the "wholly selfish way" with which Italy's leaders were considering a potential declaration of war by Italy on the side of the Triple Entente.[74]

Page's detached and critical stance changed after Italy decided to join the war. Stunned by the terrible sacrifices that soldiers and civilians were forced to make for almost four years, he felt a growing sense of sympathy for the Italians. He worked strenuously to transform an embassy that until then had been on the sidelines into an efficient forward position of American aid and his president's political message. Page organized the first American relief station, encouraged propaganda, and hired Gino Speranza to improve Americans' understanding of Italian internal affairs.

Unfortunately, even though the reports from the embassy on the Italian situation were steadily improving, Page was listened to less and less in America. He was not only largely ignored, but he was also kept insufficiently informed of new developments in Wilson's foreign policy. His opinions were discounted and thought to be excessively in line with the aims of the Italian government, which were not thought to mirror popular sentiment among the Italians. In February 1918, for instance, House wrote Wilson about the letter Page had written reporting on the views of the Italian political world about how Italy had been treated in the Fourteen Points:

> The feeling that Page describes is and has always been prevalent in certain circles in every country, . . . Sonnino as I have told you, is the worst reactionary that I know in Europe, but he does not represent Italian feeling on any subject excepting their desires of Austria. . . . Unfortunately, the reactionaries are in control of almost all the belligerent governments, but they represent the necessities of their peoples rather than their real sentiments.[75]

When it became evident that none of the American negotiators in Paris was interested in his point of view, Page bitterly resigned.

The historian John Milton Cooper claims that one of Wilson's greatest mistakes was keeping House and Lansing in influential positions in his administration.[76] Wilson supposedly understood the Colonel's true nature only too late, and for too long Wilson kept as the head of the State Department a man who, though an expert in international law, was not in tune with the fundamental direction of the administration's foreign policy, which demanded a powerful ideological commitment, a "vision." The double track on which American foreign policy ran—the official track guided by Lansing and the unofficial track under the supervision of House and, in part, Creel—is said to have hindered the United States' effectiveness in the international arena.

The problem may have been more deeply rooted. Wilson's decisions were a direct result of his general distaste for diplomacy, which he viewed as a tool of the old power politics with its balances of power and secret treaties. The sidetracking of the entire American diplomatic structure, both at home and abroad, corresponded to this basic approach. Wilson set forth, in contrast to traditional diplomacy, two new revolutionary concepts and forces: the irresistible force of a leader who knows how to appeal to the people and the plan for a new system of international relations based on a supranational organization, the League of Nations. These were the two most modern aspects of Wilson's political thinking, as well as two fundamental characteristics of international society in the twentieth century. Wilson did not believe that career diplomats could carry forward these new approaches to international political relations. To promote them, he "invented" mass propaganda based on his own words, and he organized a vast advisory organization staffed primarily by university professors, the Inquiry. He also relied on trusted individuals, first and foremost House, for his relations with the European political forces. That is, Wilson's decisions were a direct product of the central core of his way of thinking and, in that sense, were mistakes that could hardly have been avoided.

Nonetheless, the Wilsonian colossus, without the intermediation due to diplomacy, was a giant with feet of clay. The trouble began when Wilson moved from the declarations of principles and slogans of the war years to the concrete work of redesigning the map of Europe and the international order, finding points of intersections between differing, occasionally opposing political positions and demands. Unquestionably, diplomacy would have to change to keep pace with the era of mass politics, but its role remained crucial in managing international relations. Indeed, the patient work of diplomacy to bring together opposing political and cultural positions was needed more than ever in a time like the Great War. During this conflict, the whirlpool of globalization brought countries and cultures into contact that hitherto had lived in remote spheres, filled with reciprocal stereotypes.

Sonnino, Orlando, and Nitti

Let us explore in detail how the difficulties in communication manifested themselves in the relationships of the Americans with the three chief members of the Italian government: Sonnino, Orlando, and Nitti. We will focus on the period between the summer of 1918 and the spring of 1919—that is, between the last months of the war and the first months of peace, a period when the communication difficulties between Italy and the United States became evident.

As a last-ditch defender of the rights that Italy had won through its participation in the war, Baron Sidney Sonnino had become "the great untouchable" of the Italian political establishment.[77] Without doubt, Sonnino was not only the mastermind behind the conditions for Italian intervention in the world war but also, since he remained minister for foreign affairs for the entire duration of the war, he championed continuing the war, strenuously opposing both domestic pacifists and the maneuvers of the Allies in order to be able to come to the peace conference with full credentials to demand the implementation of the Treaty of London. He always considered the pact as one of his great diplomatic successes and an agreement that finally won Italy a place among the leading powers of the time. As Ambassador Page noted, "Baron Sonnino in Italy is a sort of incarnation of the idea of fighting the war through to a finish and giving Italy, through the redemption of her Irredentist provinces, and through the acquisition of defensible frontiers, the rewards of her resolution and sacrifices."[78]

The longer the war stretched out and the bloodier it became, the more Sonnino felt a sense of moral responsibility to obtain for Italy what it had been promised. He attempted to preserve this attitude even after the United States entered the war; he never liked the novelties that the United States brought either to the ideological conduct of the war or to domestic and international politics. Fearing, however, the growing influence of a partner that was not bound by the terms of the pact, Sonnino attempted for a long time to avoid any discussion of war aims, postponing the confrontation until the time of the peace negotiations. In this context, his strategy of delay was a perfect match for the American strategy. Sonnino's favorite maxim was more or less as follows: "To discuss war aims implies revision, revision implies renunciation."[79] This decision was based on two mistaken assumptions: the first was that America would have no interest in the details of purely European questions; the second was that, once victory had been won, the Allies would keep the promises made to Italy and the United States would not interfere.

Sonnino shared with the other representatives of the class that then held power the ideological foundations of nineteenth-century liberalism, which implied, among other things, an elitist view of politics: the management of public affairs was a task that devolved on only a few and certainly could not be thrown open to the ignorant masses. What Sonnino said to Malagodi in December 1914 about the possible decision to enter the war is especially illuminating: "In truth, . . . only a few want war. But if we believe it is necessary or useful to Italy, we must and we shall be able to decide over the objections of the crowd.[80] Such beliefs made it difficult for the entire Italian governing class, and for Sonnino in particular, to deal with the world that was emerging from the war, in which the masses, ideologies, and the new charismatic leaders played a leading role.

In his political career, which had been lengthy, Sonnino had always maintained a position of isolation from Italian political circles. Contributing to that stance was his closed and taciturn personality, but also the stern and intransigent moralism that derived from his personal family history. Sidney Sonnino, of Anglo-Saxon birth and upbringing (his mother was English), was the only Protestant leader in the Italian political world. A biographer described him as "decidedly British in manner and thought" and called him a "Mediterranean Victorian"; Thayer called him "the great puritan of the Chamber, the last uncorrupted man."[81] Sonnino's sterling integrity was acknowledged and universally respected, but his difficult personality, kept him distant from all forms of intimacy or comradeship with his colleagues. Those observers were correct who noted a resemblance in the personalities and intransigent moralism of Wilson and Sonnino. As Speranza wrote in mid-November 1918: "Sonnino comes nearer to Wilson in rectitude and political conscience"; Page echoed his words when he described the Italian minister as "a man of force, honesty and courage, and independent of all intrigues."[82]

During the final year of the war and then at the peace conference, the international environment became increasingly hostile to Sonnino and to his politics. A new world was emerging in which he was assigned an unpleasant role. Not only was France's and England's opposition reinforced by the United States' hostility, but international public opinion—a new and almost irresistible emerging power—went against his policy. The new reality—which was in part incomprehensible to Sonnino—took on many aspects of a nightmare in which he was unable to bring to fruition what he felt to be a moral imperative for his country and a duty to the hundreds of thousands of Italian dead and wounded in the war: to obtain a peace treaty that could justify those dead and thus pay Italy back for the immense sacrifices it had suffered. Sonnino reacted by attaching himself with increasing stubbornness to the Treaty of London, the only "talisman" capable of leading Italy toward a satisfactory peace.

Whether Sonnino's rigidity might have been smoothed out in a less unfriendly atmosphere is open to discussion—that is, if a revision of the pact had been proposed in a spirit of collaboration, a setting of full understanding of the Italian government's need to justify the war for the Italians, with an offer of valuable considerations on the international stage, if only in terms of prestige. Many observers noticed Sonnino's greater willingness to negotiate during the summer and early autumn of 1918. Two new elements encouraged dialogue: (1) the shift in U.S. policy toward the Austro-Hungarian Empire in May 1918,[83] resulting in a U.S. declaration in favor of dismantling that empire and therefore suspending negotiations with them for a separate peace; and (2) the Italian government's increasingly pressing desire to obtain American troops, both for the actual contribution they could provide to the impending, crucial offensive, and for the definitive seal of approval they would set upon the teetering Italian American alliance. Whatever the case, Speranza, Merriam, Page, and later House, in the conversations they had with Sonnino between the beginning of September and the end of November 1918, found him more open and affable ("less rigid," said House) than they expected. In a careful study of the Italian position on the Yugoslavian question, Speranza noted that the Italian government would cling to certain promises of the Treaty of London as long as it was not possible to stipulate a new agreement as solemn and binding but more liberal. Sonnino, could not give up the territories promised in the Treaty of London without some valuable consideration to make up for them.[84]

Even though this report was highly praised in Washington, it was recommended that an agreement between the Italians and Yugoslavians not be sought before the peace conference. The leadership of the State Department was advised to take Speranza's reports with a grain of salt. Military intelligence had described Speranza as "an Italian nationalist propagandist."[85] In fact, it was recommended not to pay attention to the suggestions from the embassy in Rome.

These observations show that the program that the Italian delegation presented in Paris—a program that demanded, in a contradictory manner, the Treaty of London plus Fiume (due to the groundswell of Italian nationalism, swollen by the euphoria of victory, but also to the erroneous information and impressions that Orlando and Sonnino had been given by House and by di Cellere)—was a preliminary version. From a position of strength the intention was to bargain away the necessary sacrifices, but to give away nothing if not in exchange for something else. To its astonishment, the unforgiving climate of the negotiations in which the delegation found itself froze the contradictory Italian program, which the Italians had envisioned as a favorable point of departure from which to bargain. In Paris, Sonnino lapsed into increasing isolation and silence. One prediction of Orlando's and Sonnino's behavior at Versailles had been accurate: "Sonnino will be silent in all the languages he knows, and Orlando will speak in all the languages he doesn't."[86] After the failure of the peace conference, Sonnino withdrew from political life and adopted a cloistered way of life.[87]

Vittorio Emanuele Orlando found himself in an increasingly uncomfortable position at the Paris negotiations, which he had not expected to be so fraught with problems. More than difficult, they must have struck him as profoundly disconcerting, inasmuch as he was continuously receiving assurances and tokens of Wilson's good feelings toward him while perceiving

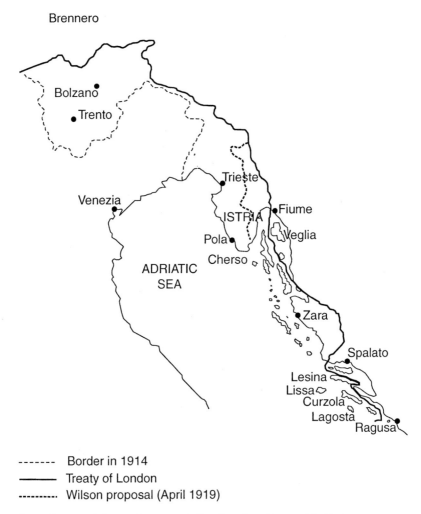

```
------- Border in 1914
——— Treaty of London
.......... Wilson proposal (April 1919)
```

Schematic map of the northeastern Italian frontiers discussed in Paris

unmistakable evidence of American indifference to his proposals. Orlando, a fluent, Sicilian-born lawyer, was a respected scholar of international law to whom any separation between the personal and official aspects of his role as a negotiator would have been incomprehensible. Like House, Orlando believed that the most sensitive international questions could be resolved with dialogue and persuasion, in an environment of open and satisfactory relations among the national representatives.

The atmosphere at the Paris negotiations must have seemed increasingly hostile and confusing to Orlando. In fact in his memoirs we find numerous passages where he seems to have fallen victim to full-fledged hallucinations and delusions of persecution. In his memoirs, which he insisted be published only after his death, he makes continuous reference to a "mysterious force" that hindered all his efforts and that was "far more powerful than any friendship that Wilson might have felt toward me." This force was "secret" and "all-powerful," "a superior force" that he could not escape, "a mysterious and occult power which deprived Wilson of the liberty to decide and act, making him into its obedient and passive instrument."[88] It is strange to see this noted jurist and statesman, accustomed to dealing with every sort of audience and debate, losing his ability to interpret the reality that surrounded him and expressing his feeling that he had become a victim of obscure, irresistible forces opposed to his plans. What more eloquent demonstration of the wall of incommunicability that separated the Italian politicians from their American counterparts than his hallucinatory vision of the peace negotiations?

Francesco Saverio Nitti was probably one of the few emerging figures in the Italian political world who fully grasped the significance of the United States entry onto the world stage, at least in economic terms. Before the war, he wrote a book entitled *Il capitale straniero in Italia* (Foreign Capital in Italy), in which he noted with regret that Italy had failed to attract American capital.[89] He hoped that this state of affairs might change and that the vast river of American resources might someday flow toward Italy as well. Nitti had a clear-eyed view of international economic relations, of American supremacy, and of Italian needs within those two realms. But his understanding did not extend far enough to grasp the new role that the masses and the mass media played in the social and political model that America was proposing. In that sense, he remained a member of the Old Guard, helplessly alien to mass politics and mass parties.

Nitti served as minister of the treasury in the Orlando government in the 1917–1919 period and succeeded Orlando as prime minister in June 1919.

Beginning with the American intervention in April 1917, he had repeatedly attempted to establish contact with the American leadership, presenting himself as an alternative to Sonnino's antiquated foreign policy.[90] He continued firmly in the belief that he had established good connections with the Wilson administration, when, as we have seen, he actually had a very poor reputation within that administration. This was in part because, without realizing it, he had established acquaintanceships with Americans who were not good channels of communication to the American political leadership. In 1917, when he took part in the official mission to the United States, he did not win the support of the American leaders, in part owing to the hostility of Sonnino's Italian ambassador, Vincenzo Macchi di Cellere, who promoted Lansing's lasting antagonism toward him. As we have already seen, the CPI's reports described Nitti as being quite similar to Giolitti: an old-school politician, skillful at palace maneuverings but devoid of an ideal and a moral vision of politics. Nitti was thought to be connected to the interests of several major banking and manufacturing groups. In short, behind him hovered the specter of the American political boss, the bête noire of so many Progressives. Especially important, Nitti thought, were his good ties with the American ambassador in Rome, Thomas Nelson Page, the American representative on the Inter-Allied Council in London, Oscar Crosby, and Fiorello La Guardia. However, those relationships meant little, for none of those three people had any influence over Wilson or House.[91]

Nonetheless, Nitti thought of himself as the vigorous and modern leader who could have led Italy in the aftermath of the war with the blessings of the Americans. In his conversations with the American ambassador in October 1918 and again in February 1919, he openly stated that he would take Orlando's place, leading a broad front that would include followers of Giolitti, Socialists, Radicals, and *Popolari*.[92] But, when he succeeded Orlando as prime minister, he did not receive the American support he was counting on.

We can conclude, that the three most important members of the Italian government, for different reasons, got off on the wrong foot in their relations with the United States, and they had almost no communications with the new ally, as powerful as it was culturally and politically distant. The worst thing was that all three failed to realize what was happening before the problems had worsened practically to the point of becoming insoluble.

— 7 —

The Paradox of the Fiume Dispute

With the arrival of autumn and the sudden proclamation of peace, Italian American diplomatic relations changed radically. Now that the war was finally won, many of the arguments in favor of a doctrine of postponement collapsed, while the impending peace negotiations were about to cast a harsh light on the contrasting objectives that the various countries in the victorious alliance had pursued in the war. In the months between the cessation of hostilities and the opening of the peace conference, there was no shortage of opportunities to work out an accord between Italy and the United States—, for instance, the armistice negotiations in October–November 1918 and Wilson's trip to Italy in January 1919. Instead, as we will see, it was precisely in this period that mutual mistrust and opposition became most accentuated. The prejudices and misunderstandings that this situation entailed, rather than any gap in political positions, made the subsequent negotiations in Paris extremely complex.

As soon as the German Prince Max von Baden asked Wilson for an armistice based on the Fourteen Points, the American president hastened to send his trusted adviser House to Paris, tasking him with wresting from the reluctant Allies an equal recognition of his principles as a basis for the peace negotiations. This time, House represented the United States officially, first at the armistice talks and later at the peace conference. In both cases, the challenge was to broker an agreement not with the defeated powers but among the nations of the victorious alliance.[1] The extended disputes among the victors showed the world just how far apart and conflicting the Allies' war aims had been. A first priority was to break the seal of silence covering the inter-Allied secret treaties in order to reach a common negotiating position that could be brought to the peace table. That was the main purpose of the meetings the Supreme War Council held in Paris between late October and early November 1918. In terms of the evolution of Italian American relations, these meetings had decidedly negative results; indeed, they increased, rather than bridged, the distance between the negotiating stances of the two countries.

On 29 October 1918, discussions began on Wilson's request for the Allies' formal acceptance of the Fourteen Points as a foundation for the armistice that would be signed with Germany. Lloyd George and Balfour were present on behalf of England, Clemenceau for France, House for the United States, and Sonnino—and later, Orlando—for Italy. To facilitate the discussions, Frank Cobb, editor of the *New York World,* and Walter Lippmann, who already happened to be in Paris, drew up an interpretation of the Fourteen Points at House's request that became the official American position once it had been approved by Wilson. In this interpretation, where Italy was concerned, a number of new positions were adopted; chief among them was the recommendation of the complete concession of the Brenner border.[2] For the Adriatic zone and the colonial possessions in the eastern Mediterranean, however, the document set forth a far more restrictive position. For Istria, reference was made to the advisability of accepting an accord, not otherwise defined, to be reached between the Italian government and the Yugoslavian state,[3] provided, however, that both Trieste and Fiume became free ports. In the Balkans, the Italian request for a protectorate over Albania and the possession of Vlorë (or Valona) was accepted, but the document recommended a solution favorable to Greece for the Aegean islands and the Dodecanese. Discussion of the partition of the Turkish Empire, made no mention of Italian ambitions.

The representatives of the four victorious nations continued discussions for a number of days. Each representative had reservations about accepting the Fourteen Points. Sonnino, while laying out his reservations, noted that Point Nine failed to satisfy all of the Italian demands in the Adriatic zone. In the days that followed, the Italian representatives withdrew this reservation, having been won over by their colleagues' arguments that it was pointless to present it at this juncture inasmuch as this was a discussion of the armistice with Germany, not Austria-Hungary. On 5 November 1918, therefore, the Allies collectively agreed to discuss the terms of the armistice with Germany on the basis of the Fourteen Points, with two reservations only: an English reservation on the freedom of the seas and a French reservation on German reparations. Despite Orlando and Sonnino's repeated, if clumsy, efforts, no mention was made of the Italian reservation in any of the notes exchanged between the Allies and Wilson or between both Wilson and the Allies and the Central Powers. Since the armistice with Austria-Hungary was later stipulated at Villa Giusti directly between the Italian and Austrian military staffs, without any reference to the Fourteen Points, the Italian reservation on the Fourteen Points was never mentioned in any official armistice-related document.

The Italian arguments were never examined openly or given substantial discussion. House's chief objective was in all cases to achieve a formal acceptance of Wilson's program by the Allies quickly and with the smallest possible number of reservations. With this goal in mind, he agreed to compromise solutions that kept the profound disagreements between the Allied nations from coming to light. By alluding to the threat of a separate peace between the United States and Germany and employing other forms of pressure, he finally attained his purpose but at the cost of postponing the unresolved difficulties into the subsequent peace negotiations. House was ready to pay any price to obtain rapid acceptance of the Fourteen Points from the European leaders. The price he paid would prove to be too high.

The armistice with the Austro-Hungarian Empire was the first to be signed. The Austrian military staff had unexpectedly asked its Italian counterpart for an armistice, without reference to the Fourteen Points. The clauses of the armistice seemed to be restricted to military issues, and that was the main reason for their rapid approval by the Supreme War Council. Colonel House, who at the time was focused on the armistice with Germany, found it convenient to sign the military armistice with Austria first, without being obliged to discuss the thorny political problems bound up with Italian ambitions. He telegraphed Wilson on 30 October:

> It was agreed that the terms of the military and naval armistice to be offered Austria should be revised by the Allied generals and admirals, and when completed should be transmitted direct through General Diaz to the Austrian Commander-in-Chief. This has the advantage of avoiding political discussion respecting Italian and other claims before capitulation of Austria is completed.[4]

Even so, House failed to prevent the inclusion of purely political clauses in the armistice. In particular, article 3 described in detail the line of withdrawal for the Austrian forces and the subsequent Allied occupation. In view of the circumstances, the occupying troops would be chiefly Italian. This line corresponded precisely to the border assigned to Italy by the Treaty of London. At the end of a highly charged meeting with Prime Minister Orlando, House had accepted the inclusion of the line from the treaty. The sole condition set was that a detailed description of the territories to be occupied should be replaced by a simple reference to the article from the Treaty of London that established Italy's new borders.[5]

These developments were not the result of House's oversight, on but rather of negotiations with Orlando. During a long meeting, House retreated in the face of the Italian prime minister's flowery and impetuous eloquence, oratory that was filled with references to the terrible price in human lives that Italy had paid during the war. The compromise they reached gave Italy the substantive contents of the Treaty of London. Orlando could understand and agree to House's reservations. The condition demanded for American approval of the Italian ambitions in the Adriatic zone was a pure formality: it would be sufficient to avoid any explicit reference to a secret treaty to which the United States had not been a party.[6]

The following day, House telegraphed Wilson: "[I] assure you that nothing will be done to embarrass you or to compromise any of your peace principles. You will have as free a hand after the Armistice is signed as you now have." All the same, House failed to report to the president on his long discussion with Orlando, nor did he mention it in his diary. He probably realized that it was not one of his shining moments as a diplomat.[7]

The concessions that House accepted on 30 October were not a momentary surrender in the face of particularly vehement oratory or strong Italian sentiment. During a subsequent meeting with Orlando on 3 November, immediately following the approval of the armistice with Austria-Hungary, House reassured the Italian prime minister, who still saw "a small cloud on the horizon," of American sympathy for Italy. House stated that Wilson had failed to make more explicit mention of Italian ambitions in the Fourteen Points only because of a "lack of information." Once Wilson arrived in Europe, he would treat those ambitions "in the most sympathetic spirit." House also observed that he was in favor of an Italian military occupation of the disputed Austrian territories. Orlando was so impressed by House's friendly and conciliatory stance that he said to Hugh Frazier, who was acting as interpreter, that "while the armistice was a cause of satisfaction to him, his conversation with Colonel House was still more satisfactory."[8] At this point, Orlando ordered the occupation of the Adriatic regions included in the Treaty of London in the confident belief that he was doing so with the blessing of the Americans.

House again failed to report his conversation with Orlando to Wilson, nor did he indicate any concern that the Treaty of London should be making an appearance in the clauses of the armistice. It was not until 11 November, when tensions began to rise in the Adriatic territories over the advancing Italian troops, that he recommended that Wilson "speak a word of caution" to Italy concerning the Adriatic problems since the United States was the only country in a position to do so. All the same, as has been noted, "House, alone with Orlando, had been in that position eight days earlier and he had spoken a word of encouragement."[9]

On 15 November 1918, it was Sonnino's turn to meet with House. During this meeting, the Colonel's recklessness reached its apex. In an unpublished passage from his diary, House described his meeting with Sonnino in these terms:

> Baron Sonnino was an afternoon caller. He contended that Italy desired nothing except to have her boundaries rearranged in a way to give protection in the event of invasion. I suggested not bringing forth Italy's plea until after Great Britain had made her plea as to why it was necessary for her safety to have control of the seas or, at least, have the largest navy in the world, and until France had explained why she should straighten out her eastern boundary to protect herself from her enemies. Sonnino was delighted with the suggestion and saw the point at once. *I did this in a spirit of sheer deviltry.* I shall enjoy being present when Sonnino and Orlando make their armument [sic] based upon the British and French claims. I did not undertake to tell Sonnino that if they would listen to our plan for a League of Nations, Italy would be amply protected, for I did not wish to start an argument at this time.[10]

In response to Sonnino's demand for more easily defensible borders, "out of pure malice," House suggested that Italy postpone making its demands until after Great Britain and France had set forth their conditions for national security. House could not have been serious in this suggestion, for he did not believe that the two leading European powers could ever obtain anything of the sort from the negotiations. But to Sonnino it appeared that the American representative, far from opposing Italian aspirations for territorial expansion, was only suggesting the best diplomatic approach for obtaining them.[11]

House's behavior on two collateral questions—the fate of the Austrian fleet and the participation of American troops in the occupation of the territories assigned to Italy by the Treaty of London—reinforced Orlando's and Sonnino's impressions that American policy was aligned with Italian policy. Once again, House had completely misled the Italian leaders, who had convinced themselves that the United States had by now accepted the substance of the Treaty of London and that a direct clash with the American president in Versailles was highly improbable. It was with these impressions in mind that they prepared to define the various points of the Italian program for the peace conference (and Fiume was one of those points).

These negotiations were conducted in such a superficial manner that they resulted in two opposing stances: the Americans interpreted Italian silence on their possible reservations with regard to the Fourteen Points as an acceptance of Wilsonian principles, whereas the Italians thought they had preserved the validity of the Treaty of London. Following these negotiations, the belief prevailed among the American representatives that the Fourteen Points had now completely replaced any preceding Allied accords that might conflict with them. That is the only way to explain American indifference to the proposal presented repeatedly by the French delegation in November 1918 that the Allies should revoke in advance all their secret agreements prior to the formal inauguration of the peace negotiations. In a memorandum regarding the French proposal, for example, David Hunter Miller, the chief American expert on international law, wrote: "It is to be supposed that any treaty engagements of the Allied Powers, particularly those with Russia, and with Italy, made during the war, which may be inconsistent with the principles enunciated by President Wilson, have been in fact, if not technically, abandoned by the Allied Powers, in view of their announced agreement with those principles above quoted."[12] As evidence that the Italians had reached the opposite conclusion, on 7 December 1918, the conservative daily newspaper, *Il Giornale d'Italia*, considered to be a vehicle under Sonnino's control, reported on the progress of the Paris talks with a front-page headline: "Treaty of London Ratified."

House's behavior on these various occasions illustrated his diplomatic style. Despite his support of "open diplomacy," he relied mostly on the traditional tools of diplomacy, that is, personal relationships and secret discussions. He replaced Wilsonian ideals with the belief that even the most difficult international problem could be solved if one could preserve a climate of friendly trust among the negotiators. Confident of his powers of persuasion in private conversation, House preferred informal meetings with just a few participants at a time. He was always careful to avoid official ceremonies and plenary sessions.[13] The other American diplomats, resentful at being excluded from these conclaves reserved for only a chosen few, called House a "whispering diplomat" and "the high priest of the mysteries" at Versailles.[14]

House's detractors accused him of being overeager to abandon principles and to accept too many compromises in order to preserve cordial relations with European leaders. Secretary of State Lansing and the head of the American experts, Isaiah Bowman, had very harsh opinions of his negotiating methods.[15] Ray Stannard Baker, too, became increasingly critical of the Colonel's style: he thought that House was basically "an arranger," not a man of strong principles.[16]

House's dealings with the Italian leaders became more frequent during the Paris negotiations. Even though, as we have seen, he had formed a substantially negative judgment of Orlando and Sonnino, from their very first meeting both of them thought House was in favor of Italian interests. The Italian leaders, had been impressed with the conciliatory approach of the American president's personal envoy beginning with the first meeting of the Supreme War Council in December 1917, immediately after Caporetto. Following the negotiations for the armistice, in which House had given them Italians practically everything they had asked for, they increasingly began to rely on his mediation and to consider him their only friend among the American negotiators in Paris. Despite his friendly manners and his desire to find compromises, House's intermediation did nothing to improve the dialogue between the two countries in the crucial months between the armistices and the peace negotiations. To the contrary, his behavior was profoundly misleading to both countries. The Italians believed that his attitude mirrored Wilson's; Wilson in turn was not informed of the Italian reservations with respect to the Fourteen Points. The two countries would thus meet at Versailles without a clear understanding of their reciprocal positions. House, who was perfectly aware of the differences, did not reveal them to either party. This was, as has been stated, "irresponsible diplomacy."[17]

Colonel House always considered the negotiations for the armistice to have been his crowning diplomatic achievement,[18] but, at least as far as Italy was concerned, it was not. It was at best a diversion, a maneuver that fed both parties a great deal of misleading information and thus merely postponed the conflict. If the two countries had been forthright regarding their disagreements at the time of the armistice, it might have been easier for them to find partial solutions to their differences, because at that point official negotiating programs and public opinion in both countries were still being formed.[19]

"Tell Me What's Right and I'll Fight for It"

To the astonishment of the experts, when the U.S.S. *George Washington* (4–13 December 1918) took Wilson and most of the American delegation to France for the peace conference, the extensive time available was not used to plan, consolidate objectives, or prepare an overall program. The disappointment of the experts was conveyed to the president, leading him to call a meeting limited to the members of the Inquiry. This meeting, which turned into a long monologue by the American president, was the only time during the entire peace conference that he met his entire staff and gave them a few general strategic lines of approach.

During that meeting, Wilson made a few statements that were particularly enlightening as to the spirit in which he was preparing for the negotiations as well as the approach he favored from his colleagues. Wilson stated that the Americans "would be the only disinterested people at the peace conference, and that the men whom [they] were about to deal with did not represent their own people." He pointed out that this would be the first international conference in which the decisions made would depend on the opinions of humanity at large rather than on previous diplomatic accords or decisions. Unless the peace conference proved able to obey the wishes of the people, instead of the governments, he said, there could be little doubt that a new war would break out before long, and that this time it would take on the proportions of a worldwide cataclysm. The meeting ended with specific reference to the attitude and role that the experts should adopt at the peace conference:

> The President concluded the conference by saying that he hoped to see us frequently, and while he expected us to work through the Commissioners according to the organization plans of the Conference, he wanted us in case of emergency not to hesitate to bring directly to his attention any matter whose decision was in any way critical; and concluded with [a] sentence that deserves immortality: "Tell me what's right and I'll fight for it; give me a guaranteed position."[20]

The territorial experts of the Inquiry remembered this invitation from Wilson to approach him directly in any especially serious case. They also remembered his request that they provide him with a "guaranteed position," when, in April of the following year, they sent him the letter that triggered the Adriatic Crisis.

Wilson's statements were symptomatic of what would prove to be one of the chief limitations of the American negotiating position in Paris. Both Wilson and his territorial experts believed that a "guaranteed position" could be taken in the context of the intricate international questions of the period. They also believed that they enjoyed a position of moral superiority over the other national delegates: the United States was not one of the litigants but set itself above them with the attitude of an arbitrator. The rigid moralism that grew out of the belief that the Americans alone were in the right proved disastrous to the outcome of the negotiations, especially with regard to Italy.

While Wilson was in part blinded by the almost religious sense of his mission in the world that emerged from the war, his experts were misled by their excessive reliance on the objectivity and utility of scientific considerations. The border issues, for instance, were analyzed mostly in terms of statistical data, with little concern for political and historical considerations. Such a trusting and positivistic determinism had been feasible only in the remote and prosperous United States, which was still immune to the schools of irrational and nihilistic thought that were sweeping across Europe. The faith of most of the experts in the absolute validity of scientific data, whether economic, ethnic, or strategic, went hand in hand with Wilson's ideological intransigence and made the American position especially rigid. Together, they provided the American delegation with arguments but deprived it of the capacity for intercultural mediation.

Most of the Inquiry experts were pleased with their private meeting with the president and were heartened as to the role the core group of the Inquiry would likely play in Paris. They began to view their future duties as those of chief technical advisers to the president.[21]

Only one expert, George Louis Beer, left the meeting dissatisfied and worried. He thought that the president, in his meeting with the experts, had shown that he had made no effort to establish how his general principles should be applied. Beer thought that this was in fact the most crucial and difficult aspect to be worked out at the negotiation table. Wilson had focused on principles, which could often be abstract and therefore danger-ous.[22] A few months later, Beer repeated his concern:

> Trouble is that there is no one near who sees the problem as a whole and
> has a fair grasp of the details. Wilson is strong on principles that a sopho-
> more might enunciate, but is absurdly weak on their application. He does
> not see, at least he did not, that the application was the difficult part.[23]

Beer was an outsider to the Inquiry, inasmuch as he came neither from
the world of academia nor from democratic political circles. Nor did he hail
from the ranks of the Progressives: he was a Republican who had acquired a
considerable reputation as a scholar of the English colonial system. In Paris,
he was appointed chief of the American colonial experts, and he came up
with the system of mandates that the conference adopted. His realistic
mind-set, together with his understanding of the international panorama,
made him skeptical about the vagueness of Wilson's program. He was especially critical of the American way of predicating the proposals to be pursued in the negotiations on general principles. He felt that this was an
impracticable approach in the intricate European territorial situation.

The actual developments of the peace conference only confirmed his
misgivings. He frequently criticized the holier-than-thou attitudes of many
Americans, who seemed to believe that everyone—except them—had
morally questionable motivations. In particular, he did not share their hostile attitude toward Italy, which he considered unjustified and based on
prejudice. He tried to help the Italian delegation throughout the conference:
"The western world cannot afford to flout Italy's feelings," he wrote. The
Italians had nearly everyone against them, even though, in his view, their
demands were "far more moderate than are those of the French, Poles,
Czecho-Slovaks and Jugo-Slavs even."[24]

As the months went by, Beer became increasingly pessimistic about the
peace treaty that was taking shape. It struck him as "a mere temporary settlement" in which "all these artificial lines in Europe are bound to lead to
another explosion." The German signature of the treaty had also embittered
him: "It was like the execution of a sentence," he commented sadly.
Nonetheless, Beer remained a devout internationalist, who was more likely
to work to develop new and more effective tools of international government than to waste time in a sterile rejection of the results of the peace conference. That set him apart from most Wilsonian intellectuals, who recoiled
at the Paris deal-making, which for them was so alien to the lofty idealism

of the war years, and became increasingly hostile to Wilson's leadership. Their caustic attacks on the results of the peace conference only strengthened the adversaries of American international engagement. In contrast, Beer did everything he could to battle the resurgent isolationism of his compatriots, until his premature death, in 1920.[25]

Wilson's Triumphal Journey to Italy

There is a great deal of evidence that Wilson carefully studied the Treaty of London during his crossing to Europe and during his first stay in Paris. Aboard ship, he had asked the Italian ambassador for information about the pact,[26] and he had also asked Lunt, the Inquiry's Italian expert, for a memo on Italian demands.[27] As soon as he arrived in Paris, the first thing he asked his experts for was a copy of the secret treaty between the Triple Entente and Italy,[28] and in the days that followed, he repeatedly focused on Italian questions.[29]

Therefore, Wilson was thoroughly briefed on Italian objectives and the opinions of American specialists on those objectives. Therefore, he made a conscious political decision to avoid any discussion with the Italian government of the thorny problems attending the peace conference. When Italian politicians, eager to discuss the most controversial points of their territorial goals, began to ask him questions, the American president blithely replied that he could not discuss the matter because he knew too little about it and he had delegated those questions entirely to his experts. The Italians, however, were convinced that he had reached conclusions of his own concerning their demands, and they interpreted his reticence as his unwillingness to consider their position. This in turn increased their mistrust.[30]

Nor did Wilson's request for a meeting with Bissolati, the interventionist Socialist who had just resigned from the government, favor mutual understanding. Wilson had been urged to request the meeting by Speranza, Ray S. Baker, and others who hoped for an alliance between the American democratic leader and the front of Italian democratic interventionism and reformist Socialism. Many different parties hoped in this way to reinforce an alternative alliance to the conservatives then in power. But the meeting had no such results, both because of Bissolati's isolation and because of Wilson's unwillingness to establish a clear link with Socialist leaders. Instead, the meeting reinforced Wilson's belief that he was correct in his plans for the Adriatic zone and in his opposition to official Italian demands.[31]

At the same time, Wilson drew from the triumphal welcome given him by the Italian people a mistaken and overblown impression of his own powers of persuasion over the Italians. During his trip to Italy (2–6 January 1919), he visited Rome, Milan, Genoa, and Turin, and everywhere he went he was greeted by cheering crowds, eager to hail him as the Messiah of the new world that was about to spring from the rubble of warfare. People displayed their devotion to him in a variety of ways: burning candles before pictures of him, scattering sand before his feet to honor him, kissing his signature, or clustering along the railroad tracks, just to watch the president's train go by. According to many witnesses, the welcomes he received in Italy were more enthusiastic than those he received in any other place he visited.[32]

The very reservations that the Italian governing class showed in prohibiting him from delivering speeches in the open piazzas convinced him even more of this powerful grip over the imaginations of the Italian masses. He had hoped to deliver a public speech in Rome, but the authorities forbade him from doing so, to his great disappointment.[33] As a result, his trip to Italy only increased Wilson's hostility toward the Italian political leadership. He saw them as the very personification of the dark forces of reaction, and they triggered in him an intransigent and doctrinaire moralism, coupled with a determination to defeat them with the power of his hold over the masses. This was Wilson's typical attitude when dealing with his political opponents: he would leave no room for dialogue and compromise.[34]

"An Infamous Arrangement"

As soon as the war ended, the Inquiry was dissolved, and about twenty of its members, along with a huge mass of studies, became part of the American delegation to the peace conference, where they served as technical consultants. With irony but also admiration, a member of the British delegation noted that "[t]he amount of material that they collected was astounding; the *George Washington* creaked and groaned across the Atlantic under the weight of their erudition."[35]

In Paris, the organizational shortcomings of the American delegation led the experts from the Inquiry to take on increasingly significant responsibilities and duties. To their own astonishment, they rapidly became the most frequently consulted experts, both for the American president and the other plenipotentiaries. Subsequently, on numerous committees, they acted as direct negotiators.

The Black Book, a lengthy, two-volume document that was prepared in Paris in January 1919 for Wilson and the American diplomats, can be considered to be the final and cumulative product of the Inquiry's work. Even if it was not an official document, it was widely distributed among the American delegates and can be considered the preliminary program that the United States presented at the peace negotiations.[36] The document thoroughly explored various Italian questions. In particular, it recommended a frontier in Trentino that, although it was described as "midway between the linguistic line and the line of the Treaty of London," differed from the frontier desired by Italy in the exclusion of a single valley, the Val Pusteria. It also conceded that the Alpine border established in the Treaty of London corresponded to the best possible strategic frontier, and it recognized that a secure frontier would allow Italy to join the League of Nations with greater confidence. The small size and irrelevance, except perhaps in strategic terms, of the area left out according to the experts, and the very content of some of their arguments, tended to encourage an attitude that was open to Italian demands regarding the Italian borders. Concerning the Adriatic zone, however, the experts, continued to reject a substantial portion of the Italian demands. Specifically, in Istria the line of the frontiers was to be modified to include Pula (the Italian Pola) and therefore Trieste as well (for the first time, there was no mention of the advisability of establishing a free port in Trieste), but it was considered essential to preserve Fiume as part of Yugoslavia for ethnic and economic reasons. All of Dalmatia should become Yugoslavian. With these modifications, "Italy is accorded on the east as much natural protection as can be permitted without giving undue weight to strategic considerations." As for the colonial areas, it was recommended that the "doubtful claim of Italy" for a zone of influence in Vlorë (Valona) be taken under consideration in the form of a League of Nations mandate, while Rhodes and the Dodecanese were to be restored to Greece. In Africa and in Asia Minor, with the sole exception of an extension of the Libyan hinterland, the document excluded the possibility of expansion of Italian possessions. On the whole, the American experts offered a negative judgment of Italy's capabilities as a mandatary state of the League of Nations, especially because it lacked the necessary "missionary spirit."[37]

Thus, even if we can describe the recommendations of the Inquiry experts as balanced,[38] we should point out their tendency to give excessive importance to economic considerations and an exaggerated faith in scientific objectivity. The resulting attitude led toward a degree of dogmatism, especially when it came into contact with Wilson's moralistic rigor, and it also kept the delegation from empathizing with the European approach, deriving as it did from a cultural context characterized by powerful emotional and irrational impulses. Ambassador Page was not wrong when he observed, with some bitterness, that in the negotiations with Italy, his lengthy experience and familiarity with the Italians had been completely discounted, while the greatest deference and attention had been accorded to the territorial "experts":

> His [Wilson's] geographical boundary experts, . . . while undoubtedly wholly honest, seem to have entirely overlooked, in their presentation of the case, the most essential factor: the human. They have reported on figures and geographic facts, but have neglected, apparently, the weightier matters—the passions of Peoples, and especially the passion of the Italian people.[39]

Even House in Paris appeared to be increasingly intolerant of the rigidity of Wilson and his geographic experts as they clung to the "American line" in the Adriatic. With some basis, House argued that politics in its highest form was nothing more than a series of wise compromises and that it was dangerous to marginalize Italy in the context of the western world. This attitude considerably heightened Wilson's incipient mistrust of House; many historians and observers believed that their divergence of opinions on the Adriatic controversy was one of the principal reasons for the break between Wilson and House.[40]

It is not the province of this work to discuss the underlying reasons for that break. The fact remains, however, that the close and intense collaboration between the two politicians, which had endured through most of two presidential terms of office, did not survive the ordeal of the peace negotiations and came to an end in the spring of 1919. This factor added a further element of confusion in the already nebulous context of the negotiations: for an extended period, House no longer knew how far his authority extended, and yet, the negotiators from other countries continued to count on him as the principal channel of access to the president.

As the controversy over the Adriatic deepened, the difference of opinions among the members of the Inquiry developed into a full-fledged split into two opposing fronts. One faction was led by House and included Mezes, Miller, Shotwell, and Beer, arrayed in favor of the Italian ambitions, while the territorial experts—Lunt, Johnson, Seymour, and Day, guided by Bowman—were sharply opposed to them.

In mid-March 1919, Mezes developed a set of recommendations on the Adriatic question, which accepted and justified nearly all the Italian demands. Mezes's document seemed to have been copied from a document from the Italian delegation.[41] The reaction from the territorial experts was immediate. In late March and early April, they wrote many letters, reports, and memoranda for the plenipotentiaries, reiterating in increasingly indignant tones their rejection of most of the Italian demands. Then they attempted to contact Wilson directly to preempt what they perceived to be an attempt to sideline their expert views on the issue, and more seriously, an effort to claim that their opinions were diametrically opposed to their actual views. Accordingly, on 17 April they sent the American president a letter from which we quote extensively, given the results that it triggered:

En route to France, on the *George Washington* in December, the President gave the territorial specialists an inspiring moral direction: "Tell me what's right and I'll fight for it. Give me a guaranteed position." We regard this as a noble charter for the new international order. We have been proud to work for that charter. At this critical moment we should like to take advantage of the gracious invitation of the President to address him directly on matters of the gravest importance. . . .

Italy *entered* the war with a demand for loot. France and England surrendered to her demand. Of all the world's statesmen the President alone repudiated a war for spoils and proclaimed the just principles of an enduring peace. The belligerent nations, including Italy, agreed to make peace on the President's principles. Italy now insists that she must carry home an ample bag of spoils or the government will fall. If Italy gets even nominal sovereignty over Fiume as the price of supporting the League of Nations, she has brought the League down to her level. It becomes a coalition to maintain an unjust settlement. The world will see that a big Power has profited by the old methods: secret treaties, shameless demands, selfish oppression. . . . Better a League of Nations based on justice than a League based on Italian participation bought at a price. . . . Never in his career did the President have presented to him such an opportunity to strike a death-blow to the discredited methods of old-world diplomacy. . . . To the President is given the rare privilege of going down in history as the statesman who destroyed, by a clean-cut decision against an infamous arrangement, the last vestige of the old order.[42]

"Loot, "selfish oppression," "infamous arrangement": the letter that the Inquiry experts sent Wilson had lost all detachment and had taken on the emotional timbre of a full-fledged war of religion.

The appeal of the experts struck a chord in Wilson. By this point, negotiations with Italy had come to a stalemate, after numerous attempts that had proved futile. Orlando's maneuvering room, moreover, was steadily diminishing since the most extremist positions were prevailing in Italian public opinion. Moreover, the Italian support that had allowed Wilson to launch the project that was dearest to his heart, the League of Nations, was no longer needed. The American president therefore faced a fairly clear choice: either yield once again to the demands of the Allies, a concession that would be especially unpleasant after the numerous compromises that had been accepted to satisfy France and Great Britain, or else openly oppose the Italian demands, in a resounding affirmation of his principles. With the second option, he could restore the gleaming splendor of his international image as a defender of justice and the freedom of peoples, an image that had been somewhat tarnished by the horse trading in Paris.

Wilson selected the second approach, and just five days after receiving the letter from the experts, he published an appeal to the Italian people, an appeal that precipitated the Adriatic crisis. To the most intransigent members of the Inquiry, the president's astonishing initiative appeared to be a clear sign of the important role that their opinions played in his effort to establish "a new standard of international morality."[43] Italy had offered a perfect occasion to demonstrate to world public opinion the high moral standing of Wilson's New Diplomacy in comparison with the discredited European power diplomacy.

Wilson's Appeal to the Italians

Wilson's appeal to the Italians on 23 April 1919 was one of the most sensational and controversial incidents of the peace conference. With his usual consummate eloquence, Wilson was asking for the support of the Italian people for his political line in opposition to the position of their official representatives. This appeal triggered Orlando and Sonnino's dramatic withdrawal from the peace conference and was rejected emotionally by Italian public opinion. Many immediately understood that the American president had committed a serious error: the Italians, far from supporting him, showed that they would not tolerate his open scorn for their national leaders, and they reacted virtually in unison with indignation.

Of course, the tone and content of Wilson's message were much more carefully calibrated than the letter that the experts wrote him, but the letter was probably more in tune with his deep personal convictions. Keenly aware of the loss of prestige that he was suffering in both America and Europe, Wilson employed the tactic that he had used successfully so many times before in his academic and political careers—a direct appeal to the people. The Americans applauded him, but the Italians condemned him. The explosion of popular anger that immediately followed the Fiume appeal made it abundantly clear that, at least where Italy was concerned, there was something profoundly wrong in Wilson's approach. The Italians, feeling they had been betrayed, succumbed to the nationalist propaganda that accused Wilson of treating Italy not as an ally but as an enemy nation. Ambassador Page, in his report on the Italians' bitter reaction to Wilson's appeal, noted ironically that the Italian government in its reply had insisted on pointing out that it was angry at the president, not at the American people. With this distinction between people and government, Page commented, the Italian leaders wished "to pay back . . . the President in his own coin."[44]

Historians have generally offered a negative judgment of Wilson's appeal. Birdsall, for instance, called it "a resounding failure and . . . one of the worst mistakes he made in Paris"; Albrecht-Carrié termed it "a capital error in judgment"; and Bailey described it as "a tremendous blunder." Others, however, such as Floto and Kernek, have made subtle distinctions, limiting the scale of Wilson's error with the argument that his main goal had not been to influence Italian public opinion but rather to give new luster to his image as a herald of liberalism and democracy, especially for American and world public opinion. After months of compromises with France and England, Wilson's reputation had declined and the dispute over Fiume offered the president an excellent opportunity to reaffirm his principles. Sonnino had a good point when he commented that Wilson, after losing his virginity with France and England, now hoped to win it back with Italy.[45]

We would suggest, instead, that the Fiume appeal represented neither a momentary error in judgment nor a tactical move in the context of the negotiations, but rather the logical outcome of Wilson's entire policy toward Italy throughout the war years. We have seen that, immediately after American intervention, Wilson began to consider the Italian government not as a partner, whose agreement should be sought through meetings and negotiations, but rather as one of the most deplorable examples of the old European order, which the new direction he had imposed on international politics was designed to combat. As a result, American action toward its Mediterranean ally was soon characterized by a marked disinterest in political dialogue with its national leaders. In the wake of Caporetto, this basic attitude was joined by the mounting of an effective propaganda campaign in Italy, which turned Wilson and America into idols of the masses. In this sense, the American policy toward Italy was more in line with the policy that had been developed for Germany than with the policy adopted toward France and England. It was based on a distinction between the "good" Italian people and their "bad" government. From the very beginning, then, the foundations had been laid to appeal to the people over the heads of their government.

We would like to emphasize that this attitude was not limited to Wilson. Indeed, it seemed to be held by most of the American president's colleagues and had been present in the Wilsonian milieu even before the American intervention.[46] We have seen, for instance, how frequently and with what passion American observers encouraged Wilson to try the path of a direct appeal. This stance was rooted in diffuse aspects of U.S. culture of the time, including Progressive moralism translated into the new context of the war, the sense of the United States' exceptionalism on the world stage, as well as the slightly naïve dogmatism of the emerging field of social sciences. These elements all rendered more intransigent the first American involvement on the international stage.

From many points of view, the peace conference was a paradox. After years of devastating war, the winners argued for months about the conditions to be imposed on the losers. The long and intensely heated dispute that developed between Italy and the United States over the fate of the small city of Fiume was also a paradox: Fiume was not "a miserable little fishing village," as André Tardieu described it,[47] but a flourishing small commercial town. Nevertheless, the inability to find a compromise on it was absurd. Concerning this episode, Thomas Bailey was right in observing that "history can offer few comparable instances where so small a matter set in train such momentous consequences."[48] This dispute produced considerable consequences for both countries, inasmuch as both in Italy and in the United States the events of the peace conference alienated public sympathies from the new international order that was being built. This order would need the support of the public of it was to grow and become strong. In Italy, American hostility contributed to the fall of the obsolete liberal governing class and fed the legend of the "mutilated victory" that assisted the rise of Fascism. In the United States, the disturbing spectacle of Versailles encouraged the reaction of disgust with European politics and international involvement among a broad swath of the American public.

Wilson's Star Sets in Italy

The explosion of the Adriatic question marked the setting of Wilson's star in Italy. The same cannot be said for the myth of America, which in various forms extended throughout Italian culture for the entire century. In the spring of 1919, the American myth which had enjoyed an extraordinary season of flourishing under the influence of Wilsonian politics and propaganda came to an end. After that time, especially with the advent of Fascism, the American myth lost the spectacular connotations that it had acquired during the war and resumed its status as a strong but underground current in Italian culture. Thus, after two years of intense and emotional exchanges, the two countries moved apart again, both culturally and politically. The two-way bond of Italian immigration and emigration also lost its grip, as the United States began in 1917 to introduce increasingly strict restrictions on immigration.[49] As a result, the paths of the two countries would not converge again until the years following the Second World War when the American myth reemerged with new vigor.

As we have seen, the gap between Italian and American positions had historical, cultural, and irrational roots. It was, however, above all the two-year period of obstinate rejection of political dialogue that crystallized that gap into the full-fledged inability to communicate in Paris. In Italy, the feeling was that Italy had not received proper appreciation for its war effort and sacrifices, and the suspicion was that Italy had been discriminated against relative to the other allies. These feelings were already present in the war years but grew sharply during the peace conference. In the spring of 1919, the majority of Italian public opinion—including even the democratic interventionists who might have been receptive to Wilson's goals in Italy—fell into line in opposition to the American approach. Gaetano Salvemini wrote in the weekly *L'Unità* of 3 May 1919: "Why did he [Wilson] want to impose what he considers to be absolute justice, but to the Italian people alone?"[50] The widespread feeling that the "victory had been betrayed" served as fertile soil for the seeds of Fascism.

Colonel House's role in Italian American relations also reveals the extent to which communications difficulties amplified the clash between the two countries. The political differences, deep though they may have been, were nonetheless no greater than those between the United States and France, Japan, or the British Dominions. The shortcomings in diplomatic structures, cultural differences, and the presence of mutually negative images contributed to construction of a wall of incommunicability between the two allies. As a result, the leaders of the two countries never fully explored with any conviction the potential paths of dialogue. Diplomacy, understood as the art of establishing communication between different cultures and of attaining compromises between diverging political stances, almost completely failed in Italian American relations in the period of the First World War.

These observations raise more general questions about American policy toward Italy. During the last year of the war, Wilson's words had reached across the ocean to respond to the ideological needs of the rising European masses. Without doubt his political approach was modern: in many ways, we are still grappling with the problems he faced and the solutions he proposed, such as leadership through mass public opinion, or preservation of world peace through the activity of a supranational organization.[51] In no country more than in Italy can we see the modernity of Wilson's political message. He was capable of reaching out to pockets of Italian society that had remained dead to the words of its governing class; this helped to make Wilson a popular idol. All the same, the colossus of Wilson's wartime foreign policy had clay feet. In particular, its traditional diplomatic tools were inadequate. Wilson increasingly relied on amateur diplomats; House was only one of them, though certainly he was the most important one. We have already seen the difficulties that the Italians encountered in trying to reach Wilson through his confused and confusing diplomatic apparatus.

In addition, the so-called doctrine of postponement—that is, Wilson's fundamental assumption that in wartime politics it was unwise to attempt to reconcile American and Allied objectives prior to the final victory—was of questionable usefulness. This position led, among other things, to the Americans' pretended ignorance of the Treaty of London. Although a discussion of war aims during ongoing combat might have threatened the unity of the Allies and the determination of the Allied bloc, it is equally certain that only a frank discussion with the American leadership would have given the Italians a clear perception of Wilson's attitude toward their objectives. Moreover, the United States was in a stronger negotiating position during the war, better able to impose its principles upon reluctant allies. As for Italy, it would have been easier for the Americans to reach an agreement with the Italian governing class in the aftermath of the disaster of Caporetto, for instance, than at war's end.

As short-sighted and tone-deaf as Italian foreign policy at the end of the war may have been, a direct appeal to the people against its government was not a practicable approach, nor was it a good way to reconcile political differences. Wilson could not replace the Italian leadership, however questionable it may have been. After all, how bad were the leaders? Considering that extreme individuals such as Mussolini or Hitler had yet to appear on the scene, the American leaders could consider Sonnino to be "a reactionary of the worst type."[52] All the same, to paraphrase George Kennan's observation about Germany, we can imagine that two decades later, in the face of the aggressive imperialism of Fascist Italy, many Americans longed for the Italy of 1918: a country governed by conservatives, antiquated but relatively moderate.[53] Perhaps these considerations can help to illuminate the strategic errors committed by the political elites on both sides of the Atlantic. A compromise could have been reached, and it need not have taken months of grueling negotiations. It could have been reached during the war they fought in common.

We may conclude that, even though Wilson's propaganda was vast and effective, the tools available to the American government to understand Italian political reality remained inadequate. Information flowed to different agencies and organizations that were insufficiently connected one with another. Among the three institutions that focused on the Italian political situation—the State Department, the Inquiry, and the CPI—the State Department was always relegated to a subordinate position. In the vacuum that came to exist, Creel's CPI took on the task of propaganda, while House's Inquiry developed specialized studies on "technical" aspects of the Italian frontiers. Wilson's foreign policy toward Italy, then, can be summarized with this formula: a great deal of propaganda, scanty and poorly coordinated political analysis, no diplomacy.

This study has sought to illustrate the most salient aspects of this Wilsonian "divorce" from policy and diplomacy with regard to Italy. The limitations of the American approach became apparent not during the war, but during the peace negotiations, when what was needed was a comprehensive political effort to encourage dialogue with the distant ally. The lack of such an effort led to the profound crisis of Italian American relations in the immediate postwar years, which had major domestic repercussions in Italy. Melograni ends his fine book on the Great War by stating that the "Italian postwar crisis . . . began to precipitate at the moment that Wilson's prestige was destroyed."[54]

The reaction to Wilson's alleged betrayal and to the fall of this beloved idol was violent; it immediately revealed the political vacuum in Italy created by the First World War. An avalanche of hatred was unleashed upon Wilson: *figlio di Wilson* (literally, "son of a Wilson") became a common insult in Italy.[55] The many squares and streets in Italy that had been named after Wilson after 1918 were hastily rededicated to D'Annunzio or to Fiume.[56] This powerful reaction brought to the surface the profound Italian malaise, which was rooted in the economic and political instability of the Italian petty and middle bourgeoisie. These were the very classes that had called for war, that had worked on behalf of the propaganda campaigns filled with Wilsonian slogans in the aftermath of Caporetto, that had hoped for a peace that would repay them for their commitment and sacrifices. Now they found themselves threatened by the instability of the postwar period. The economic crisis that resulted from reconversion, inflation, and unemployment was affecting these classes more than the high bourgeoisie or the proletariat. The petty and middle bourgeoisie reacted in ways that bespoke their desperation: internationally, they inveighed against Wilson and his internationalism; domestically, they found outlets in the violence of the emerging phenomenon of *squadrismo* (the organization of the Fascist action squads).

The way things went in Italy also helps to cast some light on the complex historic figure of Woodrow Wilson and on the positives and negatives of his general political program. Certainly, we cannot accept the totally negative judgments of Wilson that dominated the twenty-year period between the two wars. Harold Nicolson, for instance, ridiculed Wilson's personality and described him as a conceited, visionary, egocentric politician—and even questioned Wilson's intelligence.[57] Anti-Wilsonism enjoyed a long life in Fascist Italy as well as elsewhere in Europe, not to mention in the United States, where the call for a "return to normalcy" issued by the new president, Warren Harding, and enthusiastically applauded by the American populace, meant the closing of the many windows that had opened to the world at large during the war. It also meant the narrowing of the nation's—and many individuals'—goals to a short-term search for prosperity. It was a short-sighted attitude that could not endure and that laid the foundations for even greater catastrophes, including the stock market crash of 1929, the Great Depression, and the Second World War.

In many ways, however, Wilson inaugurated the politics of the twentieth century. He showed how powerful a leader can be if he knows how to appeal to the masses; he shaped a number of the instruments of mass communication available to a leader. Moreover, he was the first statesman to try to build a new international order based on the work of intermediation, led by an international organization. He believed in these new political instruments and thought that through them many of the errors of the peace treaty could later be amended. In these fields, Wilson explored and offered an answer to some of the most burning issues of the contemporary world, issues that are still being debated.

Yet, we cannot agree with those who praise every aspect of his political approach. Wilson failed to adequately encourage dialogue with the Allies or with his political adversaries in the United States. He devalued diplomacy and thus deprived himself of the valuable assistance of many of his contemporaries, at just the time when passage of his political plan to an implementation phase demanded the careful weaving of alliances, especially with European nations. At the Paris negotiations, therefore, Wilson found himself alone, and the many compromises that he was forced to accept ensured that the peace that finally emerged would be a punitive one. The map of Europe that resulted would guarantee growing tension and conflicts that would endure throughout the century.

All the same, we cannot blame Wilson for the developments that led to the outbreak of the Second World War. Wilson himself had foretold that, without the League of Nations and the involvement of the United States in the management of the world peace, it would not be long before a new war began, far worse than the one that had just ended.[58] In the twenty years that ensued, Wilson was scorned and forgotten. One American historian who has studied the role of internationalism in America between the two world wars showed that in the 1920s and 1930s, Wilsonian internationalists were reduced to no more than a small handful.[59] But with the increasingly evident and menacing emergence of the aggressive policies of the Fascist nations and then with the outbreak of the Second World War, American public opinion shifted rapidly, and the need for international engagement made itself felt again. By one of the odd ironies of history, on the same day that a monument was erected in honor of Wilson (in Geneva, at the headquarters of the League of Nations) the Second World War broke out.[60] For Wilsonian internationalists, this coincidence, with its stark symbolism, showed that the most awful predictions of this long ignored prophet were all coming true. For his detractors, however, it was clear that the all-too-many mistakes made by a politician who seemed incapable of stepping down from the plane of ideas to the world of reality had brought Europe once again to the brink of the abyss.

With the Second World War's end, the creation of the United Nations, and the United States' full assumption of a hegemonic international role, Wilson's heritage could no longer be denied. At the first meeting of the United Nations in San Francisco, President Truman told the national representatives present: "You have given reality to the ideal of that great statesman of a generation ago—Woodrow Wilson."[61] The Wilsonian heritage, in part freed from the historical and ideological limitations that we have analyzed with special reference to Italy, constituted one of the pillars of the new international order following the Second World War, which ensured the western world a long period of peace and prosperity.

Notes

Index

Notes

Abbreviations

Archivio del Risorgimento: Fondo della Biblioteca, Museo e Archivio del Risorgimento, now at the Biblioteca di Storia Moderna e Contemporanea, Rome.

Archivio MAE: Archivio Storico, Ministero Affari Esteri, Rome.

Archivio Min. Interno: Archivio Ministero dell'Interno, Direzione Generale Pubblica Sicurezza, Archivio Centrale dello Stato, Rome.

Archivio SME: Archivio Storico, Stato Maggiore dell'Esercito, Rome.

Baker Papers: Ray Stannard Baker Papers, Library of Congress, Washington, D.C.

Beer Papers: George Louis Beer Papers, Manuscripts Division, Columbia University Library, New York (NY).

Bliss Lane Papers: Arthur Bliss Lane Papers, Sterling Library, Yale University, New Haven (Conn.).

Commiss. Assistenza Civile e Propaganda: Commissariato Generale Assistenza Civile e Propaganda Interna, Archivio Centrale dello Stato, Rome.

CPI Papers: Records of the Committee on Public Information 1917–1919, RG 63, National Archives, Washington, D.C.

Creel Papers: George Creel Papers, Manuscript Division, Library of Congress, Washington, D.C.

DDI: Ministero degli Affari Esteri, I Documenti Diplomatici Italiani.

Department of State, Internal Affairs of Italy 1910–1929: Department of State, Records relating to Internal Affairs of Italy, 1910–1929, Political Affairs, M. 527, National Archives, Washington, D.C.

Department of State, WWI and Its Termination 1914–1929: Department of State, Records of the Dept. of State Relating to World War I and Its Termination, 1914–1929, Record Group 59, M. 367, National Archives, Washington, D.C.

Fondo Orlando: Fondo Presidenza del Consiglio dei Ministri, Guerra Europea, Presidenza V. E. Orlando, Archivio Centrale dello Stato, Rome.

FRUS: U.S. Department of State, *Foreign Relations of the United States.*
House Papers: Edward Mandell House Papers, Manuscripts and Archives, Sterling Library, Yale University, New Haven (Conn.).
Inquiry Collection: Inquiry Collection, American Geographical Society Archives, New York (NY).
Inquiry Papers: Records of the Inquiry, National Archives, Washington, D.C.
Lansing Papers: Robert Lansing Papers, Manuscript Division, Library of Congress, Washington, D.C.
Lippmann Papers: Walter Lippmann Papers, Manuscripts and Archives, Sterling Library, Yale University, New Haven (Conn.).
Merriam Papers: Charles E. Merriam Papers, University of Chicago Library, Chicago (Ill.).
Page Papers: Thomas Nelson Page Papers, Duke University Library, Durham (N.C.).
Polk Papers: Frank L. Polk Papers, Manuscripts and Archives, Sterling Library, Yale University, New Haven (Conn.).
Speranza Papers: Gino Speranza Papers, Hoover Institution on War, Revolution and Peace, Stanford (Calif.).
W. H. Page Papers: Walter Hines Page Papers, Houghton Library, Harvard University, Cambridge (Mass.).
Wilson Papers: Woodrow Wilson Papers, Manuscript Division, Library of Congress, Washington, D.C.

Introduction

1. A. Gramsci, *Wilson e I massimalisti russi, Il Grido del Popolo*, 2 March 1918, republished in A. Gramsci, *Scritti giovanili 1914–1918* (Turin, 1958), p. 185.
2. A. Iriye, *The Globalizing of America, 1913–1945*, vol. 3, *The Cambridge History of American Foreign Relations* (New York, 1993), pp. 107–8.

1. Reciprocal Images before the Great War

1. "The tradition of travels in Italy is perhaps the only one that is common to all schools," wrote the French painter and author Eugène Fromentin in the mid-nineteenth century, as quoted in Van Wyck Brooks, *The Dream of Arcadia: American Writers and Artists in Italy, 1760–1915* (New York, 1958), p. ix. For the themes explored in this section, see also B. MacDonald, *Henry James's Italian Hours: Revelatory and Resistant Impressions* (Ann Arbor, Mich., 1990), and K. Churchill, *Italy and English Literature, 1764–1930* (London, 1980).
2. Eighteenth-century travelers were attracted especially by the ruins and relics of the classical world, while the pilgrims of the nineteenth century added a greater

sensitivity to the natural and human landscape. Romantic artists and poets enlivened the travel experience with more dramatic tones: their contact with Italy was joyful and rewarding, but also fundamentally tragic and, in some cases, destructive. With every step, they sensed the unsettling disproportion between the immense power of man's imagination and creativity and his pathetic existential condition. The constant presence of the ruins of other civilizations and the remains of generations that had gone before only underscored the fleeting nature of human life.

3. Byron, *Childe Harold's Pilgrimage*, canto IV, 78, mentioned in Churchill, *Italy and English*, pp. 38 and 89. Browning's famous phrase "Open my heart and you will see / Graved inside of it, 'Italy,' " originally attributed by the poet to a character in the *De Gustibus*, is usually thought to be Browning's own. That is how it is taken in the inscription on a commemorative plaque on the Palazzo Rezzonico in Venice, where the poet died in 1889, after a lengthy stay in Italy. For Byron, the contrast between the grandeur of the past that emanated from the archeological ruins of Rome or the decaying façades of Venice with the poverty of Italy in his time, on the one hand encouraged the determination of the Risorgimento movement, but on the other hand basically posed the insoluble conundrum of the vanity of human life. For Madame de Staël, the necessity of the Italian experience accompanied her awareness of the impossibility of reconciling the cultural codes of northern and southern Europe. Contact between the two cultures, though initially exciting and productive, could ultimately prove destructive to each. The attitudes of these last two artists served as the foundations for two schools of thought underlying travel literature in the nineteenth century and the early twentieth century. Their works were highly influential on travelers in the Victorian Age. Byron's poetry and madam de Staël's novel *Corinne ou de l'Italie* laid the foundation for and accompanied the experiences of many foreign travelers. De Staël's popular novel, ahead of its time, was actually more of a travel guide than a novel, considering the amount of space it devoted to descriptions of places in Italy worth visiting.

4. "And the mid-nineteenth century . . . saw an unprecedented American fascination with Italy"; see MacDonald, *Henry James*, p. 13.

5. E. Amfitheatrof, *The Enchanted Ground: Americans in Italy, 1760–1980* (Boston, 1980), p. 104.

6. E. Wharton, *Italian Backgrounds* (New York, 1907), p. 179, and H. James, *Italian Hours* (New York, 1909), p. 190.

7. N. Wright, *American Novelists in Italy—The Discoverers: Allston to James* (Philadelphia, 1965), pp. 20–21. A fairly complete list of these writers appears on pp. 20–29.

8. "No other foreign country has figured so provocatively in American fiction"; see Wright, *American Novelists*, p. 29.

9. Quoted in ibid., p. 117.

10. Quoted in Amfitheatrof, *The Enchanted Ground*, p. 4.

11. Wright, *American Novelists*, pp. 124 and 136.

12. Quoted in ibid., pp. 140 and 141.

13. Quoted in Churchill, *Italy and English*, p. 149.

14. Quoted in Brooks, *The Dream of Arcadia*, p. 166.

15. Quoted in Wright, *American Novelists*, pp. 205–6. Let us mention a few other significant quotes here: George Ticknor in 1817: "Rome is worth all the other cities in the world"; Nathaniel Parker Willis: "You can exist elsewhere, but, oh! you *live* in Italy"; Ephraim Peabody of Boston: "Till a man has seen Italy and breathed it . . . he cannot be said to have lived"; Margaret Fuller: "Those have not lived who have not seen Rome"; see P. R. Baker, *The Fortunate Pilgrims: Americans in Italy, 1800–1860* (Cambridge, Mass., 1964), pp. 198–99, chapter 9.

16. Amfitheatrof, *The Enchanted Ground*, pp. 3–4.

17. J. P. Diggins, *Mussolini and Fascism: The View from America* (Princeton, N.J., 1972), pp. 5 and 11.

18. U. Ojetti, *L'America vittoriosa* (Milan, 1899), pp. 17 and 203.

19. Quoted in MacDonald, *Henry James*, p. 12. For James, Italy was a poetic world, an interior reality more than a real place. He belonged to a cosmopolitan New York family that moved to the Boston area, taking a house on the edge of the Harvard campus, where his brother, the pragmatist philosopher William James, taught for the rest of his life. At the end of the 1850s, his parents had gone to Italy on a typical "cultivated" journey. In the parlors of his home in Cambridge, adorned with views of Florence and the Tuscan countryside (as well as a bust of a Bacchante created by an American sculptor in Rome), members of Boston's intellectual aristocracy gathered. The young Henry James, in particular, had close ties with the influential Italianists of Harvard: Norton, Lowell, and Longfellow. In one of his earliest writings, in the *North American Review*, James analyzed the elements of Italy's charm for foreign writers and travelers: "We go to Italy . . . to gaze on the highest achievements of human power. . . . So wide is the interval between the great Italian monuments and the works of the colder genius of neighboring nations, that we find ourselves willing to look upon the former as the ideal and perfection of human effort, and to invest the country of their birth with a sort of half-sacred character" (quoted in MacDonald, *Henry James*, p. 34). With these beginnings, we should hardly be surprised at the sense of exaltation that took hold of James when he first saw Rome. As soon as he stepped out of the train, indifferent to his hunger and fatigue, he fell under the city's spell and wandered for hours, from one end of the city to the other, from St. John Lateran to St. Peter's, "in a fever of enjoyment": "at last—for the first time—I live!" he wrote to his brother. "For the first time I know what the picturesque is" (quoted in Brooks, *The Dream of Arcadia*, p. 157). Thus, we can at-

tribute to James himself the words and the feelings that he describes in the characters of one of his first short stories, which sprang from his experiences in Italy: an American came to Italy to find a place where nature has been "refined and transmuted into art" and where the landscape can be shaped according to the heart's content—a land where form, color, and beauty not only are evident, but also dominate over the crude natural elements. "To understand what I mean," he explains to his partner in conversation, referring to America, "you have to have lived in a land beyond the seas, barren of romance and grace." Italy "is the home of history, of beauty, of the arts—of all that makes life splendid and sweet. Italy for us dull strangers is a magic word. . . . [We see in Italy] . . . the primordial substance . . . of our consoling dreams and our richest fancies. I have been brought up in these thoughts." See *At Isella,* quoted in MacDonald, *Henry James,* pp. 66–67, and Wright, *American Novelists,* pp. 198–99; see also C. Giorcelli, *Henry James e l'Italia* (Rome, 1968).

The familiarity and the importance of the "land of romance" (Wharton, *Italian Backgrounds,* p. 23) in the life and work of Edith Wharton were, if anything, greater. Wharton lived in Italy for a number of years as a young girl, spoke fluent Italian, and went back to Italy throughout her life, exploring with taste and expertise the most famous cities and towns, but also the lesser-known Italy, which she then described in the alluring articles she published in such American periodicals as *The Century* or *Scribner's Magazine.* For her, too, the Italian experience played an important role as an artistic midwife: her first books, such as *Italian Villas and Their Gardens* and *The Valley of Decision,* grew out of time she spent in Italy. Italy served as a background for entire novels or significant sections of them. She had a profound knowledge of Italian art and history, and indeed she set one novel in eighteenth-century Italy, wrote books and articles about Italian villas and monuments, argued against the common aversion to the Baroque in popular taste, and discussed knowledgeably the attribution of a group of Della Robbia terra-cottas.

20. Wharton, *Italian Backgrounds,* p. 147.
21. Churchill, *Italy and English,* p. 155. W. D. Howells, *Tuscan Cities* (London, 1886), p. 96. Howells was the American consul to Venice from 1861 to 1865. During this stay and from his trips throughout the peninsula there emerged a stream of acclaimed articles and books, such as *Venetian Life* (1866) and *Italian Journeys* (1867), in which he described Italian life brilliantly and with an observant eye. He loved Italy for the theatrical, picturesque, and universal nature of its people. His sentiments toward Italy were echoed by the American reading public, and his books became very popular, selling in various editions over the ensuing fifty years and making him an authoritative voice on Italy.
22. Quoted in Wright, *American Novelists,* p. 139.

23. In Venice, he concluded, "The charm of the place sweetens your temper, but corrupts you" (ibid., p. 170).

24. Even though, we should point out, many of these visitors cultivated friendships with members of the Italian upper classes.

25. See, for instance, James, *Italian Hours,* pp. 110, 125, 172.

26. Thus concluded the American author of a guidebook on Rome, dated 1845: "Each day, which an American passes in Rome, adds a year to his intellectual life. . . . He finds the flood of new ideas so copious and rushing as to be actually oppressive. His mind is stimulated and heated almost to the excitement of fever. Even in the churches, he cannot find relaxation, for the striking ceremonies of the ritual are inconceivably powerful in impressing the soul through the eye and the ear. If he enters even when the altars are deserted by their officiating ministers, his eye will be caught and his admiration aroused by some master-piece of painting. . . . 'With slow, reluctant, amorous delay,' he [the American] leaves this paradise of taste; and although he has learned to prize more highly than ever the political and religious privileges of his own free land, still, when he calls to mind the proud Memories which have been inherited by the Romans—the bounties lavished by nature upon their lovely country—the genius and beauty which seem their birthright—what they have been and what they may again be, and, beyond all doubt, eventually will be—he is tempted to exclaim, in imitation of Alexander to Diogenes, 'If I were not an American, I would be a Roman.'" From W. M. Gillespie, *Rome as Seen by a New Yorker in 1843–4* (New York, 1845), pp. 204–5.

27. T. A. Bailey, *The Man in the Street: The Impact of American Public Opinion on Foreign Policy* (New York, 1948), p. 49, and Giorcelli, *Henry James,* p. 9.

28. W. D. Howells, *Impressions and Experiences* (New York, 1896), p. 279.

29. A. DeConde, *Half Bitter, Half Sweet: An Excursion into Italian-American History* (New York, 1971), p. 77. The statistics are from U.S. Bureau of the Census, *Historical Statistics of the United States: Colonial Times to 1970,* part I, p. 105.

30. L. Villari, *L'economia della crisi* (Turin, 1980), p. 4.

31. O. Handlin, *The Uprooted* (New York, 1951). For Italian immigration see also A. M. Martellone, *Una Little Italy nell'Atene d'America: La comunità italiana di Boston dal 1800 al 1920* (Naples, 1973), and D. Cinel, *From Italy to San Francisco: The Immigrant Experience* (Stanford, Calif., 1982).

32. D. W. Noble, *The Progressive Mind 1890–1917* (Minneapolis, 1981), pp. 182–86.

33. E. Foner, *The Story of American Freedom* (New York, 1998), p. 187.

34. The Italians, in particular, were "negroids," brownish, colored, or "swarthy." The dark color of their skin pointed to their defects (passionate natures, lack of respect for authority, and tendency toward criminality). So this was the place to assign them in society, as well as the place to assign Italy in the larger international community. Their substantial inability to assimilate into American soci-

ety would create problems for the wasps (white, Anglo-Saxon, Protestants), just as the Negroes had done. In a number of white schools in Louisiana, Italians were not allowed to enroll. In the north, anti-Italian prejudice was more subtle but quite similar. In 1912, for instance, Prescott Hall, son of a Boston business-man and an apostle of restrictions on immigration, claimed in the *North American Review* that southern Italians belonged to a Negroid race and were therefore undesirable; see M. H. Hunt, *Ideology and U.S. Foreign Policy* (New Haven, Conn., 1987), pp. 46ff.

35. DeConde, *Half Bitter,* p. 121.
36. W. Wilson, *A History of the American People* (New York, 1902), vol. 5, pp. 212–13.
37. "In common with Jews, Poles, Mexicans, and others, Italians were pilloried with insulting nicknames—such as wop, Dago, and guinea—abused in public, iso-lated socially, cheated of their wages, pelted in the streets, cuffed at work, fined and jailed on the smallest pretenses, lynched by nativist mobs, and crowded into slums and reeking tenements" (DeConde, *Half Bitter*), pp. 101–2, 119.
38. De Conde, *Half Bitter,* p. 102.
39. S. J. Diner, *A Very Different Age: Americans of the Progressive Era* (New York, 1998), p. 13.
40. R. Hofstadter, *The Age of Reform: From Bryan to F.D.R.* (New York, 1955), pp. 9–11 and 181–85.
41. H. Stuart Hughes, *The United States and Italy* (Cambridge, Mass., 1965) (1st ed., 1953), p. 3.
42. Margaret Fuller, a well-known writer and social reformist from the circle of the Trascendentalists led by Emerson, went to Europe in 1846, where she met Car-lyle, Wordsworth, and Mazzini. The following year she moved to Rome, mar-ried the Italian patriot Marchese Angelo Ossoli, and participated with him in the battles of the Roman Republic. The history of the Roman Republic that she wrote in 1849–1850 was lost, along with the lives of the author and her family, when her ship sank on the homeward journey.
43. James, *Italian Hours,* p. 192.
44. Amfitheatrof, *The Enchanted Ground,* p. 39.
45. W. R. Thayer, *The Life and Times of Cavour,* 2 vols. (Boston, 1911), preceded by the less important *The Dawn of Italian Independence,* 2 vols. (Boston, 1892), cited in A. W. Salomone, "The Nineteenth Century Discovery of Italy: An Essay in American Cultural History. Prolegomena to a Historiographical Problem," *The American Historical Review* 83, no. 5 (June 1968): 1359–91.
46. Salomone, "The Nineteenth Century Discovery of Italy," p. 1361.
47. Ibid., pp. 1377–78.
48. Letter from Page to House, 27 November 1917, *House Papers,* Yale [my italics].
49. G. Spini, G. G. Migone, and M. Teodori, *Italia e America dalla Grande Guerra a oggi* (Venice, 1976), p. 13.

50. In the lines that follow, Richardson, born in Mississippi, recalled that the Italians imagined that he had grown up in constant danger of being eaten by crocodiles; see N. Richardson, *My Diplomatic Education* (New York, 1923), pp. 118–21.

51. F. Colgate Speranza (ed.), *The Diary of Gino Speranza: Italy, 1915–19* (New York, 1941), vol. 2, p. 126.

52. Concerning the period 1914–1917, Ernest May wrote: "For the belligerents, . . . the American problem [was] one of unusual difficulty, delicacy, and danger. Never before had they faced a neutral so invulnerable, so awesomely powerful in potential, and so self-consciously detached from European politics. . . . No one could say for certain how much of her apparent power was real. It was arguable that her remoteness, pacifist traditions, and mixed races and nationalities condemned her to impotence. If so, a belligerent could disregard her interests. Although no sane diplomat could be cocksure of such a judgment, neither could he guarantee that America's strength should be taken at face value. The extreme alternatives were to assume that the United States could be decisive in the war or that she could have no effect upon it. Policy-makers in London and Berlin had to select some premise between these two poles." See E. R. May, *The World War and American Isolation, 1914–1917* (Cambridge, Mass. 1959), pp. 3–4.

53. On 5 January 1917, *La Tribuna* published an article headlined "The Two Americas," which commented on Wilson's recent note to the belligerent nations. The note, according to the article, was "proof of the immeasurable spiritual distance which separates his particular mentality from the European mentality, and the impossibility of the comprehension of one by the other. A Chinese from seven centuries earlier would have judged more accurately the European situation than Wilson did. The South American republics, though infinitely less advanced, are less Chinese than President Wilson." A translation of the article into English was enclosed with Page's letter to Lansing dated 6 January 1917, Doc. no. 763.72/3163, Department of State, Records of the Department of State Relating to World War I and Its Termination, 1914–1929, Record Group 59, M 367, National Archives, Washington, D.C. See also *La Tribuna*, 24 and 25 December 1916; and *Il Corriere della Sera*, 24 December 1916.

54. The war ended with the defeat of Spain and the U.S. acquisition of the former Spanish colonies of the Philippines and Puerto Rico, as well as a "protectorate" over Cuba. With this "Splendid Little War," as the American nationalist circles described it, the nineteenth-century isolation of the United States, till then focused on internal expansion, came to an end. Since then, the United States has been increasingly active on the international stage, with some interludes of quiescence.

55. The Spanish-American War lasted from February to August 1898. It was therefore simultaneous with the popular revolt that swept through Italy beginning

that spring and culminating in the insurrection in Milan in May 1898, ferociously put down by the Italian army, which fired upon the demonstrators.

56. Introduction by T. Bonazzi and R. Ruffilli to G. Spini et al., *Italia e America dal Settecento all'età dell'imperialismo* (Venice, 1976), p. 311.

57. "La repubblica decadente," *La Tribuna,* 29 December 1897, quoted in A. Olivieri, "L'immagine degli Stati Uniti nella stampa liberale a Roma e Napoli," in Spini et al., *Italia e America,* pp. 364–65.

58. "La Casa Bianca," *Il Corriere di Napoli,* 8–9 November 1888; Spini et al., *Italia e America,* pp. 353–54.

59. Concerning the attitudes of Italian Catholics toward the United States, see D. Rossini, "The American Peril': Italian Catholics and the Spanish-American War, 1898," in S. Ickringill and S. Hilton (eds.), *European Perceptions of the Spanish-American War of 1898* (Beron, Peter Lang AG, 1999).

60. *Longiqua oceani,* 6 January 1895, and *Testem Benevolentiae,* 22 January 1899.

61. "I pericoli dell'americanismo," *La Civiltà Cattolica,* no. 1184, 21 October 1899; see also "Leone XIII e l'americanismo," ibid., no. 1170, 18 March 1899, and "L'americanismo difeso da due detrattori della Santa Sede," ibid., no. 1176, 17 June 1899.

62. Ibid., no. 1149, 7 May 1898, pp. 366–69; no. 1151, 4 June 1898, pp. 622–23. See also ibid., no. 1154, 16 July 1898, pp. 236–39, and no. 1126, 15 May 1897, p. 508.

63. See *L'Osservatore Romano,* 11–12 February 1898; 21–22 March 1898; 2–3 April 1898; 24–25 August 1898; and 16–17 November 1898.

64. *L'Osservatore Romano,* 25–26 April 1898; 5–6 July 1898; 29–30 November 1898; and 14–15 December 1898.

65. "L'espansione economica degli Stati Uniti all'estero," *Il Divenire Sociale,* 31 December 1909, p. 301, quoted in A. Testi, "L'immagine degli Stati Uniti nella stampa socialista italiana (1886–1914)," in Spini et al., *Italia e America,* p. 340.

66. Theodore Roosevelt's autobiography, *The Strenuous Life* (translated into Italian in 1904 with the title *Vigor di vita*), met with an enthusiastic reception from the Italian nationalists and later from the Futurists. After the presidential elections that year, the nationalists hailed Roosevelt's victory with great favor, "a magnificent specimen of triumphant Americanism." See *Il Regno,* I, 51 (13 November 1904), quoted in Spini et al., *Italia e America,* p. 430.

67. L. D. Ventura, *I negri d'America, Cuore e critica,* 20 February 1889, p. 27, quoted in Spini et al., *Italia e America,* p. 320.

68. *Secondo dialogo politico tra Matio Zocaro e Felipo Austriacante con altre composizioni scherzevoli di don Pietro Zenari* (Verona, 1867), p. 3, quoted in E. Franzina, *La grande emigrazione: L'esodo dei rurali dal Veneto durante il secolo XIX* (Venice, 1976), p. 193. "Love of country is a sentiment entirely alien to our rural peasants," as the Inchiesta Agraria (Agrarian Inquest) noted around 1882; "most of them still yearn for Austrian rule, under which they paid less . . . the

only thing that interests them and that they greeted with joy was the abolition of the duty on grinding corn" (ibid., p. 193).

69. *Governo e pellagra, La riscossa,* 24 December 1872, quoted in Franzina, *La grande emigrazione,* p. 191.

70. P. Brunello, "Agenti di emigrazione, contadini e immagini dell'America nella provincia di Venezia," *Rivista di Storia Contemporanea* 11, no. 1 (January 1982): 98.

71. *Il Giornale di Udine,* 3 September 1878, quoted in Brunello, *Agenti di emigrazione,* p. 117.

72. "The order of the day is 'emigration to America'! and the frenzy has boiled up to such a point that neither written arguments nor clear evidence is enough to keep so many people from hurling themselves, open-armed, into almost-certain ruin." See "Le pazzie ragionanti (note d'America)," *El Visentin—Giornale del popolo,* 19 April 1877, quoted in Franzina, *La grande emigrazione,* pp. 148–49.

73. Franzina, *La grande emigrazione,* p. 206.

74. *Canti sociali e politici del Cilento* (Casalvelino Scalo, 1975), quoted in R. U. Pane, "L'esperienza degli emigrati calabresi negli Stati Uniti," in P. Borzomati (ed.), *L'emigrazione calabrese dall'unità ad oggi: Atti del II Convegno di Studio della Deputazione di Storia Patria per la Calabria* (Rome, 1982), p. 274.

75. *Notizie dell'America,* a printed sheet sold in the markets of the province of Venice in the late 1870s, quoted in Brunello, *Agenti di emigrazione,* pp. 104, 114, and 121–22.

76. Franzina, *La grande emigrazione,* p. 222, note 66.

77. "Here . . . there appeared, after being . . . 'suggested,' . . . all the characteristics of the mitemic confabulation and the interferences of the traditional popular culture, . . . which contributed to the creation of a particular image of the 'new world,' an image that was relative[ly] easy to circulate, given its specific derivation, among the country folk." See E. Franzina, *L'immaginario degli emigranti: Miti e raffigurazioni dell'esperienza italiana all'estero fra i due secoli* (Treviso, 1992), p. 69.

78. From J. Pagano, *Golden Wedding* (New York, 1943), p. 4, quoted in Franzina, *L'immaginario degli emigranti,* pp. 131–132 (my italics).

79. L. T. Mowrer, *Journalist's Wife* (New York, 1937), p. 49.

80. K. Hvidt, *Flight to America: The Social Background of 300,000 Danish Emigrants* (New York, 1975), pp. 183–94, quoted in Franzina, *L'immaginario degli emigranti,* p. 117.

81. From A. Mosso, *Vita moderna degli italiani,* p. 99, quoted in Franzina, *L'immaginario degli emigranti,* p. 154 (my italics). The literacy test was one of the first obstacles imposed to limit the entry of immigrants into the United States.

82. See Spini et al., *Italia e America,* pp. 300–310 and 314.

83. F. Engels, "Il movimento operaio in America," *Rivista italiana del socialismo* (June–July 1887), quoted in the essay by A. Testi in Spini et al., *Italia e America*, p. 313.

84. Ibid., pp. 314–20.

85. A. Kuliscioff and F. Turati, *Carteggio* (correspondence), vol. 4, 1915–1918, tome 1 (Turin, 1977), p. 426.

86. Speech by F. Turati to the Italian Chamber of Deputies on 21 November 1918, in L. Ambrosoli, *Né aderire né sabotare 1915–1918* (Milan, 1961), p. 285.

87. P. Melograni, *Storia politica della Grande Guerra 1915–1918* (Bari, 1969), p. 537.

2. Two Parallel Wars

1. France lost 20 percent of its military-age men, and the British lost an entire generation, half a million men under the age of 30. On both sides, in the single battle of Verdun, one million soldiers were lost; see E. Hobsbawm, *The Age of Extremes: A History of the World, 1914–1991* (New York, 1994), pp. 25–26. In Italy the dead in battle were some 600,000, and roughly half a million were disabled; see E. Ragionieri, "La storia politica e sociale," in *Storia d'Italia: Dall'Unità ad oggi,* vol. 4, tome 3 (Turin, 1976), p. 2058.

2. F. Fischer, *Assalto al potere mondiale: La Germania nella guerra 1914–1918* (Turin, 1965), especially pp. 5–50. Originally published as *Fritz Fischer, Griff nach der Weltmacht; die Kriegszielpolitik des kaiserlichen Deutschland 1914/18* (Dusseldorf, 1961).

3. P. Kennedy, *The Rise and Fall of the Great Powers* (London, 1989), pp. 321–30. Equally important in the process that led to war were domestic factors: all the countries of Europe were undergoing social and political crisis; see J. Joll, *Le origini della prima guerra mondiale* (Rome, 1999), pp. 133–78. Originally published as James Joll, *The Origins of the First World War* (London, 1984).

4. Kennedy, *The Rise and Fall,* p. 328.

5. B. W. Tuchman, *The Guns of August* (Milan, 1998) (1st English ed., 1962), pp. 147 and 34.

6. R. Vivarelli, *Il dopoguerra in Italia e l'avvento del fascismo* (1918–1922), vol. 1, *Dalla fine della guerra all'impresa di Fiume* (Naples, 1967), pp. 101ff.

7. For the period of American neutrality, consult E. R. May, *World War I and American Isolation, 1914–1917* (Cambridge, Mass., 1959); A. S. Link, *Wilson the Diplomatist: A Look at His Major Foreign Policies* (New York, 1974), pp. 31–90; A. S. Link, *Woodrow Wilson and the Progressive Era, 1910–1917* (New York, 1963), pp. 145–282; N. I. Painter, *Standing at Armageddon: The United States, 1877–1919* (New York, 1987), pp. 292–323. See also F. Romero, *L'impero americano: Gli USA potenza mondiale* (Florence, 1996), pp. 28–32.

8. Concerning the differences between Italian imperialism and "the forms of imperialism, properly speaking," Angelo Crespi wrote at length in the pages of *Critica Sociale:* "They develop out of a genuine surplus of capital . . . in the homeland . . . , whereas Italian imperialism, while differing from those forms not in nature, but only in degree, has no capital from which to spring, but instead steals that capital from the more urgent needs of national life . . . ; it is theft committed by a few groups to the detriment of the collective; it is not a natural development, but deranged parroting." See A. Crespi, "Politica imperialistica e investimenti capitalistici, Critica Sociale, 1914," pp. 73–75, in L. Villari, *Il capitalismo italiano del Novecento* (Bari, 1972), p. 85.

9. In chronological order of signature, aside from the Treaty of London, the following agreements were established among the Allies: (1) The Constantinople Agreement, March 1915, between Russia, France, Great Britain, and later Italy, which gave Constantinople and European Turkey to Russia in exchange for recognition of the French and British spheres of influence in Asiatic Turkey; (2) the bilateral accord between Great Britain and the Sherif of Mecca, 24 October 1915, which ratified Arab support for the Allied cause in exchange for English recognition of the independence of Arab territory; (3) the Sazarov-Paleologue treaty of 26 April 1916 between Russia and France, which promised Russia an area of northern Turkey between Persia and the Black Sea, while ceding to France the territory southwest of the newly Russian-controlled area; (4) the Sykes-Picot Agreement of 9 May 1916 between Great Britain and France, by the terms of which Great Britain would receive Mesopotamia and two Mediterranean ports while France would gain Syria and western Kurdistan. The area between the French and British possessions would be left to the Arabs, and Palestine was to be broken off from the Turkish Empire; (5) the Treaty of Bucharest, 17 August 1916, which included the conditions for Romania's entry into war on the side of the Triple Entente. In exchange for Romania's aid, the Allies promsed parts of the Austro-Hungarian Empire; (6) the Russian-Japanese treaty, 3 July 1916, which included a secret attachment in which the two powers agreed to support one another militarily in order to prevent political domination of China by a third power hostile to the two signatory nations; (7) the Anglo-Japanese accord of February 1917, which, in its final form, provided that the German islands in the Pacific Ocean south of the equator were to be given to Great Britain, while those to the north of the equator, plus the Shantung Peninsula in China, would be assigned to Japan. France, Russia, and Italy subsequently signed this agreement; (8) the Franco-Russian bilateral accord of February–March 1917, in which France and Great Britain were given complete freedom to establish the western frontiers of Germany in exchange for equal freedom for Russia to establish its boundaries with Germany and Austria. Subsequently, it was added that France would regain

Alsace-Lorraine as well as the Saar mining district. The two countries also agreed to create an autonomous and neutral buffer zone along the Rhine, temporarily occupied by French troops, and to exclude the question of Poland from the peace negotiations; (9) the Treaty of San Giovanni di Moriana, 19–21 April 1917, in which Italy was promised part of Anatolia along with the same rights in the Middle East established for France and Great Britain in the 'cot Agreement.

10. M. Toscano, *Il Patto di Londra: Storia Diplomatica dell'intervento italiano (1914–1915)* (Bologna, 1934), p. 164.

11. J. A. Thayer, *Italy and the Great War: Politics and Culture, 1870–1915* (Madison, Wis. 1964), p. ix.

12. The trenches extended over a total linear distance of about 25,000 miles. In theory, it would have been possible to walk from Belgium to Switzerland entirely underground; see P. Fussell, *The Great War and Modern Memory* (London, 1977), p. 37.

13. The best description of life at the Italian front is in E. Lussu's novel, *Un anno sull'altopiano* (Turin, 1966). The best-known description of the war on the western front was in E. M. Remarque's novel *All Quiet on the Western Front* (1st Italian ed., 1931).

14. Kennedy, *The Rise and Fall*, pp. 313–14.

15. W. LaFeber, "The American Search for Opportunity, 1965–1913," in *The Cambridge History of American Foreign Relations*, vol. 2 (Cambridge, 1993), pp. 21–44.

16. R. A. Webster, *L'imperialismo industriale italiano: Studio sul pre-fascismo 1908–1915* (Turin, 1974), pp. 4–11 and 101–15, originally published as Richard A. Webster, *Industrial Imperialism in Italy, 1908–1915* (Berkeley, Calif., 1975); A. Gerschenkron, *Il problema storico dell'arretratezza economica* (Turin, 1965), pp. 71–113, originally published as Alexander Gerschenkron, *Economic Backwardness in Historical Perspective* (Cambridge, Mass., 1962); and R. Romeo, "La rivoluzione industriale dell'età giolittiana," in *La formazione dell'Italia industriale,* edited by A. Caracciolo (Bari, 1971), pp. 115–33.

17. U.S. Bureau of the Census, *Historical Statistics of the United States: Colonial Times to 1970*, Part I, p. 225.

18. Kennedy, *The Rise and Fall*, p. 205.

19. Ibid., pp. 314, 256, and 258; A. Iriye, *The Globalizing of America, 1913–45*, vol. 3 of the *Cambridge History of American Foreign Relations* (Cambridge, 1995), p. 112; E. Foner, *The Story of American Freedom* (New York, 1998), p. 147; S. J. Diner, *A Very Different Age: Americans of the Progressive Era* (New York, 1998), pp. 3–4, and P. Melograni, *Storia politica della Grande Guerra 1915–1918* (Bari, 1969), p. 451.

20. Kennedy, *The Rise and Fall*, pp. 314 and 270.

21. G. B. Nash, J. Roy Jeffrey, et al., *The American People: Creating a Nation and a Society,* vol. 2, from 1865 (New York, 1994), p. 768.

22. Ibid., p. 617.

23. D. Pick, *War Machine: The Rationalization of Slaughter in the Modern Age* (New Haven, Conn., 1993), p. 178.

24. Melograni, *Storia politica,* pp. 292–310 and 287; Forcella and Monticone speak of approximately 3,000 death sentences, of which 729 were carried out, and 114 summary executions (without trial), which included several decimations. In total, judicial authorities received official reports of some 400,000 crimes committed under arms; see E. Forcella and A. Monticone, *Plotone di esecuzione* (Bari, 1968), pp. 442–45 and xvi–xvii.

25. Melograni, *Storia politica,* pp. 337 and 386. See also G. Procacci, "Condizioni dello spirito pubblico nel Regno," in P. Giovannini. (ed.), *Di fronte alla Grande Guerra: Militari e civili tra coercizione e rivolta* (Ancona, 1997), and A. Bravo, *Donne e uomini nelle guerre mondiali* (Rome, 1991).

26. Pope Benedict XV, with his *Note to the Heads of the Warring Nations,* a seven-point papal peace proposal, was the first leader to scorn traditional diplomatic paths in favor of a direct appeal to the peoples of the world.

27. Melograni, *Storia politica,* pp. 329–31.

28. E. A. Powell, *Italy at War* (New York, 1918), p. 6. Alexander Powell was a journalist for the *New York World,* the most widely read American newspaper in that period.

29. O. Malagodi, *Conversazioni della guerra 1914–1919,* edited by B. Vigezzi (Milan, 1960), vol. 2, p. 394.

30. Concerning the contradictions between the theory and the political reality of the Italian war, see Vivarelli, *Il dopoguerra in Italia,* pp. 1–114.

31. As early as 30 April 1917, Colonel House, Wilson's chief adviser, noted in his diary: "I can see more and more clearly the danger of friction between the Allies. Distrust lies close to the surface, and a little difference between them would bring it from under cover. This danger is not being well guarded. The Japanese, Russians, and Italians are being left out of English, French, and American calculations." Quoted in C. Seymour (ed.), *The Intimate Papers of Colonel House* (Boston, 1926–1928), vol. 3, p. 54.

32. "I recall," Secretary Lansing afterwards wrote, for example, "that . . . his attitude toward evidence of German atrocities in Belgium and toward accounts of the horrors of submarine warfare . . . [was that] he would not read of them and showed anger if the details were called to his attention." From *The Diary of Robert Lansing,* 20 November 1921, Lansing Papers, Library of Congress, Washington, D.C., quoted in Link, *Wilson the Diplomatist,* p. 35.

33. "[T]his war, unlike earlier wars, which were typically waged for limited and specifiable objects, was waged for unlimited ends. . . . the only war aim that counted was total victory." See Hobsbawm, *The Age of Extremes,* pp. 29–30.

34. P. Pieri, *Prima guerra mondiale 1914–1918: Problemi di storia militare* (Udine, 1998) (1st ed., 1947). Candeloro, too, focuses on the military causes of the defeat of Caporetto, in G. Candeloro, *Storia dell'Italia moderna*, vol. 8 (Milan, 1987), pp. 182ff.

35. "From the very first reports that filtered into Italy, despite the manipulations and half-truths of the bourgeois press, the popular masses spontaneously interpreted events in Russia as concrete manifestations of their own aspirations to peace and a genuinely democratic and just government, which might take into account the demands and desires of the humble and downtrodden. The determination to 'fare come in Russia' ('do as in Russia')—an expression that began to circulate widely as early as March—while it signified an awareness that the time of utopia was over, nonetheless charged the Russian revolution with all the contents that had built up in Italian 'subversivism,' and to a greater degree in that the specific connotations were minimal and vague." See Ragionieri, *La storia politica e sociale*, p. 2031.

36. De Felice shares this view: see R. De Felice, *Mussolini il Rivoluzionario 1883–1920* (Turin, 1975), p. 365, and L. Valiani, *Il Partito Socialista Italiano dal 1900 al 1918, Rivista Storica Italiana*, XXV, fasc. 2, 1963, p. 322.

37. "While France commenced the war with a *union sacrée* government, Italy finally found a rough equivalent by the autumn of 1917" with the Orlando government. See C. S. Maier, *Recasting Bourgeois Europe: Stabilization in France, Germany, and Italy in the Decade after World War I* (Princeton, N.J., 1975), p. 110.

38. "The year 1918 marked the second appeal for a general mobilization of intellectuals in the context of the national effort for resistance and recovery. The aftermath of Caporetto reopens the period of the 'maggio radioso': but not under the sign of . . . division and opposition . . . , but rather, under the sign of the greatest unification and cohesion of civil society wholly subsumed into the state. . . . In the army under Cadorna and Father Gemelli . . . there is no room for gratification for the professionals of intelligence and conscience. . . . Their time came later, in the last part of the war, when it became useful, and at this point it became contextually acceptable to one and all, to nourish the troops ideologically . . . And at that juncture artists, lawyers, teachers, journalists, poets, actors, shapers of public opinion and experts in the field of the mass media spread out through the improvised editorial offices [of the trench newspapers] in Mogliano and Piovene, Cittadella and Bassano, in the movable theaters, the Case del Soldato ('soldiers' homes'), the censorships offices, and the propaganda offices of each regiment . . . practically stunned by the mass consciousness [of the first two years of war] the intellectual returned to flourishing life when their patriotic passions were able to expand and find an appropriate context to its role in the cultural organization of the war: that is to say, when the

military condition itself reiterated the role and the specific prerogatives of the intellectual. . . . This would be the second ideological war campaign, after Caporetto, and it would restore their privileges in terms of role and their usual functions while multiplying the sense of their social utility: work done, not in a classroom or behind a lectern, but in the dynamic center of a struggle that involved millions of men, a struggle for life or death, where the paragon of the word was practice and the recipient extended to include, in an illusory manner, a sort of universal audience: it was here that they would exercise their mission, from then on, their social duty." See M. Isenghi, *I Giornali di trincea (1915–1918)* (Turin, 1977), pp. 6–8 and 98. Outside of the army, though, the government encouraged the formation of private associations and new national agencies for relief and propaganda, so as to engender the emergence of a new ruling class alongside the local prominent citizenry: "the lists of the Commissioners of the Opere Federate," Fava notes, for instance, "do feature the names of landowners, notaries, and parish priests, but they are especially crowded with schoolteachers, lawyers, professors, town secretaries, and provincial journalists; and the same phenomenon can be observed with the swelling of their numbers, especially in smaller towns, in the relief committees. In a profoundly altered social context, sheltered, that is, from the competition of a free expression of the demands of the masses, the activation of the petite bourgeoisie and the middle classes moved to seek out a direct relationship with the populace, and gave origin, on the concrete terrain of civil mobilization, to the myths and the watchwords that hailed in the war the great occasion to text national solidarity." See A. Fava, *Assistenza e propaganda nel regime di guerra (1915–1918)*, in M. Isenghi (ed.), *Operai e contadini nella Grande Guerra* (Bologna 1982), p. 192.

39. Concerning this development in the major European countries, except for Italy, see A. J. Mayer, *Political Origins of the New Diplomacy, 1917–18* (New Haven, Conn., 1959).

40. Both of these aspects of Italian-American relations during the war will be analyzed in the chapters that follow.

41. As Ambassador Page pointed out as early as spring 1918: "The United States was . . . greatly respected and appreciated. At first this appreciation was only of America's power, but later the spirit in which the United States entered the war came to be generally recognized, and this had an effect on the Italian spirit itself." See [T. Hinckley], "Quarterly Report no. 2: Italy, April 1, 1918–June 30, 1918," enclosed with Page's letter to Lansing on 30 July 1918, Doc. no. 865.00/70, Department of State, Internal Affairs of Italy, 1910–1929.

42. Ragionieri, *La storia politica e sociale*, p. 2047.

43. Phrase by Guglielmo Ferrero, quoted in Vivarelli, *Il dopoguerra in Italia*, p. 14.

3. Woodrow Wilson, World Leader

1. S. J. Diner, *A Very Different Age: Americans of the Progressive Era* (New York, 1998), p. 29.
2. Arthur Link called it "a variety of progressive movements." See A. S. Link and W. B. Catton, *American Epoch: A History of the United States since 1900,* vol. 1: *The Progressive Era and the First World War, 1900–1920* (New York, 1973), pp. 50–78. Foner called it "a fluid and complex set of beliefs . . . , [b]ut at its core stood a coalition of middle-class reformers, male and female, . . . who sought to humanize capitalism." See E. Foner, *The Story of American Freedom* (New York, 1998), p. 141. See also, in addition to the previously mentioned works by Hofstadter, Noble, and Diner, L. Fink, *Progressive Intellectuals and the Dilemmas of Democratic Commitment* (Cambridge, Mass., 1997); R. L. McCormick, "Evaluating the Progressives," in L. Fink (ed.), *Major Problems in the Gilded Age and the Progressive Era* (Lexington, Mass., 1992), pp. 316–18; the classic study by B. P. De Witt, *The Progressive Movement* (Seattle, 1968) (1st ed., 1915); and A. Testi (ed.), *L'età progressista negli Stati Uniti* (Bologna, 1984), pp. 7–98.
3. R. Hofstadter, *The Age of Reform: From Bryan to F.D.R.* (New York, 1955), p. 144.
4. Ibid., pp. 131–73; Link, *American Epoch*, p. 56.
5. R. N. Current, T. H. Williams, and F. Freidel, *American History: A Survey* (New York, 1975), p. 570.
6. See C. F. Casula, *Storia e storie tra Otto e Novecento* (Cagliari, 1994), especially the two chapters entitled "Incunabuli culturali e ideologici del Novecento" and "La prima guerra mondiale da mito a tragedia," pp. 158–212.
7. McCormick, "Evaluating the Progressives," pp. 316–17.
8. D. M. Kennedy, *Over Here: The First World War and American Society* (Oxford, 1980), pp. 92 and 143. See also Neil A. Wynn, *From Progressivism to Prosperity: World War One and American Society* (New York, 1986).
9. A. S. Link, *Woodrow Wilson and the Progressive Era, 1910–1917* (New York, 1963), p. 22.
10. S. Ricard, *Theodore Roosevelt: principes et pratique d'une politique étrangère* (Aix-Marseille, 1991), pp. 395–402.
11. Link, *Wilson and the Progressive Era*, p. 18, and J. M. Cooper, *The Warrior and the Priest: Woodrow Wilson and Theodore Roosevelt* (Cambridge, Mass., 1983), pp. 206–12.
12. J. W. Schulte Nordholt, *Woodrow Wilson: A Life for World Peace* (Berkeley, 1991), pp. 3–5.
13. A. S. Link, *Wilson the Diplomatist: A Look at His Major Foreign Policies* (Baltimore, Md., 1957), p. 5.
14. H. A. Turner, "Woodrow Wilson and Public Opinion," *Public Opinion Quarterly* 21, no. 4 (Winter 1957–1958); 508.

15. W. Wilson, *Constitutional Government in the United States* (New York, 1961), p. 77.

16. Link, *Wilson the Diplomatist*, p. 23.

17. Turner, *Woodrow Wilson and Public Opinion*, pp. 509–10.

18. Tumulty "was the President's interpreter of public opinion, his guide to mass psychology." See J. M. Blum, *Joe Tumulty and the Wilson Era* (Boston, 1951), p. 60. Edward House, one of the president's closest friends and advisers, kept Wilson informed through his network of contacts as to the views of Wall Street, the major industrialists, the radical intellectuals, and a number of American and European leaders.

19. A. S. Link, *Wilson the Diplomatist*, in Earl Latham (ed.), *The Philosophy and Policies of Woodrow Wilson* (Chicago, 1958), p. 153.

20. T. J. Knock, *To End All Wars: Woodrow Wilson and the Quest for a New World Order* (Princeton, N. J., 1995), p. 165.

21. These errors were carefully avoided in the Second World War, which required no long months of peace negotiations; instead the fundamental agreements were made while the war was still being waged.

22. Quoted in Schulte Nordholt, *Woodrow Wilson*, pp. 34–35. This type of religious nationalism remained a basic feature of Wilson's political thinking. Nearly twenty years later, in a speech during the campaign for the elections of 1912, he stated: "I believe that God presided over the inception of this nation; I believe that God planted in us the vision of liberty. . . . I cannot be deprived of the hope that is in me—the hope not only that concerns myself, but the confident hope that concerns the nation—that we are chosen, to show the way to the nations of the world how they shall walk in the paths of liberty" (ibid., p. 38).

23. Vaughn notes that at the time most Americans believed, as an article of faith, that the American system was a model for the world: "In this sense," he adds, "internationalism as expressed through the CPI was a manifestation of American nationalism." See S. L. Vaughn, *Holding Fast the Inner Lines: Democracy, Nationalism, and the Committee on Public Information* (Chapel Hill, NC, 1980), p. 97.

24. "Wilson . . . began his mediation by adopting a very ambiguous position, one that in the long run was impossible. He wanted America to play a great role in the international order, but without it having anything to do with the conflict of interests in Europe. America would participate and still remain unique, it would stay pure and yet bear responsibility. It would participate in the wicked world and yet keep its hands clean. That curious paradox continued to define his position for a long time; indeed, it can be said that he never really broke away from it, and it was this that made his relations with the Old World so complex." See Schulte Nordholt, *Woodrow Wilson*, p. 172.

25. Letter from Lippmann to Frankfurter, 28 July 1919, b. 10, f. 420A, Lippmann Papers. In an article published that same month, Lippmann, already openly critical of Wilson's policies, observed: "Mr. Wilson knew what a network of

commitments, arrangements, notes, and treaties would confront him when the time for making peace finally arrived. He had resolved to take part in the making of that peace, and to pledge America to guarantee the results. Yet he refrained from interfering in the decisive stages of the preliminaries. This is a central point in the Wilsonian diplomacy, and the answer to it is perhaps the chief clue to his action." W. Lippmann, "The Peace Conference," *The Yale Review* (July 1919): 718.

26. W. Lippmann, "Assuming We Join," *The New Republic*, 3 September 1919, p. 145.

27. C. Seymour, "Woodrow Wilson in Perspective," in Latham, *The Philosophy and Policies of Wilson*, p. 184.

28. R. A. Divine, *Second Chance: The Triumph of Internationalism in America during World War II* (New York, 1967), pp. 167–83.

29. A. Link, *The Higher Realism of Woodrow Wilson and Other Essays* (Nashville, Tenn., 1971), pp. 127–39; A. Iriye, *Cultural Internationalism and World Order* (Baltimore, Md., 1997), pp. 51–90.

30. This section is a revised version of my essay "Nuovi rapporti tra città e campagna nell'America in armi: la nascita della propaganda, 1917–18," published in C. Giorcelli, C. Cattarulla, and A. Scacchi (eds.), *Città Reali e Immaginarie del continente americano* (Rome, 1999), pp. 695–711.

31. See J. Tebbel and S. M. Watts, *The Press and the Presidency: From George Washington to Ronald Reagan* (New York, 1985), p. 391, and J. M. Cooper, "Fool's Errand or Finest Hour? Woodrow Wilson's Speaking Tour in September 1918," in J. M. Cooper and C. E. Neu (eds.), *The Wilson Era: Essays in Honor of Arthur S. Link* (Arlington Heights, Ill., 1991), p. 218.

32. H. D. Lasswell, *Propaganda Technique in the World War* (New York, 1938), pp. 216–17.

33. E. R. May, *World War I and American Isolation, 1914–1917* (Cambridge, Mass., 1959), p. 155.

34. George Creel, director of the CPI, nicely described the spirit with which many American intellectuals devoted themselves to propaganda work for the CPI, when he wrote: "Our effort was educational and informative throughout, for we had such confidence in our case as to feel that no other argument was needed than the simple, straightforward presentation of facts," G. Creel, *How We Advertised America, The First Telling of the Amazing: Story of the Committee on Public Information that Carried the Gospel of Americanization to Every Corner of the Globe* (New York, 1920), pp. 4–5. "For publicity is the life blood of democracy," claimed Ray Stannard Baker; see R. S. Baker, *American Chronicle: The Autobiography of Ray Stannard Baker* (New York, 1945), p. 387.

35. D. Frezza, "Informazione o Propaganda: il dibattito americano tra le due guerre," in M. Vaudagna (ed.), *L'estetica della politica: Europa ed America negli anni '30* (Bari, 1989).

36. "Publicity, the hope of the Progressive Era, became propaganda: the scourge of the twenties." L. W. Huebner, "The Discovery of Propaganda. Changing Attitudes Toward Public Communication in America 1900–1930," unpublished doctoral thesis, Harvard University, 1968, p. 200.

37. Creel, *How We Advertised,* p. 225.

38. R. C. Hilderbrand, *Power and the People: Executive Management of Public Opinion in Foreign Affairs, 1897–1921* (Chapel Hill, N.C., 1981), p. 164. Creel talks of 150,000 people involved in the work of the CPI; see Creel, *How We Advertised,* p. 13.

39. "George Creel Replies," *The New Republic,* 27 March 1915, p. 210.

40. J. R. Mock and C. Larson, *Words that Won the War: The Story of the Committee on Public Information, 1917–1919* (Princeton, N.J., 1939), p. 338.

41. On these topics, see F. Fasce, *La democrazia degli affari: Comunicazione aziendale e discorso pubblico negli Stati Uniti, 1900–1940* (Rome, 2000), chapter 2.

42. On American moviegoing, see note 46 below.

43. Creel, *How We Advertised,* p. 150.

44. Ibid., pp. 84–98; and Vaughn, *Holding Fast the Inner Lines,* pp. 116–17 and 120. For a description of the organization, see also the historic issue of the bulletin, the *Four Minute Men News,* F edition of December 1918, CPI 11A-A2, Sc. 3, CPI Papers.

45. See, for instance, Bulletin no. 1, dated 22 May 1917 and no. 29, dated 6 April 1918, CPI 11A-A1, Sc. 2, fasc. *Four Minute Men Bulletins,* CPI Papers.

46. Mock and Larson, *Words that Won the War,* pp. 113–14. Statistics on public attendance of movie theaters began to be gathered only in 1922. That year, some 40 million moviegoers (out of a total national population of about 110 million) saw a film every week. Average weekly attendance per family was one-and-a-half times, and the number was the same in the 1950s, after the peak of the 1930s and 1940s. "The United States was literally transformed into a nation of moviegoers between 1900 and 1930." See M. L. De Fleur and S. J. Ball-Rokeach, *Theories of Mass Communication,* 4th ed. (New York, 1982), pp. 62–64.

47. Bulletin no. 17, 8 October 1917, CPI 11A-A1, Sc. 2, fasc. *Four Minute Men Bulletins,* CPI Papers.

48. Creel, *How We Advertised,* p. 3.

49. Saying of Confucius, taken from T. A. Bailey, *The Man in the Street: The Impact of American Public Opinion on Foreign Policy* (New York, 1948), p. 302.

50. F. L. Mott, *American Journalism: A History of Newspapers in the United States Through 250 Years, 1690 to 1940* (New York, 1941), pp. 546–49. Statistics on the average daily circulation of newspapers in the United States are 1.36 copies per family in 1910 and 1.34 in 1920; see De Fleur and Ball-Rokeach, *Theories of Mass Communication,* p. 40.

51. CPI, Bureau of Cartoons, *Bulletin for Cartoonists*, no. 4, 29 June 1918, no. 17, 5 October 1918, and no. 22, 9 November 1918, Sc. 1 and 2, Executive Division, CPI 1-C5, CPI Papers.

52. Bulletin no. 5, 6 July 1918, no. 9, 3 August 1918, no. 14, 14 September 1918, and no. 22, 9 November 1918, CPI Papers.

53. U.S. Bureau of the Census, *Historical Statistics of the United States: Colonial Times to 1970*, Part 2, table R 244–257: "Newspapers and Periodicals—Number and Circulation: 1850 to 1967," p. 810.

54. Let us take as an example the edition of the *New York World* for Sunday, 14 January 1917: aside from the main section of the newspaper, which was eighteen pages long, as it was generally on weekdays, there were two sections with more specialized news (finance, real estate, etc.), each eight pages long, an insert of classified ads, eighteen pages, an op-ed section, four pages, a New York section called "Metropolitan Section," ten pages, a literary section, sixteen pages, the "Funny Side," a four-page funnies section, and finally an entirely photographic section, four pages. Total ninety pages.

55. Mock and Larson, *Words that Won the War*, pp. 109–11, and Vaughn, *Holding Fast the Inner Lines*, p. 30.

56. "My dear Creel: I have a proposition to put up to you. . . . I am writing a novel designed to hold the support of the radicals for the war. The title of the story is: 'Jimmie Higgins Goes to War'. It tells the story of a Socialist workingman, one of the rank and file, who believes what the leaders tell him and goes on opposing war regardless of everything. He finds himself in the hands of the German propagandists and little by little he comes to see how he has been used. In the end he goes to France as a mechanic, is drawn into the fighting in a sudden emergency and gives his life for democracy. . . . I suppose I hardly need point out to you that my name is known to workingmen, to foreign working men as well as to American. The Jungle was translated into seventeen languages, and it is today the best known American novel in every country in Europe. . . . I have been twenty years building up a reputation and an influence with these workingmen, and why should not the Government use it in this crisis? I don't want anything out of it, of course; I will gladly make the book my contribution to the cause. All I ask is the satisfaction of knowing the book is doing its work." Letter from Sinclair to Creel dated 16 September 1918, General Correspondence of George Creel, Sc. 22, fasc. 33, CPI 1-A1, CPI Papers.

57. Creel, *How We Advertised*, p. 111.

58. Vaughn, *Holding Fast the Inner Lines*, pp. 102–3, and Creel, *How We Advertised*, pp. 92–193, 111–12.

59. Ibid., p. 112.

60. Vaughn, *Holding Fast the Inner Lines*, p. 112.

61. Creel, *How We Advertised*, pp. 213 and 217–19.

62. G. Creel, *Complete Report of the Chairman of the Committee on Public Information, 1917:1918:1919* (Washington, D.C., 1920), p. 1.

4. Propaganda in Uniform

1. H. Stuart Hughes, *The United States and Italy* (Cambridge, Mass., 1965), p. 7.

2. A. Gramsci, "Wilson e i Socialisti," *Il Grixdo del Popolo*, 12 October 1918, republished in *Scritti giovanili 1914–1918* (Turin, 1958), p. 318.

3. "There is no part of Italy that has not sent its quota of citizens to the United States. . . . Everywhere in Italy, America is known at first hand and admired as a land of power and plenty and loved as a land of freedom. . . . Everywhere our delegates went they were continually running across odd bits of American atmosphere." C. M. Bakewell, *The Story of the American Red Cross in Italy* (New York, 1920), pp. 57 and 59.

4. See "L'opera della American Red Cross in Italia," in *Il Giornale d'Italia*, 25 November 1917.

5. "Another great event followed on the international stage with the United States' declaration of war against Austria-Hungary. . . . And while our soul still quickens with gratitude and admiration for the magnificent impulse with which the American Red Cross has lent us a powerful hand during our recent disaster, we also attribute great value to the assistance that will be provided to us in the battle against our common enemy by the prodigious activity and the conscientious and energetic efforts of the american people." "Le dichiarazioni del Presidente del Consiglio sui recenti accordi internazionali," *Il Tempo*, 13 December 1917.

6. See, for instance, a number of instructions issued by the Ministry of War to liaison officers to the American Red Cross: "The American Red Cross, in contrast with other Red Crosses, is an integral part of the American army: as such it has come here as a vanguard [underlined in the text,—author's note] of as much of the American army as will be able to come to Italy." Italian Ministry of War, General Secretariat, *Divisione Stato Maggiore*, "Direttive per l'opera degli ufficiali coadiutori della Croce Rossa Americana" ("Instructions for the Work of Liaison Officers for the American Red Cross"), 4 February 1918, Fondo F3 "Carteggio Sussidiario Prima Guerra Mondiale," racc. 255, Archivio SME. The American side also claimed: "When we entered the war we were completely unprepared, and we realized that it would require a certain period of time before we could take a strong position in the fighting lines. During this interval— through the work of the Commissions of the American Red Cross—we hoped to manifest, if only to a small degree, our profound appreciation for everything that had been done, our most sincere sympathy, and our ardent desire to offer our help in the best way possible." Speech delivered by Mr. Henry P. Davison,

President of the War Council of the American Red Cross in Florence—at Palazzo Vecchio—on 17 April 1918, pamphlet published by the Department of Public Information of the ARC, Rome n.d. [prob. 1918], Fondi Vari—Fondo Scotti/ Croce Rossa, racc. F.V. 25, Archivio SME.

7. Working alongside them were the Administrative Department and, later, the Division for the Fight Against Tuberculosis.

8. In his memoirs, Norval Richardson, first secretary of the American embassy, remembered: "These last [the ARC professional staff] appeared on the Roman horizon with considerable—as the Italians said—*slancio*. They were a fine-looking lot, smartly uniformed and with an impressive air of efficiency. . . . They were very soon installed in a large building, organized departments to cover the whole of Italy, and went to work in a way that had much to do with creating an impression of unlimited funds and capacity for undertaking and carrying out anything. . . . As a matter of fact, Rome and the whole of Italy received them with open arms; and a Britisher said soon after they arrived: 'There is no use of our organization remaining any longer in Italy. Your Red Cross is so tremendously rich that it makes our efforts appear entirely puerile. We are going to close up and let them handle the whole situation.' . . . In Italy we had very few soldiers; and for a long time Italians had to judge of what we could do solely by the Red Cross. One Italian frankly confessed that the style in which the Red Cross went about had more to do with bracing up the morale in Italy than anything that had appeared during the war." N. Richardson, *My Diplomatic Education* (New York, 1923), pp. 171–73.

9. Instead, the novel is set in the months before and after Caporetto. Hemingway worked for the ambulance service, but for a short period he assisted in the distribution of creature comforts to the soldiers on the front lines. At the end of July 1918, while he was working in that second capacity, he was wounded by the explosion of an enemy bomb. For this episode, the Italian government awarded him a medal for valor.

10. C. A. Fenton, "Ambulance Drivers in France and Italy: 1914–1918," *American Quarterly* (Winter 1951): 337. See also A. J. Hansen, *Gentlemen Volunteers: The Story of the American Ambulance Drivers in the Great War, August 1914–September 1918* (New York, 1996), p. vi.

11. G. Cecchin, *Americani sul Grappa: Documenti e fotografie inediti della Croce Rossa Americana in Italia nel 1918, Magnifica Comunità Pedemontana* (Asolo, 1984), p. 36.

12. Fenton, "Ambulance Drivers," p. 326, and M. Cowley, "Hemingway's Wound—and Its Consequences for American Literature," *The Georgia Review*, no. 2 (Summer 1984): 223–39.

13. H. James, *The American Volunteer Motor-Ambulance Corps in France* (London, 1914).

14. Statistics taken from [ARC], *Report of the Department of Military Affairs, January to July, 1918,* pamphlet printed in Rome, 1 August 1918, p. 6, Fondo F3, "Carteggio Sussidiario I Guerra Mondiale," racc. 255, Archivio SME. In the first half of 1918, the ambulances of the American Red Cross transported more than 140,000 injured men over a total distance of some 846,000 kilometers.

15. See the report of the *Generale Medico dell'Intendenza Generale dell'Esercito Italiano,* 25 July 1918, concerning the arrival of the American ambulances in Genoa, Fondo F1-Carteggio Sussidiario Comando Supremo, Vari Uffici, racc. 250, Archivio SME.

16. Report of the Department of Military Affairs, pp. 7–14.

17. "The heat is unbearable. On the edge of the road, in the shade of a clump of trees, there is something beneath an Italian flag and another flag filled with white stars on a deep blue field, crossed by red and white stripes. The soldiers hurry toward it. It is a refreshment post of the American Red Cross. There are many of these as you get closer to the lines, at the main points of traffic, where it is hardest to get a cool drink or a bite to eat. There our great American allies bring an endless bounty of good things to eat and drink; they set up a table, they stretch out the Stars and Stripes and the Italian tricolor, and there they stand, with shaven faces, khaki uniforms, and big round hats—offering freely an abundance of delights to all the soldiers who go by: coffee, milk, cool, thirst-quenching drinks, sandwiches, chocolates like they had in the good old days, cookies and biscuits like they don't make anymore. . . . Manna from heaven. And they offer the food with such good-hearted, such cordial brotherhood! The soldiers have already given a name to these Posts: they cheerfully call them 'American Bars.' And when they see far down the road an Italian tricolor and the white stars in a deep blue sky, they say: 'Let's go to America!'" From Arnaldo Fraccaroli, "Il grano e il sangue," *Il Corriere della Sera,* 21 July 1918.

18. H. S. Villard, "Red Cross Driver in Italy," in H. S. Villard and J. Nagel (eds.), *Hemingway in Love and War: The Lost Diary of Agnes von Kurowsky* (New York, 1989), p. 23.

19. Report of the Department of Military Affairs, pp. 16–22.

20. See Table 1, p. 90.

21. Bakewell, *Red Cross in Italy,* p. 36.

22. Letter from T. N. Page to Wilson, 29 January 1918, Series 2: Correspondence, Wilson Papers.

23. John Dos Passos, *The Best of Times: An Informal Memoir* (New York, 1966), pp. 59 and 63.

24. Statistics from Bakewell, *Red Cross in Italy,* p. 60.

25. Telegram from the Carabinieri Lieutenant (Tenente RR CC) Carini, Avigliano, to the Ministry of the Interior, 12 April 1918, Div. Affari Generali e Riservati,

Cat. A5G (Prima Guerra Mondiale), fasc. 66, sf. 1 (Croce Rossa Americana, Missione in Italia), Archivio Min. Interno.

26. See, for instance, this telegram from the prefect of Sassari, dated December 1917: "Delegates from the American Red Cross have arrived in this provincial capital. . . . The city provided guests with enthusiastic welcome stop civilian and military authorities, clubs, associations, schools, and committees all came to the station with flag, as well as many thousands of ordinary citizens stop arrival of train greeted with great ovations and notes of royal march, to the cry of 'Viva l'America' stop during procession through streets of city, flags flying, ovations repeated stop at hotel delegates obliged appear at window thank cheering crowd and Captain Stevens spoke to thunderous applause stop delegation toured Red Cross hospital, city hospital, reserve military hospital, and garrison military hospital stop afterward went to city hall where presentation of authorities and members of civilian relief committees followed stop royal commissioner extended greetings to delegates with response from Captain Carrol to enthusiastic acclaim stop after visit to headquarters of civilian mobilization committee delegates came to my house to confer regarding operation of hospitals and committees stop they said they were moved at the greeting they received—gave me check for ten thousand lire to distribute to relief agencies with the possibility of further generous aid to come stop delegates leave for Cagliari tomorrow morning 9 o'clock." Telegram from the Prefect Serra Caracciolo (Sassari) to Ministry of the Interior, 18 December 1917, ibid., fasc. 66, sf. 1. The same file contains telegrams from the prefects of Genoa (16 December 1917 and 13 April 1918), Cagliari (19 December 1917), Parma (7 April 1918), Alessandria (9 April 1918), Cuneo (11 April 1918), Ancona (Recanati, 14 April 1918), Turin (15 May 1918), and Forlì (1 September 1918). See also *Il Messaggero* of 18 and 19 December 1917.

27. Bakewell in his book on the ARC's work in Italy describes similar ceremonies and atmospheres: "The plan was simple and direct. It was to send at once to every part of Italy men in the American uniform to carry the message of American friendship and sympathy and of her determination to spend all of her resources in men and means in order to insure victory, and to give the people tangibie evidence of her determination through a gift of money to the neediest and most deserving of the families of soldiers at the front. . . . The Premier, keenly alive to the possibilities of the undertaking, promptly set in motion the elaborate governmental and municipal machinery to determine which families of soldiers were to be aided. Meanwhile, Red Cross agents were dispatched to every city, town, and village. Telegrams were sent to delegates in distant fields to leave at once by the most rapid means of conveyance and travel night and day without stopping until every hamlet in their territory had received the message from America. . . . Relief must be carried immediately to those to whom the

war had brought the greatest distress, and it must be shown by the actual presence of American officers in uniform that America was at hand with aid. . . . The itineraries were carefully planned notwithstanding the haste necessary. The Government telegraphed ahead the news of the expected arrival of the delegate. At each provincial capital the Prefect would meet the American representative and at each town he was given a gratifying demonstration—a spontaneous response from the people which showed their confidence and trust in their friends in the United States. Generally, he was met at the city gates by the Mayor, the town doctor, the parish priest, and other dignitaries, and a large crowd of people, and escorted to the city hall, showered with flowers and notes of welcome, while the band played and barefooted children ran ahead waving American flags. Then in the public square the delegate would deliver his message, the Mayor and the Prefect respond, and the meeting turn into an enthusiastic patriotic rally." See Bakewell, *Red Cross in Italy*, pp. 57–59.

28. Letter from Chester Aldrich, Managing Director of Civil Affairs for the ARC to Colonel Apolloni, Ufficio di Collegamento alla Croce Rossa Americana (ARC Liaison Office), 27 August 1918, and letter from Colonel Marzocchelli, head of that liaison office, to the Commander in Chief of the Divisione Militare Territoriale (Territorial Military Division) of Rome, 4 September 1918, Fondo F3—"Carteggio Sussidiario Prima Guerra Mondiale," racc. 255, Archivio SME.

29. G. Prezzolini, *Tutta la guerra—Antologia del popolo italiano sul fronte e nel paese* (Florence, 1921), p. 363.

30. Bakewell, *Red Cross in Italy*, p. 154.

31. "The pompous, bombastic, and boring speeches that the soldier was obliged to listen to, standing, following an 'attention, at ease,' often during his few hours of leave, awaiting another 'attention, at ease, break ranks,' without any chance to talk or personal contact," Prezzolini, *Tutta la guerra*, pp. 361–62.

32. See, for instance, the Bollettino no. 6 del Comando della I Armata, Sezione P, 30 August 1918, "Informazioni per propaganda e Spunti di conversazione coi soldiers—L'assicurazione gratuita ai Combattenti," in which an effort was made to discredit three "defeatist" claims circulating among the enlisted men: (1) The free life insurance policy represented blood money; (2) the free life insurance policy was a soldier's last will and testament; and (3) the policy was an ill omen for the soldier. See Fondo E1—"Carteggio Sussidiario Armate," racc. 303, Archivio SME.

33. Prezzolini, *Tutta la guerra*, p. 359.

34. Ibid., p. 301.

35. Circular letter on the organization of the propaganda from the Headquarters of the Italian Second Army, 22 March 1918, no. 736/P of Prot. Uff. Inf., Fondo E1—"Carteggio Sussidiario Armate," racc. 115, Archivio SME.

36. Here are a few examples of *spunti di conversazione*: Section P of the Headquarters of the Italian First Army, "What American help means" and "The Sacrifice of Rice"; Section P of the Headquarters of the Italian Eighth Army *(Sezione P del Comando dell'VIII Armata)*, "American intervention," "Free Life Insurance for Combatants," and "The War Is Also for Our Daily Bread," Fondo E1— "Carteggio Sussidiario Armate," racc. 303, Archivio SME.

37. Headquarters of the Italian Twelfth Army—Centro V. P., *Bollettino Settimanale* (*Weekly Bulletin*) no. 2, 30 July 1918, Fondo E1—"Carteggio Sussidiario Armate," racc. 303, Archivio SME.

38. One Italian *bersagliere* (sharpshooter) observed, "The greatness of America lies in the fact that the undersigned was always treated with respect." See [G. Volpe], *Per la storia dell'VIII Armata, dalla controffensiva del giugno alla vittoria del settembre–ottobre 1918* (Rome, n.d.), pp. 99–107 passim.

39. The pay for American Red Cross personnel is mentioned in the pamphlet of the ARC Report of the Department of Military Affairs, mentioned above; the pay for Italian soldiers is reported in Bakewell, *Red Cross in Italy*, p. 55.

40. R. W. Lewis, "Hemingway in Italy: Making It Up," *Journal of Modern Literature* 9, no. 2 (1981–1982): 215 and 225. The list of those decorated is found in the previously mentioned ARC pamphlet, Report of the Department of Military Affairs. As often happens, behind the evident spectacle of the differences between the two countries, there lurked a fairly pronounced prejudice. In a description of the qualities that workers in ARC canteens at the front needed to have, for instance, in the official ARC pamphlet it was stated that they would need to be able to get along with men of another race. See ARC, *Report of the Department of Military Affairs*, pp. 14–15.

41. YMCA, *1919 Calendario Y.M.C.A. del Soldato*, Fondo Scotti-Fondi Vari, Archivio SME. Francis B. Sayre, Wilson's son-in-law and a member of the association's board of directors, led one of the YMCA's first missions to Italy in late 1917.

42. Most of the information about the YMCA's activity in Italy is taken from the pamphlet published in 1919 by the executive headquarters of the YMCA: *Opera di Fratellanza Universale, L'opera dell'YMCA presso l'esercito italiano, febbraio 1918–dicembre 1919* (Rome, 1919), Archivio Museo Risorgimento.

43. One of the main reasons for the Comando Supremo's mistrust and fear had to do with the possibility that the American association might carry out Protestant religious propaganda among the soldiers. At the insistence of Father Semeria and Monsignor Bartolomasi, there was a specific prohibition of religious propaganda in the convention signed by the YMCA and the Intendenza Generale (General Superintendency) of the Italian army on 8 February 1918; see Fondo F1—"Carteggio Sussidiario Comando Supremo," racc. 257/5, Archivio SME.

44. Father Giovanni Minozzi founded and operated the Case del Soldato before the Americans arrived.

45. For example, in a report dated 21 April 1918 by the Intendente Generale (general superintendent) of the Italian army, General Zaccone, to the Comando Supremo (Italian chiefs of staff), we can clearly discern his amazement at the "truly substantial sum" of half a million lire that the YMCA budgeted to help in the operation of the existing case del soldato. One should keep in mind that in a previous memo from the Intendenza Generale (general superintendency) from September 1917, it was pointed out that the 50,000 lire budgeted for the operation of the case (homes) by under secretary Dall'Olio had already largely gone to cover previous purchases. The gap between Italian and American resources in this area was enormous; see Fondo F1—"I Guerra Mondiale, Carteggio Sussidiario Comando Supremo," racc. 257, fasc. 5, Archivio SME.

46. G. Minozzi, *Ricordi di guerra* (Amatrice, 1956–1959), vol. 2, p. 172. A bit further down, he added bitterly: "We shall have the Americans open the 'Case' ('homes'), in any case. The General Superintendent has absolutely no interest in putting up any money, to spend anything himself, and he has said very clearly that either I find the money as I did in the past, or we'll ask the Americans to pay for everything, we'll let them do it all, we'll fall into their arms. And that was the end of that" (ibid., p. 175).

47. "This struggle for personnel and supplies is the dominant note in all early reports from the army fronts. . . . [T]he remarkable cooperation of Italian officers enabled the few Americans to multiply their capacity for accomplishment. The secretaries were always facilitated in every personal matter, becoming members of the officers' mess whenever stationed in the field away from regional headquarters. Each was usually assigned an orderly. The regional headquarters were manned by a full personnel of soldier assistants. Chauffeurs were often drawn from the ranks for the 'Y' cars. A group of reliable soldiers was detailed to serve at every *casa*. A competent and energetic American in khaki, with the triangle on his sleeve to authorize his movements at the front, and a military pass in his pocket—seldom called for—could supervise a number of wdely separated 'soldiers' houses,' provided he had means of locomotion, and they would function under their sergeants and soldiers as if he were present. Only, there was a certain indefinable value in the presence among the friendly and responsive troopers of a live representative of America, a personal symbol of American comprehension and right evaluation of Italian courage, sacrifice, and blood. This human symbol gave full significance to the Italian name of the 'Y'—the Fratellanza—to the triangle on the soldier's letter paper, and even to the American flag whipping with the wind of a speeding motor truck loaded with supplies for a new 'soldiers' house.'" See O. D. Wannamaker, *With Italy in Her Final War of Liberation: A Story of the "Y" on the Italian Front* (New York, 1923), pp. 142–45.

48. F. Vismara, *L'Anima Americana: Lecture* [delivered in Turin on 22 February 1919], published by the Opera di Fratellanza Universale-Corpo Americano (YMCA), n.p., n.d. [1919], Fondo F1—"Carteggio Sussidiario del Comando Supremo," racc. 303, Archivio SME.

49. Minozzi, *Ricordi di guerra*, pp. 174–75.

50. See C. M. Panunzio, *The Soul of an Immigrant* (New York, 1921), pp. 319–22, and Wannamaker, *With Italy*, pp. 182–84 and 190–91.

51. Panunzio recalled in particular the troops' reactions following one of his speeches near Messina: "The address over, we exchanged greetings with the officers in charge of the occasion and returned to our car. Then followed a scene which will forever remain indelibly imprinted upon my memory and consciousness. The soldiers, even before being ordered to do so, spontaneously broke ranks and made a mad dash toward the road, where our car was waiting. Wave upon wave of 'Evviva l'America' swelled. They massed themselves along both sides of the road, as our car began to move slowly down the serpentine way. The standards were still waving triumphantly. The band was now playing 'The Star Spangled Banner.' We moved on. The sun was just going down into the sea. The waves of cheers followed us, growing fainter and fainter like an echo. We gradually lost sight of the soldiers, their uniforms blending with the earth. But still we could see a mass of white in the distance; the boys with their handkerchiefs were waving the last possible farewell, the last 'evviva' to America." See Panunzio, *The Soul*, pp. 325–26.

52. [YMCA], *La Y.M.C.A. (Opera di Fratellanza Universale) americana in Italia* (n.p., n.d. [approximately late 1918]), Archivio del Risorgimento.

53. Byron Nester, who worked for the Italian branch of the CPI, wrote to his superior, Commissioner Merriam: "American chewing gum is a great success among all Italians who have tried it. 10,000,000 pieces in American flag wrappers could be distributed with great effect." Memo from B. M. Nester to C. Merriam, n.d. [around spring–summer 1918], sc. 20-B3, CPI Papers.

54. Aside from the repeated requests from Ambassador Page that fill the diplomatic archives, there were other interesting communiqués from the American consuls in Venice and Milan: see, for instance, the dispatches to the secretary of state and the ambassador from the American consul in Milan on 15 January, 26 February, and 1 March 1918, reporting on the growing Italian impatience for the arrival of American troops and the importance of that arrival in terms of keeping up Italian morale and fighting the German propaganda that claimed that the United States had no intention whatever of sending troops to Italy. The consul in Milan believed that at least 100,000 soldiers should be sent to Italy before April 1918; Department of State, *Internal Affairs of Italy, 1910–1929*, reel 4, doc. 865.oo/52–63–65. The consul in Venice wrote an interesting document urging the American leadership to focus the attack on the

Italian-Austrian front with half a million soldiers. See Harvey B. Carroll, Jr., *Why Half a Million American Soldiers Are Immediately Needed on the Italian Front,* 17 September 1918, Doc. No. 763.72/11898, Department of State, *WWI and Its Termination, 1914–1929.* Diaz, as we will see, also asked for troops through La Guardia and Merriam. Nitti claimed credit for bringing about the arrival of that regiment through the mediation of Oscar Crosby. See O. Malagodi, *Conversazioni della guerra 1914–1919* (Milan, 1960), vol. 2, p. 395. For an overall description of the Italian request for American troops, see also H. J. Burgwyn, *The Legend of the Mutilated Victory: Italy, the Great War, and the Paris Peace Conference, 1915–1919* (Westport, Conn., 1993), pp. 178–80.

55. In his memoirs, Joseph Lettau, a sergeant in the 332nd Infantry Regiment, recalls that at the end of June 1918, when he was still in training in France, "a rumor went forth that we were scheduled to go to Italy as a propaganda regiment to encourage the Italians." J. L. Lettau, *In Italy with the 332nd Infantry* (privately published, 1921), p. 12.

56. Ministero della Guerra-Stato Maggiore Esercito, *Le Grandi Unità nella guerra italo-austriaca 1915–1918* (Rome, 1926), vol. 2, p. 605.

57. Telegrams from Orlando to His Majesty the King on 27 and 28 July 1918, b. 68, "Contingente Usa in Italia," Fondo Orlando.

58. Fondo F1—Carteggio Sussidiario Comando Supremo, racc. 304 (Comando Supremo Vari Uffici), Archivio SME, translated from English.

59. T. N. Page, *Greetings to the American Soldiers in Italy,* pamphlet, n.p. and n.d., Collection Pamphlets from the First World War, Widener Library, Harvard University (Cambridge, Mass.). Concerning the celebration of the fourth of July in Italy, see the following chapter.

60. Dispatch from P Section of the Third Army to the P Subsections, 16 September 1918, and P Section of the Eighth Army, "L'intervento Americano," 24 September 1918, Fondo E1—"Carteggio Sussidiario Armate," racc. 303, Archivio SME.

61. Lettau, *In Italy,* pp. 21–24.

62. Ibid., pp. 23, 29, and 17.

63. "His Excellency Diaz requests that in the list of troops singled out for positive mention in the report on the battle of Vittorio the American regiment should be mentioned, placing the mention in question among the citations for the Army units to which that regiment belonged." *Fonogramma* from Captain Visconti of the Comando del Corpo di Stato Maggiore ("General Staff—Rome Headquarters"), 2 January 1919, Fondo F1—I Guerra Mondiale—"Comando Supremo Vari Uffici," racc. 295, Archivio SME.

64. L. Elliott, *Little Flower: The Life and Times of Fiorello La Guardia* (New York, 1983), p. 238.

65. Ibid., p. 11.

66. "During his first two administrations, before the World War put an end to large-scale domestic programs, New York became a vast demonstration project for federal assistance yielding hundreds of thousands of jobs for the unemployed and providing La Guardia with the 'hammers and chisels' to reconstruct the physical city." T. Kessner, *Fiorello H. La Guardia and the Making of Modern New York* (New York, 1989), p. xiv.

67. "Insurgent" was the term that La Guardia used to describe himself in his autobiography: F. H. La Guardia, *The Making of an Insurgent." An Autobiography, 1882–1919* (Westport, Conn., 1985); (1st ed., 1948).

68. "In the Balkans he met his future immigrant constituents and acquired their languages. There, too, the ambitious youth wielded power for the first time and liked it. Ambition for power and solicitude for poor uprooted people would be the two most creative impulses in his career." A. Mann, *La Guardia: A Fighter Against His Times, 1882–1933* (Chicago, 1969), p. 35.

69. Mann, *La Guardia,* p. 81.

70. La Guardia, "America's Congressman-Aviator," *New York Times,* 30 June 1918; "A Violinist and a Congressman," *The Literary Digest,* 13 July 1918.

71. Elliott, *Little Flower,* p. 187.

72. "The difference between La Guardia the campaigner and La Guardia the legislator was like the difference between Mr. Hyde and Dr. Jekyll, and would always be so. In running for office he cunningly played the jungle-like game established by the [Tammany Hall] Tiger, but once in office he was an uncompromising moralist who measured legislation by the standards of democracy, which was for him a religion." Mann, *La Guardia,* p. 83.

73. La Guardia, *The Making of an Insurgent,* p. 183; Mann, *La Guardia,* pp. 91–92.

74. La Guardia, *The Making of an Insurgent,* pp. 187–88.

75. Mann, *La Guardia,* p. 93.

76. Ibid., p. 86.

77. Albert Spalding, who accompanied him to Spain, described this undertaking at length in his autobiography: A. Spalding, *Rise to Follow: An Autobiography* (New York, 1943), pp. 232–45.

78. Letter from Page to Lansing dated 29 December 1917, letter from Wilson to Lansing dated 1 January 1918, and letter from Lansing to Page, 5 January 1918, in Mann, *La Guardia,* pp. 346–47.

79. S. Crespi, *Alla difesa d'Italia in guerra e a Versailles (Diario, 1917–1919)* (Milan, 1938), p. 119.

80. Mann, *La Guardia,* p. 90.

81. "Forgive me if, since I must speak in the Italian language, I shall fail to achieve the perfection of form; but I am here to guarantee the sincerity of our feelings: I have something to say and I want to say it. . . .

"*America joined this war, not to prolong it, but to bring it to an end* (thunderous applause). They say that we are a people of dollars, a people without feelings or ideals. Well, it's true that we have dollars, but we also have feelings and ideals; with this difference, that we know how to put those feelings and ideals into practice, while others are contented with singing them in the form of poetry (laughter, cries of approval).

"Why did we join the war? We were safe from danger; our soil was not threatened; we could have simply sold everything we could produce and developed our commerce and increased our wealth. *But when we saw the smaller peoples overwhelmed and the liberty of Europe threatened; when we saw that German barbarity intended to crucify Europe on the iron cross, we felt that under those conditions we could not live* (great applause). We seek no territorial conquests in Europe, we want no African colonies; we do not desire annexations or indemnities; we only wish to bring aid to the civilized nations of the world (ovation). . . .

"Now as an American, as a practical man, I want to talk to you about your national debt. Every Italian must do his duty. . . . *I know that the Italian soldier in the trenches is giving one hundred percent!* (acclaim, cries of *bravo! bravo!*). *You must give everything you have. The boys born in 1898 and 1899 have been called to duty; . . . now the hundred and five hundred and thousand lire must answer the call* (laughter, applause).

"The Hon. Orlando summarized in a phrase the country's duty: resist! resist! resist!; the Hon. Nitti adds: give! give! give! so that General Diaz can say to the soldiers: forward! forward! forward! and the Hon. Sonnino can then say to the Allies: Istria! Trieste! Trento! (enthusiastic, prolonged applause). . . .

"And let me conclude by reaffirming what I said at the beginning. 'We joined this war because we love peace, because we want it to be the last war. For that reason, soon American soldiers will fight side-by-side with Italian soldiers. America has renounced all its interests, it has offered money and materiel, and it has made sacrifices, and it wants to do its full duty: it sends its finest sons to die for civilization.' (The huge crowd filling the immense theater leaps to its feet and applauds the speaker while all the senators and deputies and authorities cluster around him. The military band plays the American national anthem and the demonstration of support continues, massive and at length)." Pamphlet printed by the Unione Generale degli Insegnanti Italiani—Comitato Lombardo, Il Discorso del Deputato Americano Lionetto [*sic*] La Guardia—Il significato e il valore dell'intervento Americano, CPI 20-C2 "Italian Newspaper Clippings," CPI Papers. Italics in original.

82. Let us examine, for instance, a passage from a speech delivered on 8 April 1918 by a teacher, Professor Eteocle Lorini, in Pavia in honor of the American Red Cross: "He [Wilson] is the true Caesar of the heroic age of ancient Rome. . . . Wilson's 'sic volo et jubeo' ('This I will, this I command') should cause the grim Kaiser's haughtiness to tremble, his long-taloned feudal centralization." Unione

Generale degli Insegnanti Italiani, Pavia Section, op. no. 13: *Il poderoso contributo americano,* Misc. C. 64–109, Archivio del Risorgimento.

83. Quoted in Unione Generale degli Insegnanti Italiani, Pavia Section, op. no. 15, *L'Intervento dell'America (Discorso pronunciato a Bologna il 9 June 1918 dal Deputato Americano La Guardia),* Misc. C. 64–109, Archivio del Risorgimento. Italics in original.

84. Report from Merriam to Creel, 25 June 1918, CPI 20-B1, CPI Papers.

85. Colgate Speranza, *The Diary of Gino Speranza,* vol. 2, pp. 156–57 and 144, corresponding, respectively, to 24 April and 26 March 1918.

5. The Arrival of the Professional Propagandists

1. G. Creel, *Complete Report of the Chairman of the Committee on Public Information, 1917:1918:1919* (Washington, D.C., 1920), p. 5.

2. "J. R. Mock and C. Larson, *Words that Won the War: The Story of the Committee on Public Information, 1917–1919* (Princeton, N.J., 1939), pp. 235–47; Creel, *Complete Report,* pp. 108–12, 127–29, 137–40; and G. Creel, *How We Advertised America: The First Telling of the Amazing Story of the Committee on Public Information that Carried the Gospel of Americanization to Every Corner of the Globe* (New York, 1920), pp. 237–302.

3. Creel, *Complete Report,* pp. 6 and 5.

4. Letter from Merriam to Creel, 15 April 1918, Office of the Commissioner at Rome, CPI 20-B2, Reports, CPI Papers. The letters of introduction from Creel for Merriam, all dated 11 March 1918, addressed to T. N. Page (Rome), J. F. Kerney (at the embassy in Paris), R. W. Flournoy (State Department, Washington, D.C.) and "To Whom It May Concern," are all in the archives of the Executive Division, General Correspondence of George Creel, Chairman, July 1817–March 1919, CPI 1-A1, sc. 16, f. 17, CPI Papers.

5. Report from Merriam to Creel, 13 August 1918, "Report for the week ending Aug. 12, 1918," Executive Division, Propaganda Records, CPI1-C4: Articles, Correspondence, and photographs in regard to propaganda abroad, file of G. Creel, January–November 1918, collection "Italy," CPI Papers.

6. Confidential very private letter, 25 August 1918, from Col. Aymonino, Group Leader of the Missions to the Allied Army, Comando Supremo, to Prime Minister V. E. Orlando, fasc. 19.3.35, "Invio di una missione militare e tecnica nord America in Italia" ("Sending a Military and Technical North American Mission to Italy"), Fondo Orlando.

7. Karl D. Barry, *Charles E. Merriam and the Study of Politics* (Chicago, 1974), pp. 89–95.

8. See, for instance, G. Wolper, "Wilsonian Public Diplomacy: The Committee on Public Information in Spain," *Diplomatic History* 17, no. 1 (Winter 1993):

17–34, and his doctoral thesis at the University of Chicago (1991), The Origins of Public Diplomacy: Woodrow Wilson, George Creel, and the Committee on Public Information.

9. The impossibility of closing the gap between the embassy and the CPI in Italy emerges from the reports Page and Merriam sent to Washington. Ambassador Page wrote: "Upon my return to Rome I find serious friction and the usefulness of the Embassy impaired by actions of Charles E. Merriam, who has usurped functions pertaining solely to Military and Naval Attaches offices, and even my own. He gives himself the title of 'High Commission' [sic] and his manner and actions are such as to convey the impression to the Italians that he is a kind of secret special plenipotentiary having extraordinary powers in Washington. He has made considerable personal impression in Rome owing to his pretension and his large appropriation. I have learned that he told some Italian officials at Grand Headquarters that if they wanted to get anything through with promptness, without using the ordinary channels, they should come to him. He has made the statement that as a result of his representations, General Swift was recalled. Merriam is now industriously criticizing Swift's successor. . . . I am indeed sorry that he seems to have lost his head, for I consider him very energetic and I heartily approve of a great many things that he does"—telegram from T. N. Page to the State Department, quoted in a letter from P. N. Patchin to G. Creel, dated 28 September 1918. Merriam responded in a report to Creel: "The Ambassador objects to my sending political information; the Naval Attaché to my sending naval information and the Military Attaché to my sending military information. If these three subtractions were successfully carried out, it is a little difficult to see what I could send. It is absolutely vital that I have free communication with you, otherwise the office might as well be closed." Report from Merriam to Creel, 17 September 1918; CPI 1C4, Executive Division, Propaganda Records, Sc. 1, f. 11: Italy, CPI Papers.

10. The amount of the monthly budget is recorded in the report from Merriam to Sisson, 2 September 1918, CPI 20-B1, Office of the Commissioner at Rome, Reports, CPI Papers, and also in the letter from Rickey to Hearley, 21 January 1919, CPI 17-A1, Director's Office of the Foreign Section, General Correspondence, sc. 9, fasc. "John Hearley," CPI Papers.

11. Creel, Complete Report, p. 191.

12. Ibid., pp. 137–40 and 192.

13. Ibid., pp. 192–93.

14. Report from Merriam to Creel, 13 August 1918, "Report for the week ending Aug. 12, 1918," Executive Division, Propaganda Records, CPI-C4: Articles, Correspondence, and photographs in regard to propaganda abroad, file of G. Creel, January–November 1918, racc. "Italy," CPI Papers.

15. Report from Merriam to Creel, 19 August 1918, ibid.

16. Report from Merriam to Creel, 17 September 1918, ibid.

17. Agents' Reports from Paris, 11 September 1918, Director's Office of the Foreign Section, Record Cards, CPI 17-H2, Sc. 1, I and II fasc. "Italy," CPI Papers.

18. Record of Distribution in Italy of Postcards, Bow Flags, Posters, Pamphlets, and Booklets, 11 June, 1918–14 January, 1919, CPI 20-E1, 1 vol., CPI Papers.

19. Report from Byron N. Nester to Merriam for the week ending 9 September 1918, CPI 1-C4, Executive Division, Propaganda Records, Sc. 1, f. 11: Italy, CPI Papers.

20. Creel, *Complete Report*, p. 47.

21. Ibid., p. 7 and Creel, *How We Advertised*, pp. 276–77.

22. Creel, *Complete Report*, p. 148.

23. The documentaries were about, the training of soldiers, American arsenals, the "response of America to Germany," cooperation with the French, the fourth of July in America and in Paris, the "industries" of fir trees, apples, and oranges, submarines, the Naval Academy, the presidents of the United States, liberty loans, the cities of New York, Boston, Minneapolis, Indianapolis, San Francisco, and Santa Fe, the Great Lakes, the wheat fields, and so on.

24. We have already discussed the YMCA's movie activity. As for the CPI, in the areas around Rome, there are mentions, for instance, of Tivoli, Bolsena, Palestrina, Velletri, Terracina, Marino, Magliano, Civitavecchia, Albano, Viterbo, Fiuggi, Avezzano, Spoleto, Segni, Castelgandolfo, Alatri, Terni, Frascati, Rieti, Foligno, L'Aquila, Soriano, Anagni, Amelia, Artena, and Poggio Mirteto; in the north and the south of Italy, movies were sent to Genoa, Perugia, Bologna, Turin, Naples, Ancona, Catania, Palermo, Rosburgo (Teramo), Bari, Florence, and Milan, as well as to the propaganda offices of the army and the YMCA of Bologna. See the Record Book Showing Distribution in Italy of Films of the Committee. July 4–October 20, 1918, CPI 20-E2, CPI Papers.

25. Report of Speakers' Department No. 7, week ending 4 August, 1918, CPI 1C4, sc. 1, fasc. 11 "Italy," CPI Papers.

26. From Merriam, Italy (Report of Speakers'Dept.), 11 August, 1918, Director's Office of the Foreign Section, Abstracts of Agents' Requests, CPI 17-H2, sc. 1, III fasc. "Italy," CPI Papers.

27. Report for Speakers' Department, week ending 28 July 1918, 30 July 1918, CPI 1-C4, Executive Division, Propaganda Records, sc. 1, fasc. 11 "Italy," CPI Papers. See also the memoirs of S. A. Cotillo, *Italy during the World War* (Boston, 1922), pp. 24–31.

28. Concerning San Gimignano, which he visited on 25 August, Altrocchi wrote: "I never saw a worse place to speak in, but I hope I did some good," Report of Speakers' Department, week ending 1 September, 1918, ibid.

29. Ferdinando Fasce mentions Arthur Benington in his essay, "L'Ansaldo dei Perrone e gli Stati Uniti," in *Storia d'Italia: Le regioni dall'Unità a oggi* (Turin, 1994), pp. 715–16.

30. *Intelligence Report no. 6—Concerning Feeling Prevalent among Certain Italian Peasant Classes Concerning the War* by Arthur Benington, n.d. [but end of August 1918], CPI 1-C4, Executive Division, Propaganda Records, sc. 1, fasc. 11 "Italy," CPI Papers.

31. Report of Speakers' Department, 11 August 1918, CPI 1-C4, Executive Division, Propaganda Records, sc. 1, fasc. 11 "Italy," CPI Papers.

32. *Strictly Confidential Report by Mr. Benington,* Rome, 30 November 1918, Office of the Commissioner at Rome, CPI 20-B3, Reports, CPI Papers.

33. During the summer of 1918, Samuel Gompers and the American Federation of Labor were the targets of virulent attacks by *l'Avanti!,* which considered them to be allies of the capitalists and among the most determined opponents to Italian immigration to America. Gompers, with his grating, arrogant attitude and his evident interest in meeting with the top Italian leadership rather than the Italian masses, only aggravated the hostility of the Socialists. "The visit of Mr. Gompers to Rome has not been a success," Gino Speranza commented in his diary on 12 October 1918. The same judgment emerged from various CPI reports. Spargo pointed out, for instance, in one of his reports: "The agitation of 'Avanti' during the last week has been almost exclusively confined to attacks against Mr. Gompers, whose intention to visit Italy has been announced in the press, and upon the American Federation of Labor mission which is now touring Italy. . . . It is practically impossible for the Italian unionists to understand such men, and these, in turn, fail to understand the Italians." See Colgate Speranza, *The Diary of Gino Speranza,* vol. 2, p. 198, and *Observations on the Italian Socialist Situation,* week ending 21 September, 1918, report from Spargo to Merriam, Office of the Commissioner at Rome, Reports, CPI 20-B4, CPI Papers. "The chief event of the week was the visit of the mission from the American Federation of Labor, led by Samuel Gompers," Report of Speakers' Department No. 17 for the week ending 13 October, 1918, ibid. Concerning the figure of Gompers, see M. R. Stabili, *America: Verso una società corporata. La AFL di Gompers* (Bari, 1984).

34. *Democratic Issues of the War* (n.d.), Office of the Commissioner at Rome, Reports, CPI 20-B4, CPI Papers. Russell's name is written by hand on the first sheet. Thompson, too, emphasized that the cooperation of the prowar Socialists, such as Spargo and Russell, was invaluable to the Wilson administration; see J. A. Thompson, *Reformers and War: American Progressive Publicists and the First World War* (Cambridge, 1987), pp. 179–82.

35. Letter from Creel to Sisson dated 26 August 1918, Executive Office, General Correspondence of G. Creel, CPI 1-A1, sc. 22, fasc. Sisson, Edgar G., CPI Papers. The letter went on: "Not only do I send it to you for your own guidance, but I want it sent also to Mr. Poole and his associate[s] for their information. As I tried to explain to you, we must stand fast at all times against imperialism and jingoism. . . . As completely as possible I want to avoid any effect of intrusion

in class quarrels; just as I did not think it wise for us to indorse [sic] the right wing of the labor movement in Great Britain, just so did I think it unwise to be put in the attitude of incurring favor with the left wing. We have our own aims to present and this is task enough."

36. *Defeatism in Tuscany,* report by A. Benington from the beginning of November 1918, Office of the Commissioner at Rome, CPI 20-B3 Reports, CPI Papers.

37. Many reports from Merriam appear in Creel's personal archives. Creel's correspondence with Wilson shows that news was given to the president and that Merriam and his suggestions were given great credence and followed more than once. Creel also forwarded a number of Merriam's reports to House; for instance, see the letter from Creel to House dated 25 September 1918 in which Creel forwarded the report on Merriam's talks with Sonnino, *House Papers.* On a number of Merriam's reports, Sisson wrote by hand: "For Creel" and sometimes also "Submit to Secretary or President."

38. Ambassador Page completely subscribed to—and conveyed to Washington— the thesis of the "military work-stoppage" that was first put forth by the commander-in-chief of the Italian army, General Cadorna, who insisted that the defeat was due to the collective betrayal and cowardice of the enlisted men, who had fallen prey to enemy, pacifist, and Socialist propaganda; see the letter from Page to Wilson dated 4 November 1917, Page Papers, and the letters dated 4 and 15 December 1917, Wilson Papers, Series 2, Correspondence (reel 93); see also the letter from Page to Lansing dated 14 November 1917, *House Papers.* Merriam also observed: "What made the situation [in early 1918] still more serious was the fact that the Italian defeat at Caporetto had been caused to a large extent by enemy propaganda." Moreover, "the combination of Giolittians, Socialists powerful in rural as in urban districts, and underground business interests, was a powerful one, and made itself felt in weakening the war will of Italy." See C. Merriam, "American Publicity in Italy," *The American Political Science Review,* no. 13 (1919): 542–43.

39. Ibid., p. 544.

40. C. Merriam, Analysis of the Italian Situation and Leadership in Italy, sc. 10, fasc. 5, Merriam Papers; G. Speranza, Report Relative to the Imperialist, Liberal, and Social Revolutionary Forces in Italy, n.d. [but around the end of August 1918], Speranza Papers.

41. Jacini identified the main case as the excessive centralization of the Italian political system. For an analysis of this aspect of Jacini's work, see J. A. *Thayer, Italy and the Great War: Politics and Culture, 1870–1915* (Madison, Wis., 1964), pp. 39–42. For an analysis of the CPI's work in Italy, see the doctoral thesis of L. J. Nigro, Propaganda, Politics, and the New Diplomacy: The Impact of Wilsonian Propaganda on Politics and Public Opinion in Italy, 1917–1919, Vanderbilt University, Nashville, Tenn., 1979, UMI 1980.7926620, pp. 114–66.

42. The distinction between the real Italy and the legal Italy touched an open wound in the Italian social and political body. The idea had become one of the favored grievances of those disappointed by the outcomes of the Risorgimento. This aspect of Italian cultural history should not be overlooked because it helps explain the widespread malaise that many observed in the educated classes of Italy at the turn of the twentieth century, a malaise that proved to offer fertile ground for the budding nationalist, vitalist, and irrationalist schools of opinion. In the immediate aftermath of the unification of Italy, two schools of thought developed concerning the young nation. On the one side were those who recognized the immense problems facing the postunification political class, but who were willing to roll up their sleeves and set to work on tasks that were more prosaic than the real and ideal battles of the Risorgimento in order to build painstakingly the new unified Italian nation. For them, the age of heroes was over, and now Italy needed a long quiet period of good administration. At the opposite extreme were, those who felt fully invested in the heroic past of the Risorgimento and who were disillusioned by the drudgery and the closed atmosphere, devoid of ideals, of the post-Risorgimento period. They scorned the prosaic nature of the new world; their heads were filled with libertarian rhetoric and literary romanticism. These two fronts of the governing class also had opposite attitudes toward Italian intervention in the First World War. For the first group, the gradualists, the war only served to interrupt, if not entirely overturn, the slow but constant process of modernization that the liberal class then holding power, led primarily by Giolitti, had carried on till then. For the second group, the motivations for intervention might harken back to the great ideals of the Risorgimento.

    Intervention was an act of redemption, a form of catharsis from the drudgery—if not corruption—of the postunification years. The glorification of Italy's entry into war, then, contained a rejection of the entire postunification era. The war once again restored glorious ideals to Italian political life and, with its call for discipline, sacrifice, and idealism, would lead to a new unification of the "legal Italy" with the "real Italy." The war would finally "make Italians"; that is, it would encourage the fusion of Italy's regions and classes, which would make it possible to achieve the potential of the heroic Risorgimento. On these themes, see J. A. Thayer, *Italy and the Great War,* pp. 38–56, and A. Lyttelton, *The Seizure of Power: Fascism in Italy 1919–1929* (1973; Princeton, N.J., 1987), pp. 2–5.

43. For the speeches in which Wilson sets forth this distinction between peoples and governments, see *For Declaration of War Against Germany,* 2 April 1917; *Our Objects in Going into the War,* 22 May 1917; *This Is a People's War,* 14 June 1917; *The Four-Point Speech,* 4 July 1918; also see R. S. Baker and W. E. Dodd (eds.), *War and Peace: Presidential Messages, Addresses, and Public Papers*

(1917–1924) by Woodrow Wilson (New York, 1927), vol. 1, pp. 12, 47–48, 61–62, 232–33.

44. *Democratic Ideals*, attachment to letter from Merriam to Creel, 4 June 1918, CPI 20-B2, CPI Papers.

45. Even though he was never contacted, Gino Speranza's name was included in the Inquiry's list of potential sources of information on Italian affairs who lived in the United States. The address that accompanied Speranza's name was a New York address, even though Speranza had already been living in Italy for five years; see *Confidential Memorandum of Persons Having Information in Regard to Special Subjects* [stamped received 28 January 1918], Inquiry Doc. no. 991, Inquiry Papers. In the Inquiry document, Speranza was described as "a conservative lawyer and a strong Italian nationalist."

46. John Hearley also thought that "what will prove to be a Wilsonian party is quietly growing up around Bissolati. It is composed of liberals, radicals and reformed socialists. Even the Turati stripe of official socialists may be attracted and many in the clerical group." See the letter from J. Hearley to R. S. Baker, 30 December 1918, Baker Papers.

47. "Even if Mr. Turati has not passed the Rubicon, as the 'Piccolo' of Rome puts it, a profound change has taken place in his mental attitude"; see *Mr. Turati and the Commission for after the War*, 31 July 1918. For Turati, see also Weekly Report, 5 August 1918; letter from Merriam to Sisson, 14 September 1918; all are in CPI 1-C4 Executive Division, sc. 1, fasc. 11: Italy, CPI Papers. Speranza described him as the intellectual leader of the Socialist Party, at risk of being expelled for his recent independent and patriotic statements; see Speranza, *Report Relative to the Imperialist*, p. 19.

48. A. Mann, *La Guardia: A Fighter Against His Times, 1882–1933* (Chicago, 1969), p. 86. Page regarded him as a likely leader for the new party being formed in Italy. In October 1918 he reported to Lansing that there were growing rumors of "a new party with Nitti as its leader. . . . He is said to be working with both Socialists and Catholics." Letter from Page to Lansing, 2 October 1918, quoted in Nigro, *Propaganda, Politics, and the New Diplomacy*, p. 65.

49. Page to [House], [but November 1917], *Miscellaneous n.d.*, Page Papers.

50. The American diplomatic archives are filled with negative views of Nitti: Lansing called him "one of the chief fomentors of trouble at Rome"; see the letter from Lansing to Wilson, 19 October 1918, Doc. no. 763.72.119/2223, in Department of State, *WWI and Its Termination, 1914–1929*. "As a perfect type of Italian intriguer, Nitti demands careful study and watching"; see *Italy's Trusts*, April 1918, CPI report, in CPI 20-B2 Reports. Speranza described him as an intelligent but intriguing politician, ambitious beyond all limits, and devoid of solid ideals; see Colgate Speranza, *The Diary of Gino Speranza*, vol. 2, pp. 141–42, 175, and 213. Concerning the Nitti mission to America, see also

A. Monticone, *Nitti e la grande guerra (1914–1918)* (Milan, 1961), pp. 59ff.; F. Barbagallo, *Francesco S. Nitti* (Turin, 1984), pp. 189–99 and 222–27.

51. Speranza described him as "a man of vision"; see Speranza, *Report Relative to the Imperialist,* p. 19.

52. Speranza, *Report Relative to the Imperialist;* and Colgate Speranza, *The Diary of Gino Speranza,* vol. 2, pp. 168–89.

53. Letter from J. H. Hearley to R. S. Baker, 30 December 1918, Baker Papers.

54. Letter from T. N. Page to House, 14 April 1919, *House Papers.*

55. Letter from R. S. Baker to House, 6 December 1918, *House Papers.* The reference to the article Massingham published in *The Nation* shows that the same invitation had been extended to Wilson as well in the press.

56. The *Bollettino delle Opere Federate d'Assistenza e Propaganda Nazionale,* no. 32, 14 July 1918, contains a list of about sixty small towns that held celebrations on the fourth of July: "The list," the bulletin states," could continue because there are countless reports. . . . All the far-flung districts of Italy, all the small townships and villages of the peninsula had a wave of sympathy for the commemoration of American independence." See Commissione Assistenza Civile e Propaganda, b. 15, fasc. 1093.2. Many mayors, especially in the south, also sent telegrams describing the celebrations; see Fondo Orlando, b. 19.3.53.

57. S. Crespi, *Alla difesa d'Italia in guerra e a Versailles (Diario, 1917–1919)* (Milan, 1938), p. 119.

58. Merriam's Report to Creel, 9 July 1918, CPI 20-B2 Reports, CPI Papers.

59. Telegram from Will Irwin to the American Embassy, 6 June 1918, doc. no. 103.93/370f and telegram from Merriam to Irwin, 19 June 1918, Doc. no. 103.93/406, in Department of State, Internal Affairs of Italy, 1910–1929. The text of D'Annunzio's poem, dedicated to America on the occasion of the fourth of July 1918, and in which the poet calls the Americans *i novelli Argonauti* (literally, latter-day Argonauts), is quoted in the letter from Merriam to D'Annunzio on 7 July 1918, CPI 20-A2, CPI Papers.

60. See, for instance, *La Tradotta* (1 August 1918), *La Giberna* (21 July, 6 and 29 August, and 16 October 1918), *Il Razzo* (25 July and 5 September 1918). The headquarters of the Italian Third Army wrote to the Propaganda Office of the Italian chiefs of staff, *Comando Supremo,* on 5 October 1918: "The American intervention itself, upon which minimizing comments of dismissal were made before, now takes on outsized proportions in the popular imagination," Report on the Morale of the Troops and the Population in the Second Half of September 1918 *(Relazione sullo spirito delle truppe e della popolazione nella seconda metà di settembre 1918),* Fondo F1 (Prima Guerra Mondiale), racc. 296, Archivio SME.

61. Italy's Censorship (Week Ending 31 July) and the Trial of Turin, 30 July 1918, CPI 1-C4, CPI Papers.

62. Report from Merriam to Creel dated 13 August 1918, CPI 1-C4, CPI Papers.

63. Letter from Hearley to Creel, 25 October 1918, Sc. 20-B2, CPI Papers. Merriam wrote to the CPI headquarters: "It is impossible to overstate the importance of the position held by the President here. . . . he stands in the position of a super man and all his uterances are read with the greatest interest." Letter from [Merriam] to Creel, 7 May 1918, CPI 20-B2, CPI Papers. In another report, Merriam claimed: "The President . . . is an idol among the Italian people. He has inspired their confidence in a wonderful way and they cling to his words in an amazing fashion. For that reason all of his speeches have the very greatest value." See [C. Merriam], *Democratic Ideals,* b. 10, f.5, Merriam Papers.

64. Harvey B. Carroll Jr., Why Half a Million American Soldiers Are Immediately Needed on the Italian Front, 17 September 1918, Doc. no. 763.72/11898, Department of State, WWI and Its Termination, 1914–1929.

65. A. Bliss Lane, unpublished autobiography, Bliss Lane Papers Yale University Library, New Haven, Conn.

66. Letter from Page to Frazier, 5 November 1918, and letter from Page to Wilson dated the same day; *Diplomatic Papers, 1915–18,* Page Papers.

67. N. Richardson, *My Diplomatic Education* (New York, 1928), pp. 179–81 and 196.

68. A. J. Mayer, *Politics and Diplomacy of Peacemaking: Containment and Counterrevolution at Versailles 1918–1919* (New York, 1967), pp. 212–13.

6. Wilson's Diplomacy toward Italy

1. For a detailed analysis of the American attitude toward the Treaty of London, see D. Rossini, "Wilson e il Patto di Londra nel 1917–18," *Storia Contemporanea* 22, no. 3 (June 1991): 473–512.

2. See Chapter 2, note 9.

3. The principal compromises to the Fourteen Points that Wilson was forced to accept were as follows: agree for Germany to accept the burden of war reparations for $56 billion, lose many of its richest coal- and oil-producing regions, and accept responsibility for having started the war. Through the mandate system, England and France were allowed to take possession of parts of the Midde East, while Japan was allowed *de facto* to occupy the Shantung Peninsula and the German colonies north of the equator; the German colonies to the south of the equator went to England and to the dominions of Australia and New Zealand. France and England (and South Africa) were given the German colonies in Africa. Opposed by England, Wilson was unable to win recognition of freedom of the seas.

4. U.S. Senate (Sixty-sixth Congress, First Session), Hearings before the Committee on Foreign Relations on the Treaty of Peace with Germany, signed at Versailles on June 28, 1919, and submitted to the Senate on July 10, 1919, by the

President of the United States, Senate Doc. no. 106, Washington, D.C., 1919 (hereafter *Versailles Hearings*), p. 525.

5. *Manchester Guardian*, 12 December 1917, 18 and 19 January, 1, 7, 8, and 22 February, and 12 March 1918; *Washington Evening Star*, 30 November 1917; *New York Times*, 2 December 1917; *Current History Magazine of the New York Times*, 7, March 1918; *The New Europe*, 20 and 27 December 1917 and 17 January 1918; *New York Evening Post*, 25 January 1918; *New York Tribune*, 1 and 2 December 1917.

6. *Versailles Hearings*, Lansing Testimony, 6 August 1919, p. 190.

7. In connection with his meeting with Balfour on 28 April 1917, during which they had carefully explored the future arrangement of Europe together, House noted in his diary that "he [Balfour] had a large map of Europe and of Asia Minor and we began this most important and interesting discussion, the understanding being that he and I would go through with it first, letting me convey our conclusions to the President before the three of us had our conference on Monday." Concerning Italy, House remembered: "We came to no conclusion as to Trieste. I did not consider it best or desirable to shut Austria from the Adriatic. Balfour argued that Italy claimed she should have protection for her east coast by having Dalmatia. She has no seaport from Venice to Brindisi, and she claims that she must have the coast opposite in order to protect herself. . . . This led me to ask what treaties were out between the Allies as to the division of spoils after the war." In a footnote, C. Seymour, as the Editor of House's diary, added a comment: "House later wrote that this map had the secret treaty lines traced on it and that Balfour left it with the Colonel. It is not to be found among the House Papers, and was doubtless handed over to The Inquiry and later sent to the State Department." See C. Seymour (ed.), *The Intimate Papers of Colonel House* (Boston, 1926–1928), vol. 3, p. 43–44.

8. American ignorance of the secret agreements to partition the Far East seems to have lasted quite a while and, along with other shorter-term aspects of the negotiations, might have influenced the more conciliatory attitude that the American president showed in Paris toward Japan's imperialistic aims. See *Versailles Hearings*, Lansing Testimony, 11 August 1919, pp. 216–18; see also letter from House to Seymour, 9 April 1928, Seymour, *The Intimate Papers*, vol. 3, p. 62, and C. Seymour, *American Diplomacy during the World War* (Baltimore Md., 1934), p. 268.

9. House recalled that "Balfour spoke with regret at the spectacle of great nations sitting down and dividing the spoils of war or, as he termed it, 'dividing up the bearskin before the bear was killed.' I asked him if he did not think it proper for the Allies to give copies of these treaties to the President for his confidential information. He thought such a request entirely reasonable and said he would have copies made for that purpose. He was not certain they had

brought them over, but if not, he would send for them." Seymour, *The Intimate Papers,* vol. 3, p. 44.

10. Ibid., pp. 48–49.

11. "[During] the evening of April 30th, . . . after a family dinner at the White House, the President and Balfour entered upon an informal conversation about War Aims, Colonel House acting as steersman in the conversation. Then it was that Balfour disclosed to the President the existence and the character of certain 'Secret Treaties' concluded between the Allied Powers." See B. E. C. Dugdale, *Arthur James Balfour, First Earl of Balfour* (London, 1936), vol. 2, pp. 200–201.

12. *Versailles Hearings,* Lansing Testimony, 11 August 1919, p. 219.

13. In January 1918, Balfour returned to the topic of the treaty with Italy in a letter to Wilson at the urging of the British Colonel William Wiseman, who had conveyed to him the American president's concern over the contents of the Treaty of London: "That treaty (arranged of course long before I was at the Foreign Office) bears on the face of it evident proof of the anxiety of the Allies to get Italy into the war, and of the use to which that anxiety was put by the Italian negotiators. But a treaty is a treaty; and we—I mean England and France (of Russia I say nothing)—are bound to uphold it in letter and spirit. The objections to it indeed are obvious enough: It assigns to Italy territories on the Adriatic which are not Italian but Slav; and the arrangement is justified not on grounds of nationality but on grounds of strategy." See Seymour, *The Intimate Papers,* vol. 3, p. 50.

14. Sonnino wrote as follows to the Italian ambassador in Washington, Macchi di Cellere: "It would be necessary for Your Excellency to keep a careful watch and be aware if the Adriatic question looks like it will become an object of discussion between this government and the French and English missions. If you were to observe indications suggesting this were the case, Your Excellency might, in appropriate manner, point out to your French and English colleagues that it would be best for those exchanges of views with the American government not to develop past a certain limit, beyond which they might create in this government the mistaken impression, fraught with consequences, that our allies could be induced to undercut the scope and effectiveness of the commitments undertaken." Letter from S. Sonnino to V. Macchi di Cellere, 16 April 1917, DDI, Quinta Serie 1914–1918, vol. 8 (1 January–15 May 1917), p. 549.

15. Letter from Wilson to House, 21 July 1917, in R. S. Baker, *Woodrow Wilson: Life and Letters* (New York, 1939), vol. 7, pp. 180–81.

16. Letter from House to Wilson, 22 April 1917, in Seymour, *The Intimate Papers,* vol. 3, pp. 37–38.

17. In the face of the insistence of the Russian ambassador to Washington, "in 1917 . . . Lansing protested that it was better for him to be ignorant of the treaties, since he could not ask Europeans to wipe them out without danger of

embarrassing the conduct of the war." From A. C. Walworth, *Woodrow Wilson* (New York, 1958), vol. 2, p. 146 n. 8.

18. Letter from Wilson to House, 21 July 1917, mentioned in note 15 above.

19. See V. Grandi, "I limiti dell'internazionalismo wilsoniano," *Comunità*, no. 183 (1981): 122–24 and 142–44.

20. Seymour, *The Intimate Papers*, vol. 3, p. 62.

21. Ibid., p. 323.

22. Baker, *Woodrow Wilson: Life and Letters*, vol. 8, p. 253.

23. Letter from Lippmann to Frankfurter, 28 July 1919, Lippmann Papers.

24. House's role in Italian American relations during the war and the peace conference is analyzed in my article, " 'Alleati per caso': il Colonnello House, la diplomazia americana e l'Italia durante la Grande Guerra," *Storia delle relazioni internazionali* 11–12 (1996–1997/2 June): 3–38.

25. Seymour, *The Intimate Papers*, vol. 1, p. 114.

26. Ibid., pp. 7 and 115. See also the *New York Times* of 16 December 1917, which featured a lengthy article on "The E. M. House mystery," while House was in Europe as the chief of the American delegation to the inter-Allied conference. The article was headlined "The Real Col. House." It opened: "If Colonel House were Secretary of State in name, as he almost is in fact, or if he were an ambassador, . . . there would be no mystery about him. Nor would he be doing so much for the country as he now is as the unpaid adviser to the president. . . . House is doing what he is doing now, and what he has been doing since 1892, for the love of doing it, and for nothing else. That is, he is an artist in high politics, a dilettante, a connoisseur of statesmen and public policies."

27. Seymour, *The Intimate Papers*, vol. 3, p. 217 and J. T. Shotwell, *At the Paris Peace Conference* (New York, 1937), p. 18. More importantly, House considered himself a "Super-Secretary of State"; see House's diary, 14 December 1918, in A. S. Link (ed.), *The Papers of Woodrow Wilson* (Princeton, N.J., 1983), vol. 53, p. 390.

28. W. B. Fowler, *British-American Relations, 1917–1918: The Role of Sir William Wiseman* (Princeton, N.J., 1969, p. 12. Fowler describes House's political influence in these terms: "Before and during the war House's Manhattan apartment had the aspect of a super foreign office. Unencumbered by any official position, he received ambassadors and unobtrusively gave guidance to the State Department, kept in touch with Republican leaders, and gave the 'right steer' to newsmen. Pilgrimages to his home became *de rigueur* for visiting dignitaries."

29. H. Nicolson, *Peacemaking 1919* (Gloucester, Mass., 1984; 1st ed., 1933), p. 15.

30. I. Floto, *Colonel House in Paris: A Study of American Policy at the Paris Peace Conference, 1919* (Princeton, N.J. 1980; 1st ed., Copenhagen 1973), passim.

31. This latter sardonic definition is mentioned in E. R. May, *The World War and American Isolation, 1914–1917* (Cambridge, Mass., 1959), p. 40.

32. Letter from W. Lippmann to S. E. Mezes, 5 September 1918, Lippmann Papers.

33. In 1938, Walter Lippmann sketched this description of the complementary relationship between Wilson and House: "The things which Colonel House did best, meeting men face to face and listening to them patiently and persuading them gradually, Woodrow Wilson could hardly bear to do at all. The President was an intellectual, accustomed to acquiring knowledge by reading and to imparting it by lecturing and by writing books. . . . Wilson spared himself personal contact whenever he could, and said what he had to say in speeches, notes, and writt memoranda. . . . Thus Colonel House brought to Wilson a faculty which Wilson lacked, though it is essential to a statesman. No one can be President of the United States without having a great variety of personal contacts. . . . The Colonel kept open the channels of understanding between the solitary man in the White House and representatives of all sorts of influential and indispensable men. . . . And, as everyone knows, he made personal contact with the leading personalities in Germany, France, and Great Britain." See W. Lippmann, *Public Persons,* edited by G. A. Harrison (New York, 1976), pp. 135–37.

34. House likely he considered his judgment and negotiating skills were superior to those of the president. In 1920, for instance, House said to Lansing: "He [President Wilson] has no creative genius. He adopted the ideas of others and then after a while he honestly believed them to be his own, and took credit for them." He added (rather bitterly, I believe): "If it had not been for you and me and some others *with* imagination I wonder how many constructive measures and foreseeing policies would have been produced during this administration." See Interview with Colonel House at the Biltmore, 11 October 1920, Confidential memoranda and Notes (1 January 1920–23 May 1922), Lansing Papers. See also G. Creel, *Rebel at Large* (New York, 1947), pp. 245ff.

35. "The strangest friendship in history," as George Viereck called it in his book, entitled, appropriately enough, *The Strangest Friendship in History: Woodrow Wilson and Colonel House* (New York, 1932), attracted the attention of psychologists as well as historians. See, among other books, S. Freud and W. C. Bullitt, *Thomas Woodrow Wilson, Twenty-Eighth President of the United States: A Psychological Study* (Boston, 1966); A. L. George and J. L. George, *Woodrow Wilson and Colonel House: A Personality Study* (1964) (1st ed., 1956). See also C. E. Neu, *Woodrow Wilson and Colonel House: The Early Years, 1911–1915,* in J. M. Cooper and C. E. Neu (eds.), *The Wilson Era: Essays in Honor of Arthur S. Link* (Arlington Heights, Ill., 1991), pp. 248–78.

36. C. T. Grayson, "The Colonel's Folly and the President's Distress," *American Heritage,* no. 15, October 1964, pp. 96 and 98. In an interview with Malagodi on 8 April 1919, Orlando called House a "true friend of ours"; see O. Malagodi, *Conversazioni della guerra 1914–1919,* edited by B. Vigezzi (Milan, 1960), vol. 2, p.

614. Orlando held this opinion for a long time; see the correspondence between House and Orlando until 1936, *Selected Correspondence, House Papers,* as well as Orlando's memoirs: V. E. Orlando, *Memorie (1915–1919),* edited by R. Mosca (Milan, 1960), pp. 460–65.

37. Letter from H. White to R. Lansing, 8 November 1919, quoted in Floto, *Colonel House in Paris,* p. 216.

38. R. Lansing, *The Peace Negotiations: A Personal Narrative* (Boston, 1921), pp. 229–30.

39. Shotwell, *At the Paris Peace Conference,* p. 11. For a more detailed analysis of the Inquiry's work on Italy, see D. Rossini, *L'America riscopre l'Italia: L'Inquiry di Wilson e le origini della Questione Adriatica 1917–1919* (Rome, 1992).

40. The Council of Four, composed of Wilson, Lloyd George, Clemenceau, and Orlando, was the highest decision-making structure at the Paris peace conference.

41. Concerning yet another of House's missions to Europe, he wrote in his diary: "There's an amateur touch at Washington as regards foreign affairs. Else of course Lansing would come here himself. The President would send him instead of sending House. The civilian members of the House Commission [i.e., The Inquiry] have no coordination with the State Department. . . . In a very important sense, there is no State Department. . . . The whole management of foreign relations has an uncoordinated, amateur touch." See Walter Hines Page, *Journal,* 24 November 1917; see also W. H. Page, *Diaries and Embassy Notes, 1913–1918,* 13 April 1918, W. H. Page Papers.

42. Letter from Wilson to House, 23 August 1917, in Baker, *Woodrow Wilson: Life and Letters,* vol. 7, p. 231.

43. "I am beginning to think that we ought to go systematically to work to ascertain as fully and precisely as possible just what the several parties to this war on our side of it will be inclined to insist upon as part of the final peace arrangements, in order that we may formulate our own position either for or against them and begin to gather the influences we wish to employ,—or, at least, ascertain what influences we can use: in brief, prepare our case with a full knowledge of the position of all the litigants. What would you think of quietly gathering about you a group of men to assist you to do this? I could, of course, pay all the bills out of the money now at my command. Under your guidance these assistants could collate all the definite material available and you could make up the memorandum by which we should be guided." Letter from Wilson to House, 23 August 1917, in Baker, *Woodrow Wilson: Life and Letters,* vol. 7, p. 231. On 2 September, concerning his response to the message from the pope, Wilson wrote to House: "I did not dare to submit it to our Associates across the sea more than twenty-four hours before I made it public. I felt morally certain that they would wish changes which I could not make. . . . The differences of opinion will be less embarrassing now than they would have been if I had invited

them beforehand." See ibid., p. 254. The Allies never formally ratified Wilson's note probably because both the French and the Italians feared that such a ratification would have committed them to move toward a revision of the secret treaties.

44. For an examination of the overall influence of the Inquiry on the Fourteen Points, see L. E. Gelfand, *The Inquiry: American Preparations for Peace, 1917–1919* (New Haven, Conn., 1963), pp. 134–53.

45. W. Lippmann, *The Reminiscences of Walter Lippmann,* Oral History Collection, Columbia University, New York, pp. 108–9 (the interview with Lippmann was done in 1950). As soon as he learned the content of the Fourteen Points, Lippmann supposedly exclaimed: "This is the second time that I have put words into the President's mouth"; see letter from Bowman to Seymour, 24 May 1928, Inquiry Collection. See also R. Steel, *Walter Lippmann and the American Century* (Boston, 1980), pp. 138–39.

46. Seymour, *The Intimate Papers,* vol. 3, pp. 322–23. William Wiseman, the chief of the British secret service in the United States, noted in his account of the conversation he had with Wilson on 23 January 1918: "The President said the Italian Ambassador called on him directly after his speech to thank him for his reference to Italian aspirations. He now hears from Rome that ORLANDO has gone to Paris and London to protest against his and Lloyd George's speeches, and demand that the Allies live up to the full terms of their secret treaties. He would like to know what Lloyd George proposes to do about it. His judgment is not to commit himself any further. He is evidently not much in sympathy with Italian war aims, or particularly pleased with the part they have taken in the war." From "Interview with the President, January 23rd, 1918," W. Wiseman Papers, Yale University Library, New Haven, as published in the appendix to Fowler, *British-American Relations 1917–1918,* pp. 254–58.

47. Wilson's notations are reported in R. S. Baker, *Woodrow Wilson and the World Settlement* (Garden City, N.Y., 1923), vol. 3, pp. 23–41.

48. The Present Situation: The War Aims and Peace Terms It Suggests, 22 December 1917, FRUS, 1919, *The Paris Peace Conference,* vol. 1 (Washington, D.C., 1942), pp. 41–53.

49. Telegram from T. N. Page to Lansing, 21 January 1918, FRUS, 1918, Suppl. 1, vol. 1, p. 35.

50. For instance, Lansing wrote to Wilson on 25 January 1918: "I presume you have read the telegrams from Rome indicating a measure of dissatisfaction or at least of disappointment on the part of the Italian Government and people with the statement in your address of January 8th relative to Italy and presumably the statement in regard to Austria-Hungary. . . . There is no doubt but that Italy's position in the Adriatic is more or less precarious and that it is one which the Italian government seeks to make more stable in the final peace. . . . Manifestly

an adjustment of the Italian frontiers along line of nationality will in no way cure this situation or make Italy's position more secure than it is at present. I think that this is the ground for Italian dissatisfaction, and it is not entirely without justification. . . . I fear that if Italy gains the impression that she is not to strengthen her position in the Adriatic, the Italian people will become discouraged and feel that the war has no actual interest for them, that they will be disposed to make peace provided the Germans and the Austrians retire from Italian territory, and that they will consider themselves to have been abandoned by this country and the Allies. With the present political situation in Italy and the depression following their military reverse, such an impression would be most unfortunate and might be disastrous." See letter from R. Lansing to Wilson, 25 January 1918, in *Personal and Confidential Letters from Secretary of State Lansing to President Wilson, 1915–1918*, Lansing Papers. See also the telegrams from T. N. Page to Lansing dated 10, 11, 21, 31 January 1918, and the letter from Lansing to Wilson dated 18 February 1918, with, enclosed, a letter from T. N. Page to Lansing, dated 29 January 1918, FRUS, 1918, Suppl. 1, vol. 1, pp. 18–98 passim.

51. "This [the Italian dissatisfaction with the Fourteen Points] is a very delicate matter; but while you were away from your office I took occasion to say to the Italian Ambassador (who, oddly enough, had called to thank me in the name of his Government for what I *had* said), that I had limited my statement about Italian rights as I did because I was taking my programme as a whole, including the league of nations through which mutually defensive pledges were to be given and taken which would render strategic considerations such as those affecting the Adriatic much less important. I told him that, failing a league of nations, my mind would be open upon all such matters to new judgments. I am clear that I could not pledge our people to fight for the eastern shore of the Adriatic; but there is nothing in what I have omitted to say to alarm the Italian people, and it ought to be possible for Orlando to make that plain to his own followers." See letter from Wilson to Lansing, 29 January 1918, ibid., p. 94. The Italian ambassador had this to say about his conversation with the president: "Wilson is an incorrigible utopian, and he likes to preserve a great indeterminacy with respect to a number of the issues of peace. . . . it would be childish to persist in the belief that Italy's security should and could be devolved to a hypothetical League of Nations." See A. A. Bernardy and V. Falorsi, *La Questione Adriatica vista d'oltre Atlantico (1917–1919)* (Bologna [1923]), p. 36.

52. Miller's monumental 21-volume diary on the conference in Paris is still an invaluable source of information for scholars of the period. See D. H. Miller, *My Diary at the Conference at Paris*, 21 vols. (Washington, D.C., 1928).

53. Gelfand, *The Inquiry*, appendix no. 7, p. 354.

54. Walter Lippmann's influence on American politics was even greater in the decades that followed, when he became one of the most famous journalists in the

United States and an assistant to many presidents; see the biography of Lippmann by Ronald Steel, *Walter Lippmann and the American Century* (New York, 1980).

55. Wilson wrote to House in September 1917, at the time of the original organization of the Inquiry: "I do not think that anyone could reasonably criticise your associating President Mezes with you in the work of preparing data for the final settlement, and I should be glad to see you get Lippman [*sic*] too, if he can be spared from the work he is now doing in the War Department. You certainly can do the work best with the assistance of men you know and trust." See letter from Wilson to House, 24 September 1917, in *House Papers.*

56. See letter from Wilson to House, 31 August 1918, *House Papers.*

57. As early as March 1919, Lippmann described Wilson's recent, short return to the United States as "Parsifal's visit to this country." See letter from Lippmann to Berenson, 18 March 1919, Lippmann Papers.

58. See the *Reminiscences of James T. Shotwell,* Oral History Collection, Columbia University, New York, microfiche 1, pp. 81–82. The interview is from 1951–1952.

59. "On many of the problems of first-rate importance there is a real famine in men and we have been compelled practically to train and create our own experts. This is especially true of problems connected with Russia, the Balkans, Turkey and Africa. Those are lands intellectually practically unexplored." See letter from Lippmann to the Secretary of War Newton Baker, 16 May 1918, in FRUS, 1919, *The Paris Peace Conference,* pp. 97–98.

60. In the so-called Black Book of Draft Exemptions, compiled by the executives of the Inquiry and dated 26 September 1918, in order to secure exemption from military service for certain of their colleagues, we read: "William Lunt—It is exceedingly difficult to find a historian who is not already engaged in one form of war work or another who has knowledge of Italian. Lunt possesses knowledge of Italian He has gone into the problem of the Trentino with enthusiasm and has produced results that indicate that he will be master of the problem in time for the peace conference." From Gelfand, *The Inquiry,* p. 70. Gelfand concludes: "The majority of Inquiry workers were not in 1917 specialists or experts on their assigned topics. Experts were the exception rather than the rule" (ibid., p. 78).

61. W. Lunt, *The Italian Tyrol,* delivered on 13 November 1918; Inquiry Doc. no. 353, Inquiry Papers.

62. In a letter to Bowman dated 18 November 1918, Lunt stated: "So far I have done nothing about Dalmatia, since Gray has reported upon it." See letter from Lunt to Bowman, 18 November 1918, Fasc. Lunt, General Correspondence, Inquiry Papers.

63. The Italian negotiations with the Central Powers, in particular with Austria-Hungary, during the period of neutrality were published in 1915 in the so-called

Libro Verde: Documenti Diplomatici, presented to the Italian parliament by the Ministry for Foreign Affairs during the 20 May 1915 session, Milan [1915]. In it were published the concessions regarding "Italia Irredenta" that the empire was willing to concede in exchange for Italian neutrality. These concessions included the Trentino, but not Alto-Adige, and a number of zones in the Venezia Giulia, with the exclusion of Trieste.

64. W. Lippmann, "For a Department of State," *The New Republic,* 17 September 1919, p. 195.

65. Notes dated 30 December 1918, 10 January 1918, and 11 January 1919, in *Confidential Memoranda and Notes,* Lansing Papers.

66. The President's Draft of a Covenant for a League of Nations, 11 January 1919, ibid.

67. Another fascinating character who played a significant role in the crowded group of improvised Wilsonian diplomats was George Herron, whom many Europeans considered a Wilson emissary and spokesman. Herron was a Socialist as well as a former Congregationalist minister and a professor of theology; during the war years he moved from Italy, where he had lived since 1904, to Geneva. From Switzerland he maintained a vast network of contacts with Italian, American, German, and Austrian diplomats. We know that Wilson, flattered by the book that Herron published in 1917, *Woodrow Wilson and the World's Peace,* asked the State Department to request that Herron write reports about Europe. The Herron Papers at the Hoover Institution in Stanford (California) revealed his ties with Italy. At the peace conference, the Italians asked him for help. For more information on Herron, see L. Valiani, *La dissoluzione dell'Austria-Ungheria* (Milan, 1966), pp. 400–5.

68. Letter from di Cellere to Sonnino, [19] April 1917, DDI, Quinta Serie 1914–1918, vol. 7 (1 January–15 May 1917), pp. 571–72.

69. On 29 January 1918, Wilson wrote to Lansing that the Italian ambassador "oddly enough, had called to thank me in the name of his Government for what I *had* said." See Department of State, FRUS, The Lansing Papers, 1914–1920, vol. 2 (Washington, D.C., 1940), p. 94.

70. Letters from di Cellere to Sonnino, 10 and 14 November 1918, DDI, VI, I, pp. 49 and 81. While still on the ship taking him to Europe with Wilson and the American delegation, di Cellere wrote: "Either I am much mistaken or these people will come to the Conference with us and support our legitimate claims." See Bernardy and Falorsi, *La Questione Adriatica,* p. 199.

71. Letter from di Cellere to Sonnino, 4 February 1915, *Archivio Politico Ordinario e di Gabinetto,* b. 192 (1917–1918), f. 9 *(Missione in Germania del Col. House),* Archivio MAE. From the diary of Polk, State Department Counselor, we note the frequency of di Cellere's visits to the State Department; see Diaries 1917–1918, Polk Papers.

72. Seymour, *The Intimate Papers,* vol. 1, pp. 180–84.

73. In 1915 di Cellere confided to Sonnino that House knew Ambassador Page but did not consider him very highly. See letter from di Cellere to Sonnino, 4 February 1915, as mentioned in note 71.

74. Seymour, *The Intimate Papers,* vol. 1, p. 412. See also the letters from Page to House, 5 February 1915 and 11 March 1915, *Selected Correspondence, House Papers.*

75. Letter from House to Wilson, 1 February 1918, Link, *Papers of Woodrow Wilson,* vol. 46, 16 January–12 March 1918, p. 207.

76. J. M. Cooper, *The Warrior and the Priest: Woodrow Wilson and Theodore Roosevelt* (Cambridge Mass., 1983), p. 296.

77. H. J. Burgwyn, *The Legend of the Mutilated Victory: Italy, the Great War, and the Paris Peace Conference, 1915–1919* (Westport, Conn., 1993), p. 163. Even democratic interventionism was in some sense linked to that political approach, given the impossibility of accepting compromises similar to Giolitti's *parecchio.* Leo Valiani recalled: "for those who, like Bissolati, had battled strenuously to reject Giolitti's 'parecchio' and had wanted Italy to join the war at any cost, acceptance . . . of a compromise similar to that which they had thrown in Giolitti's face as a betrayal of national interests would have been a political impossibility." See Valiani, *La dissoluzione dell'Austria-Ungheria,* p. 223. Page also wrote to Wilson, commenting on the Italian reactions to the Fourteen Points: "The Government, or at least the Foreign Minister, who has held this post since before the war, will . . . be held responsible for having gained by war less than Giolitti was promised without war." See letter from Page to Wilson, 29 January 1918, Wilson Papers.

78. Letter from Page to House, 29 October 1918, *House Papers.*

79. Burgwyn, *The Legend of the Mutilated Victory,* p. 117.

80. Malagodi, *Conversazioni della guerra,* vol. 1, p. 32.

81. See B. F. Brown, Sidney Sonnino, 1847–1922: The Stranger in Two Worlds, doctoral thesis, unpublished, Harvard University, 1966, pp. 9, 37, 488, and 492. Subsequently, Brown edited and oversaw the publication of Sonnino's diary. See also J. A. Thayer, *Italy and the Great War: Politics and Culture, 1870–1915* (Madison, Wis., 1964), p. 368.

82. Letter from Page to House, 29 October 1918, in *House Papers,* and F. Colgate Speranza (ed.), *The Diary of Gino Speranza: Italy, 1915–1919* (New York, 1941), vol. 2, p. 213. Speranza claimed that Sonnino, however unpopular he might have been, was one of those honest men to whom a nation turns in emergencies (ibid., p. 175).

83. See A. Ara, *L'Austria-Ungheria nella politica americana durante la prima guerra mondiale* (Rome, 1973), pp. 139–40, and V. S. Mamatey, *The United States and East Central Europe, 1914–1918* (Princeton, N.J., 1957), pp. 252–60.

84. Merriam, in the conversation that he had with Sonnino at the beginning of September 1918, had received the impression that "certain claims in the London treaty may be waived." See report from Merriam enclosed with the letter from Creel to Wilson dated 25 September 1918, Creel Papers. House wrote to Page: "I found his views less rigid than I had been led to suppose they would be." From House's letter to Page, 20 November 1918, *House Papers*. Speranza wrote that "it may reasonably be asserted that the majority of the men at the government, including Sonnino, are willing to recede from the claims of the London Treaty but on condition of an equally binding agreement, substantially recognizing legitimate Italian national aspirations. . . . On the side of practical politics we must not overlook that if Sonnino should recede from the Treaty of London without *'substitute of equal quantity and better quality,'* all his now quiescent enemies (Clericals, official and reform Socialists and Giolittians) would arise and destroy him. For example, Sonnino has kept the Giolittians in subjection by his very insistence on the Treaty of London which gives Italy far more than the *"parecchio"* which Giolitti contended would be obtainable from Austria merely by Italian neutrality. . . . So Sonnino . . . cannot renounce anything under the Treaty of London unless he can submit to his country an equally strong guarantee." See G. Speranza, *Italian Attitude with Reference to the Jugo-Slavs,* 17 September 1918, Department of State, *WWI and Its Termination, 1914–29,* R. 109, Doc. no. 763.72/11730.

85. Letter from William Bullitt to Phillips, 18 October 1918, which accompanied the earlier report by Speranza, ibid.

86. S. Crespi, *Alla difesa d'Italia in guerra e a Versailles (Diario 1917–1919)* (Milan, 1938), p. 242.

87. This is how Sonnino commented on the failure of the Paris negotiations: "As far as I am concerned, in all this I see my death, I mean to say, my moral death: I have ruined my country in the belief that I was doing my duty," as quoted in P. Alatri, *Nitti D'Annunzio e la questione adriatica (1919–1920)* (Milan, 1959), p. 31.

88. Orlando, *Memorie,* pp. 465–84.

89. F. S. Nitti, *Il capitale straniero in Italia* (Bari, 1915), p. 49. Page wrote to House: "Nitti is the only one of the three [the other two were Orlando and Sonnino] who has ever visited America or has any idea of what we are. . . . he has been spoken of in the press as 'l'Americano.'" See letter from Page to House dated 27 November 1917, *House Papers*.

90. Concerning Nitti's mission in America, see A. Monticone, *Nitti e la Grande Guerra* (Milan, 1961), pp. 59–110, and F. Barbagallo, *Francesco S. Nitti* (Turin, 1984), pp. 222–31.

91. Nitti considered Crosby to be "the general representative of the United States in Europe," a clear exaggeration of his merely technical role; see Nitti's conversa-

tion with Malagodi on 27 September 1918 in Malagodi, *Conversazioni della guerra 1914–1919*, vol. 2, p. 395. A number of documents show that Wilson was displeased by Crosby's meddling in the political aspects of American relations with Italy; see Department of State, *WWI and Its Termination, 1914–29*, Doc. no. 763.72/13437–8. Gordon Auchincloss, Polk's assistant and Colonel House's son-in-law, pointed out in a letter to Polk: "From all accounts, Crosby is regarded with particular dislike by everyone." See letter from G. Auchincloss to F. Polk, 28 August 1918, Polk Papers.

92. See letter from Page to Lansing, 5 October 1918, Doc. no. 763.72. 11644, Department of State, *WWI and Its Temination, 1914–29*, and letter from Page to House, 24 February 1919, *House Papers*.

7. The Paradox of the Fiume Dispute

1. The representatives of the enemy nations were not summoned to Versailles until months of grueling negotiations had gone on among the Allies, and they were presented with the text of a treaty that they could only accept or reject as a whole, without discussion.

2. Looking back on this document and the Black Book of the Inquiry, which we will soon examine, we can understand how readily Wilson accepted the Italian demands in Trentino-Alto Adige in one of his first conversations with Orlando. In Trentino, Lippmann advised adopting the border desired by Italy and agreed to by the Triple Entente in the Treaty of London, although he acknowledged that it was in open contradiction of the principle of nationality, as it would place a large number of ethnic German inhabitants under Italian sovereignty. This border, however, formed the best strategic frontier, and it was advisable for it to be accepted, especially in view of the possibility that Italy, after the war, might find itself a neighbor of a Germany enlarged by the addition of German Austria. The greater sense of safety that would derive from that concession would allow Italy to reduce its armaments, while the establishment of an autonomous administration could at the same time make it possible to respect to the greatest degree possible the diverse cultural roots of the population. From telegram from the Special Envoy (House) to the Secretary of State, 29 October 1918, in FRUS, 1918, Supplement I, Part I, *The World War* (Washington, D.C. 1933), p. 410.

3. There was no agreement between the Italian government and the Yugoslavian state. Lippmann was probably referring to the understanding reached by the Congress of Rome (8–10 April 1918), within which the territorial problems of the frontiers had never been addressed. Instead, the discussion had been limited to determining what principles would be invoked in their discussion; moreover, that congress had never received the official participation of the Italian government.

4. Telegram from House to Wilson, 30 October 1918, A. S. Link (ed.), *The Papers of Woodrow Wilson* (Princeton, N.J., 1982), vol. 51, 14 September–8 November 1918, p. 517 (my italics).

5. That same day, House telegraphed the text of the armistice to the State Department, still containing explicit reference to the Treaty of London dated 26 April 1915; he had added by hand, however, that the territories involved were to be described in detail, telegram from House to the Secretary of State, 30 October 1918, *House Papers*.

6. V. E. Orlando, *Memorie (1915–1919)* (Milan, 1960), pp. 461–63.

7. Telegram from House to Wilson, 31 October 1918, Link, *The Papers of Woodrow Wilson,* vol. 51, 14 September–8 November 1918, p. 534. In another telegram sent the same day, House stated: "Fortunately I was able to prevent discussion of political questions. I regard this feature as most favorable" (ibid., p. 532).

8. Referring to the meeting on 3 November 1918 of the Supreme War Council, House wrote in his diary: "As the sitting was breaking up word came that Austria had accepted the terms of the armistice laid down for her. There was great excitement and clasping of hands and embraces. I said to Orlando, 'Bravo, Italy' which brought him near tears. . . . When Clemenceau and Lloyd George left, Orlando remained behind for a conversation upon purely Italian affairs. Frazier reported this and it is attached." See manuscript diary of House, 3 November 1918, *House Papers*. Frazier, in his summary of the conversation, reported: "Senior [*sic*] Orlando began by saying that while all of Italy was delighted by the signing of the armistice, there was a small cloud on the horizon; they realized that the enemy was beaten but at the same time did not feel victorious. President Wilson had stated as a condition of peace that Alsace-Lorraine must be restored to France; he had, however, made no corresponding declaration regarding that part of Austria which Italy had always considered her own. Colonel House replied that this was due to lack of information in the United States, and that when President Wilson came over he would deal with the entire matter in the most sympathetic spirit. Senior Orlando requested that the Italian troops be at least allowed to take possession of this disputed territory from the time of the signing of the armistice until the meeting of the Peace Conference. Colonel House expressed himself in favor of this and stated that as soon as the organization which he had created for the purpose of discussing peace problems could arrive in Europe, it would be placed at the disposal of Senior Orlando; he fully assured that all Italian claims would be entered into most fully and sympathetically by this organization." Conversation between Senior [*sic*] Orlando and Colonel House, 3 November 1918, 5 P.M., *House Papers*.

9. House to Wilson, 11 November 1918; Link, *The Papers of Woodrow Wilson,* vol. 53, 9 November 1918–11 January 1919, pp. 43–44; and J. W. Gould, Italy and

the United States, 1914–1918: Background to Confrontation, doctoral thesis, Yale University 1969, UMI, Ann Arbor, 1970, no. 70–16.275, p. 197.

10. House's manuscript diary, 15 November 1918, *House Papers* (my italics).

11. Upon his return from Paris at the end of November 1918, Sonnino's personal secretary, De Morsier, confided to Malagodi that Sonnino's long conversation with Wilson's representative, Colonel House, had shown him that the Americans were not hostile to Italian aspirations but actually supported them. The attitudes of the Americans toward the Italians were "excellent." "Out of a sense of justice," the Americans intended to help the Italians in their troublesome interactions with the European allies. Italian fear of possible American opposition was "exaggerated" because Wilson's principles should be interpreted "loosely" and were important in particular with application to the more general questions, such as the League of Nations, open diplomacy, or the freedom of the seas rather than to more specific territorial questions. He commented: "These criteria [Wilsonian criteria], far from opposing our aspirations, favor them" see O. Malagodi, *Conversazioni della guerra 1914–1919,* edited by B. Vigezzi (Milan, 1960), vol. 2, pp. 453–54.

12. Memorandum on the French Note of 21 November 1918; D. H. Miller, *My Diary at the Conference at Paris,* 21 vols. (Washington, D.C., 1928), vol. 2, p. 37, and R. S. Baker, *Woodrow Wilson and the World Settlement* (Garden City, N.Y., 1927), vol. 1, p. 33.

13. Letter from House to Page, 28 October 1918, *House Papers.*

14. Letter from Lansing to Polk, 1 May 1919, quoted in I. Floto, *Colonel House in Paris: A Study of American Policy at the Paris Peace Conference, 1919* (Princeton, N.J., 1980) (1st ed., Copenhagen, 1973), p. 216, and *Colonel House as the President's Substitute on the Council of Four,* 8 April 1919, in *Confidential Memoranda and Notes (Jan. 2–Dec. 27, 1919),* Lansing Papers.

15. Bowman's Views as to Colonel House, 21 August 1919, in Confidential Memoranda and Notes (2 January–27 December 1919), Lansing Papers.

16. "He is a liberal by instinct, though not at all a thinker. He is a conciliator, an arranger. He likes human beings—and so they like him. And he has a shrewdness, too!" Notebook XXV, Series II, Baker Papers, as quoted in Floto, *Colonel House in Paris,* p. 28.

17. Gould, *Italy and the United States, 1914–1918,* p. 202.

18. C. Seymour, "End of a Friendship," *American Heritage,* August 1963, no. 14.

19. Reproducing Salvemini's thoughts, Alatri wrote: "What would have happened if the agreement had been attempted at least at the end of 1918, immediately after Vittorio Veneto, or in early 1919, when Wilson needed the support of the Italian diplomats to withstand the political activity of Clemenceau and Lloyd George, when the Italian people still had a sense of a victory that had not yet been sabotaged, depressed, and scattered by the errors and exasperating delays

of the negotiations in Paris, when Yugoslavia was going through the early, difficult phase of its formation?" See P. Alatri, *Nitti D'Annunzio e la questione adriatica (1919–1920)* (Milan, 1959), p. 23.

20. Notes on the conversation taken by Isaiah Bowman, reported both in Miller, *My Diary at the Conference,* vol. 1, pp. 370–73, and in J. T. Shotwell, *At the Paris Peace Conference* (New York, 1937), pp. 75–78.

21. G. L. Beer, *Diary* (15 December 1918); *Beer Papers;* and Shotwell, *At the Paris Peace Conference,* p. 88.

22. Beer, *Diary* (10 December 1918), *Beer Papers,* and Shotwell, *At the Paris Peace Conference,* p. 75. Concerning Beer, see D. Rossini, "George Louis Beer and the British Influence on the American Peace Program, 1917–1919," in S. Ricard and H. Christol (eds.), *Anglo-Saxonism in U.S. Foreign Policy: The Diplomacy of Imperialism, 1899–1919* (Aix-en-Provence, 1991).

23. G. L. Beer, *Diary* (5 April 1919), Beer Papers.

24. Ibid., 20 March and 4 April 1919.

25. Ibid., 21 March, 9 May, and 28 June 1919.

26. Justus [pseud.], *V. Macchi di Cellere all'Ambasciata di Washington: Memorie e testimonianze* (Florence, 1921), p. 179.

27. W. Lunt, Memorandum dated 12 December 1918, attached to the letter from A. A. Young to Wilson, 13 December 1918, Wilson Papers.

28. Miller, *My Diary at the Conference,* vol. 1, p. 45, and Shotwell, *At the Paris Peace Conference,* pp. 88–89.

29. Beer, *Diary* (22 December 1918), Beer Papers.

30. See R. Albrecht-Carriè, *Italy at the Paris Peace Conference* (New York, 1938), p. 85. According to Lloyd George's memoirs, Wilson already had a strongly anti-Italian attitude during his trip to Great Britain immediately prior to his trip to Italy. For the British premier, that was the result of meetings that he had just had with Sonnino in Paris; see D. Lloyd George, *The Truth about the Peace Treaties* (London, 1938), vol. 1, p. 193.

31. For a description of the conversation between and Bissolati, see A. J. Mayer, *Politics and Diplomacy of Peacemaking: Containment and Counterrevolution at Versailles, 1918–1919* (New York, 1967), pp. 212–13; L. Valiani, *La dissoluzione dell'Austria-Ungheria* (Milan, 1966), pp. 433ff., and H. J. Burgwyn, *The Legend of the Mutilated Victory: Italy, the Great War, and the Paris Peace Conference, 1915–1919* (Westport, Conn., 1993), pp. 245–46.

32. Dr. Grayson, Wilson's personal physician, who accompanied him everywhere he traveled, thought that the welcome Wilson received in Rome outdid any other; see letter from Grayson to Tumulty, 7 January 1919, quoted in A. Walworth, *America's Moment: 1918. American Diplomacy at the End of World War I* (New York, 1977), p. 168. See also C. T. Grayson, "Memories of Woodrow Wilson," *Atlantic Monthly,* November 1959, p. 65.

33. Various American observers mention it in their memoirs: see in particular the account offered by Wilson's wife: "It seemed that the Government, seeing the outpouring of the people, and especially the soldiers, feared that if the President addressed them he would say something which would enlist their support for his Fourteen Points. Though Italy had agreed to the Points as the basis of the Armistice, she had no intention of standing by her word in the Peace Conference. So, before my husband had left the Vatican the police were instructed to disperse the crowd. To do this without consulting the President was a gross discourtesy, and when I got back to the Quirinal he was already there and fairly blazing with anger." See E. Bolling Wilson, *My Memoir* (Indianapolis, Ind., 1938), p. 217. George Creel, a member of the American delegation, also recalled Wilson's "deep and bitter resentment" (p. 170) over the obstacles constantly thrown in the way of his speaking directly to the Italians; "that added to his distrust of Sonnino" (pp. 170–71). "It was told to me later, by a sympathetic member of court circle, that the reason for it all was Sonnino's fear that the President, speaking extemporaneously to the people, might bring up the Fiume proposal. This would have been fatal to the plans of the politicians, for they had not yet commenced their propaganda campaign, and all Italy was thinking in terms of peace and justice, not in terms of annexation and renewed hostilities." See G. Creel, *The War, the World and Wilson* (New York, 1920), pp. 170–71. Gino Speranza recalled in his diary: "all the obstructive measures taken by the Italian Government to prevent the President from speaking to the people. It succeeded! . . . Page told me that, when Sonnino first heard of the plan [for Wilson to address the people], he said 'Porcheria! Porcheria!' The officials in charge of Wilson's visit even lied to him." See F. Colgate Speranza (ed.), *The Diary of Gino Speranza: Italy, 1915–1919* (New York 1941), vol. 2, pp. 238–39.

34. This attitude became more pronounced with the passing of the years, and in the end, in the struggle to persuade the American Congress to ratify the peace treaty, it proved fatal. See T. A. Bailey, *Woodrow Wilson and the Great Betrayal* (New York, 1945), pp. 254–87.

35. Harold Nicolson, *Peacemaking 1919* (Gloucester, Mass., 1984) (1st ed., London, 1933), p. 27.

36. Outline of Tentative Report and Recommendations, prepared by the Intelligence Section, in accordance with instructions, for the President and the Plenipotentiaries: The volume for 21 January 1919, for the most part focused on European territorial questions and is in the Wilson Papers (Series 5B: Peace Conference Correspondence). The second volume, completed on 13 February 1919, concerning colonial questions, is in the House Papers. In Paris they were generally known as the Black Book and Red Book or as the Black Book, numbers 1 and 2.

37. The Inquiry, *Black Book*, pp. 47–49 and 56–58.

38. Albrecht-Carriè, *Italy at the Paris Peace Conference*, p. 94.

39. Letter from T. N. Page to E. M. House, 26 May 1919, *House Papers.*

40. Alatri, *Nitti D'Annunzio e la questione adriatica*, p. 28; P. Birdsall, *Versailles Twenty Years After* (New York, 1941), p. 277; T. A. Bailey, *Woodrow Wilson and the Lost Peace* (Chicago, 1944), p. 261; Shotwell, *At the Paris Peace Conference*, p. 200.

41. Albrecht-Carriè, *Italy at the Paris Peace Conference*, pp. 119–20, n. 18.

42. I. Bowman, W. E. Lunt, C. Day, D. W. Johnson, C. Seymour, and A. A. Young, Letter to President Wilson, 17 April 1919, published in Baker, *Woodrow Wilson and the World Settlement*, vol. 3, pp. 278–80.

43. Letter from Johnson to House, 26 April 1920, *House Papers.*

44. Letter from T. N. Page to House, 25 April 1919, *House Papers.*

45. Birdsall, *Versailles Twenty Years After*, p. 283; Albrecht-Carriè, *Italy at the Paris Peace Conference*, p. 144; Bailey, *Woodrow Wilson and the Lost Peace*, p. 267; Floto, *Colonel House in Paris*, p. 231; S. J. Kernek, "Woodrow Wilson and National Self-determination Along Italy's Frontier," *Proceedings of the American Philosophical Society* 126, no. 4 (1982).

46. As early as 12 January 1917, for instance, the *New York World*, considered to be a vehicle for Wilson's views, had written that the war aims of the "sordid" Italian government were "immoral" and called for the acquisition of territories that had never been Italian.

47. Burgwyn, *The Legend of the Mutilated Victory*, p. 302.

48. Bailey, *Woodrow Wilson and the Lost Peace*, p. 266.

49. As understood by its sponsors, the legislation was meant to target immigration from southeastern Europe in general and from Italy in particular.

50. The article concluded: "Italy rebelled against this difference in treatment." See *L'Unità*, 3 May 1919, republished in G. Salvemini, *Dal Patto di Londra alla Pace di Roma* (Turin, 1925), pp. 270–74.

51. On these topics, see R. C. Hilderbrand, *Power and the People: Executive Management of Public Opinion in Foreign Affairs, 1897–1921* (Chapel Hill, N.C., 1981), pp. 93–164, and T. J. Knock, *To End All Wars: Woodrow Wilson and the Quest for a New World Order* (New York, 1992).

52. House's manuscript diary, 30 November 1917, *House Papers.*

53. G. F. Kennan, *American Diplomacy, 1900–1950* (London, 1952), pp. 55–56.

54. P. Melograni, *Storia politica della Grande Guerra 1915–1918* (Bari, 1969), pp. 559–60.

55. L. T. Mowrer, *A Journalist's Wife* (New York, 1937), p. 77. Dos Passos talks about it as well, as quoted in W. L. Vance, *America's Rome* (New Haven, Conn., 1989), vol. 2, p. 304.

56. R. S. Baker, *What Wilson Did at Paris* (New York, 1919), p. 75.

57. Nicolson, *Peacemaking 1919*, pp. 52, 94, 195–96.

58. W. Wilson, speech on 5 September 1919 in St. Louis, Missouri, in R. S. Baker and W. E. Dodd (eds.), *War and Peace: Presidential Messages, Addresses, and Public Papers (1917–1924) by Woodrow Wilson* (New York, 1927), vol. 1, p. 633.

59. R. A. Divine, *Second Chance: The Triumph of Internationalism in America during World War II* (New York, 1967). On the survival of internationalism in America in the years between the two world wars, see E. S. Rosenberg, *Spreading the American Dream: American Economic and Cultural Expansion, 1890–1945* (New York, 1982), pp. 112–17, and A. Iriye, *Cultural Internationalism and World Order* (Baltimore, Md., 1997), pp. 65–130 passim.

60. Divine, *Second Chance,* p. 29.

61. Ibid., p. 4.

Index

Adams, Henry, 7

Adriatic zone: Sonnino and, 140–41, 237n14; American peace policy and, 152–53, 155–57, 170, 241–42n50–51; map of, 166; occupation of, 172–73; territorial experts and, 181–84; Wilson's appeal on, 184–87

Agenzia Stefani, 117

Agriculture: European, 12, 34; American vs. Italian, 44

Alatri, Paolo, 249–50n19

Albania, 39, 137, 170

Albertini, Luigi, 142

Albrecht-Carriè, René, 185

Allies, 42, 50; peace negotiations and, 169–71, 174, 184, 247n1–2. *See also* Triple Entente

Alsace-Lorraine, 63, 248n8

Alto Adige, 39, 155, 247n2

Altrocchi, Rudolph, 120–22, 229n28

Ambulance service (ARC), 84–85, 87–88, 218n14

American Academy in Rome, 6

American Field Service (AFS), 84

American Films Division (CPI), 119

American Red Cross (ARC), 2, 17, 81, 83–90, 93; Italian morale and, 83, 85–87, 217n8; as vanguard of U.S. army, 83, 216–17n5–6; ambulance service of, 84–85, 87–88, 218n14; canteens and hostels of, 85–86, 218n17; Italian enthusiasm for, 88, 216n5, 219–20n26–27; cash rewards of, 88–89;

expenditures of, 90t; CPI and, 115, 118, 121

American travelers, 5–10, 196–97n1–3, 200n26

America's Answer (film), 119

Amfitheatrof, Erik, 8

Andrew, A. Piatt, 84

Anglo-Japanese accord, 206n9

ARC. *See* American Red Cross (ARC)

Arcadia, dream of, 5, 8, 11

Armistices, 248n5; with German, 169–71; with Austria-Hungary, 171–73, 248n8

Artists, in Italy, 5–6, 196–7n2–3, 200n26

Auchincloss, Gordon, 247n91

Austria-Hungary, 36, 38, 39, 49, 53; armistice with, 171–73, 248n8

Avanti!, L', 230n33

Baden, Max von, 169

Bailey, Thomas A., 185–86

Baker, Ray Stannard, 131–32, 175, 179, 249n16

Bakewell, Charles M., 89–90, 216n3, 219–20n27

Balfour, Arthur James, 139–40, 170, 236n7, 236–37n9, 237n11–13

Bartolomasi, Angelo, 221n43

Bass, John, 116

Beer, George Louis, 156, 177–79, 182

Belgium, 36, 63

Bellanca, Giuseppe, 105

Benedict XV, 46, 208n26

Benington, Arthur, 116, 121–25

255

governments vs. peoples and, 127–33, 161, 176, 179–80; Italian popularity of, 133–36; diplomacy of, toward Italy, 137–68, 186, 240–41n43; peace conference and, 176–77, 212–13n25; journey of, to Italy, 179–80, 251n33; Fiume appeal of, 184–87; impact of failed diplomacy of, 187–90; final assessment of, 190–92

Wiseman, William, 237n13, 241n46

Women's War-Work Division (CPI), 72, 78–79

Work with the Foreign Born Division (CPI), 72

World War I, 3, 33–55; outbreak of, 36; U.S. and, 36–38, 41–42, 50–51, 54, 100; Italy and, 38–42, 46–50; economic front of, 41–42; as war of exhaustion, 41–43, 46–50, 205n1, 207n12, 208n25; divergent objectives in, 48, 150, 169, 208n33, 240–41n43; ideology in, 48, 50–55; governing classes and, 51–55; middle classes and, 59–60; as "peoples' war," 128; secret treaties and, 138–40, 151–52, 206–7n9, 236–37n7–11; domestic factors in, 205n3. *See also* Diplomacy; Propaganda

Writers: in Italy, 6–11, 197n3, 198–99n21; CPI and, 77, 215n56

Young Men's Christian Association (YMCA), 81, 83, 93–100; soldiers' homes (case del soldato) of, 94–97, 222n45–47; support of by Italian military, 96, 222n47; materials distributed by, 97, 98–99; CPI and, 115, 118–19

Yugoslavia, 3, 155, 170, 181, 247n3, 250n19

Zaccone (General), 222n45

Zoppoloni, Federico, 107